BLACK POWER
AND BLACK RELIGION

BLACK POWER
AND BLACK RELIGION
Essays and Reviews

Richard Newman

Foreword by
Robert A. Hill

LOCUST HILL PRESS
West Cornwall, CT
1987

Library of Congress Cataloging-in-Publication Data

Newman, Richard.
  Black power and black religion.

  Includes index.
  1. Afro-Americans—Politics and government.   2. Black
power—United States.   3. Black nationalism—United
States.   4. United States—Race relations.   5. Afro-
Americans—Religion.   I. Title.
E185.615.N39   1987   305.8'96073   86-20906
ISBN 0-933951-03-5 (lib. bdg. : alk. paper)

Printed on acid-free, 250-year-life paper

Manufactured in the United States of America

To the Memory of
Addie Mae Collins
Denise McNair
Carole Robertson
Cynthia Wesley
September 15, 1963

Contents

Foreword

Amazing as it seems, twenty years have passed since the original appearance of the opening essay in this valuable restrospective collection. More important than a convenient chronological marker, however, the essay, "Black Power: A New Direction for the Movement," reminds us of a different kind of demarcation, the line separating complicity and conscience.

The present collection shows its author, Richard Newman, to be a man of moral and intellectual courage as well as a richly creative scholar. A colleague for whom I have the liveliest affection and admiration, he has given generously of himself in the past; the materials compiled here evince a person of extraordinary persistence and dedication.

We can be thankful that he did not succumb to the trepidation, for which even the most seasoned scholar can be forgiven, that always accompanies the prospect of reprinting work spanning several years, especially work that was originally addressed to rather different audiences. The material presented here does bear up under critical scrutiny, and is inherently valuable as the testament of a personal and professional quest that originated in the course of one of America's greatest social crises and is still being pursued.

I find great pleasure in recalling my meeting with the author. Quite by accident, we found ourselves standing across from each other on the steps of the former building of the Schomburg Center for Research in Black Culture (known better and more simply as "the Schomburg"). Sharing the stoop, as it were, we were taking a smoke outside, when the much-admired Blyden scholar, Hollis Lynch, a mutual friend, approached on his bicycle. (With more than a tinge of envy, I noticed how nattily attired was the good gentleman in fashionable summer shorts, a sure sign, by my still ingrained colonial standards, of the freedom possible in the land of opportunity.)

Ebullient as ever, Professor Lynch no sooner ascended the steps than he saw to our introduction. Whereas just a moment before we were strangers, suddenly Richard Newman and I discovered, much to our mutual delight and amazement, that we were working on very similar historical lines of inquiry. Richard was then researching the still-undocumented career of Archbishop George Alexander McGuire, West Indian patriarch and founder of the frequently mentioned but very little understood African Orthodox Church (AOC). McGuire had also served as the first elected chaplain-general of Marcus Garvey's Universal Negro Improvement Association (UNIA). Since Garvey and the UNIA were the major foci of my own research, we found that we had, to put it mildly, a whole lot to talk about.

Richard Newman and I have been engaged, it would be fair to say, in a nonstop conversation ever since that summer day in 1970 on the steps of the old Schomburg building in Harlem. Shortly after that first meeting I went to visit him in Boston (he was at the time on the faculty of Boston University). I remember well how our discussion (it still amazes me how much one is able to learn simply by talking with Richard) lit upon the idea of our collaborating on a scholarly reprint edition of Archbishop McGuire's official AOC journal, *The Negro Churchman*. Richard had located what to our knowledge at the time was the only extant source (in the possession of the then head of the AOC, the late Archbishop Gladstone Nurse) of the complete original run of this important historical source.

It took several years for our goal to be realized. However, when I was invited by the Kraus-Thomson Organization to be the general editor for its African Diaspora Series, I moved with dispatch to revive the idea, and with the blessings of Archbishop Nurse the reprint of *The Negro Churchman* was published in 1977. By way of a historical introduction to the reprint, Richard Newman produced what is still the outstanding reconstruction of "The Origins of the African Orthodox Church." I am very pleased to see this important essay form part of the present volume.

Richard was not content, however, to leave the story there. He proceeded to offer an entirely new reconstruction of the story of the AOC in South Africa, which necessitated a special research trip to the Union of South Africa. The result was another remarkable piece of scholarship, documenting the career of McGuire's early South African disciple Daniel William Alexander. As the head of the South African AOC, Daniel Alexander was responsible not only for building his congregation within the boundaries of South Africa: he also brought the AOC's gospel to Zimbabwe and as far away as Kenya and Uganda with important consequences. Once again I am pleased to see the essay on Alexander made available to a wider audience.

Both these essays are classics in the historiography of African church independence, forming as they do the basic point of reference for all subsequent inquiries on the subject of the AOC in the United States and South Africa and the lives of its two greatest leaders. When the day of freedom dawns eventually in South Africa, Richard Newman's work will be certain to hold an honored place.

It was as the historian of the AOC that I knew the author. The present collection testifies, however, to Richard Newman's extraordinary commitment to the struggle for social justice in the 1960s. I had not realized, until reading his essays from this period, how profound for him was the movement toward the articulation of Black Power.

Richard Newman is to be numbered among that band of courageous Americans who, under the impact of the spontaneous education that the struggle for human rights afforded, sought to rethink the dynamics of institutional racism and its effects upon blacks and whites alike. It was inevitable that, once embarked upon this process of elucidation and clarification, he would soon discover how amazingly little even educated whites, including himself, knew about the lives of black Americans. The present collection is the fruit of what he has learned along the way.

In the relatively short number of years since his intervention on behalf of the cause of black education, Richard Newman has become, by dint of dedication and ever increasing fascination with the subject, a leading bibliophile of the Afro-American experience. In the best tradition of enlightened scholarship, he has been generous to a fault in sharing his rapidly accumulating knowledge with countless fellow researchers. The reader can observe an aspect of this generosity of spirit in the book reviews that comprise the final section of the present collection. He never fails to find some original aspect of a work to draw attention to; in this way, and unlike the average reviewer, he offers important encouragement to fellow scholars. In addition, he seems to be always at pains to notice the out-of-the-way publications that are forever in danger of being overlooked in scholarly journals. All in all, these reviews are a boon to the profession.

This collection is an important document revealing a quest in the best tradition of American social and religious thought. It also documents the satisfaction to be gained from working through the peculiar challenges inherent in pursuing the study of Afro-American history and culture, not the least of which satisfactions is in the people whom we meet in the process.

Robert A. Hill
Editor, The Marcus Garvey and
  UNIA Papers Project
African Studies Center
UCLA

Introduction

Those who participated in the Civil Rights Movement of the late 1950s and 60s were confronted by a crisis of belief and action in the summer of 1966. It was then that Stokely Carmichael, following the attempted assassination of James Meredith in Mississippi, first began to speak of Black Power. The public articulation of that phrase signalled important changes in the direction of "The Movement." There was a shift from white or interracial leadership to black leadership, from integration to a kind of nationalism as the movement's goal, and from moral suasion to militancy as the means to achieve it.

Some whites saw these changes as logical and necessary developments, as we began to realize that our own involvement in the struggle of black people was itself, at least in significant part, a dimension of white paternalism and oppression. As our consciousness was raised concerning the depth and pervasiveness of racism, it became increasingly clear that "Civil Rights" had gone as far as it could go, and now needed to be superseded by a more radical ideology and action. It became evident that the anatomy of black liberation was a matter for black people themselves to determine, and that white people, as a phrase of the time said it, were part of the problem rather than of the solution.

For some whites, this realization was immediate and intuitive. For others, it was a slow and difficult process of learning. Still others—of good will, it must be said—were never persuaded, believing that the abandonment of integration as either means or end was an indefensible sacrifice of a great social ideal. It must be remembered, in the context of the time, that for most whites and a good many blacks, there was little awareness of the whole separatist tradition in black protest. Names like Delany and Garvey were little known, African repatriation schemes had been largely forgotten, and Malcolm X was looked upon by liberals as a contemporary aberration.

In this setting, my own response was to attempt to take seriously Carmichael's admonition to whites to direct their efforts toward those who constituted the problem, and among whom we supposedly had some influence, namely our fellow white people. As a result, I wrote several articles intended to explain and defend the new Black Power phenomenon. At the beginning these were published in religious journals. Since the churches had been among the foremost white institutions to participate in the Civil Rights Movement, I assumed them to be the most likely organizations to be able to transcend their own insitutionalism in support of the new black consciousness. This is only one illustration of how naive it was possible to be in 1966.

Those articles are published here in chronological sequence. It feels strange to me to read them after twenty years. They move from theoretical statements seeking to interpret and support the concept of Black Power, to some later attempts to deal with particular and local issues as these came to light in the face of heightened black expectations and more militant black action. At the time I was a professor at Boston University, and we were struggling with domestic questions about admissions policy and the retention of black students. While dated, these essays do reflect one white man's wrestling with the ideological and practical dimensions of the Black Power movement. They also reveal other naivetés, and I might well say different or additional or better things if I were writing them today.

As I have suggested, a central problem among people who supposed themselves broadly educated was the general ignorance of black history in general and its nationalist tradition in particular. As a consequence, the Afro-American's paradoxical identity in being both a black and an American—the "two-ness" of which Du Bois wrote in a classic statement—was not at first clear. Only when that bifurcation is in focus, it seems to me, is it possible for non-blacks to begin to perceive the dilemma of personal and group identity for Afro-Americans, and therefore the inevitable ambiguity in the ways black people and organizations have struggled historically to come to grips with it. And this, of course, within the given framework of a dominant white society and a schizophrenic white culture that invite with their democracy and standard of living, and reject with their racism and exploitation.

The dawning realization of this ignorance of the black past as well as my own personal and professional interests as an academician led me to an investigation of what was then available in black history. The first clues as to what to look for came from the insights of Harold Cruse's sometimes brilliant and sometimes inchoate *The Crisis of the Negro Intellectual.* What I eventually found were the largely uncharted worlds of slavery, Reconstruction, and urbanization; the accounts of movements struggling with the contradictions of integration and separation; and the stories of incredibly valiant, eloquent, and steadfast men and women who are still largely ignored or misrepresented in what passes for American history.

I was particularly struck by several discoveries: the dramatic importance of Marcus Garvey and the Garvey Movement, the historic role and vitality of the black church, and the way every expression of black consciousness in America was led to the necessity of coming to terms with Africa—with African history and culture, with colonialism, and with the relationship of Americans and West Indians of African descent to the idea of Pan-Africanism. In addition to extensive reading in these areas, I was immeasurably aided in my thinking by the work, the ideas, and the encouragement of three friends—Prof. Robert A. Hill, then of Northwestern University; Prof. Malcolm McVeigh, sometime of the University of Nairobi; and Prof. George Shepperson of Edinburgh University.

The major impact on my thinking was Shepperson's extraordinary book *Independent African: John Chilembwe and the Origins, Setting and Significance of the Nyasaland Native Rising of 1915,* first published by Edinburgh University Press in 1958. Here was everything: the link between Africa and America, the link between religion and revolution, and, perhaps most important, the link between past and present. That is to say, Shepperson presents the information which makes possible the link between history and understanding. His remarkable unearthing of the material for his study shows that the data for Afro-American historiography is *there*; it is true that it simply has been neglected and ignored. Shepperson's ability and willingness to go, to search, and to find, combined with the informed daring of his imaginative connections, the rigor of his scholarship, and the elegance of his style in presentation created an intellectual excitement from which, happily, I have not yet recovered.

I combined my interests by undertaking a study of the African Orthodox Church, an expression of black consciousness in the United States which was originally related to the Garvey Movement and which spread to Africa to play a significant part in the development of African nationalism. Research trips to Africa and the Caribbean were powerfully instructive experiences. I never did write the book I intended, but several articles in the area of black religion constitute the second portion of this book.

As I left academia for the publishing business, my interests were broadened to encompass Afro-American books, bibliography, and libraries. About the same time I became involved in the Afro-American Religious History Group of the American Academy of Religion and the Northeast Seminar on Black Religion. These associations with authors, editors, and publishers; librarians and bibliographers; book dealers and collectors; and the members of the Northeast Seminar have all been collegial, stimulating, and enriching and I am very grateful for them. Randall K. Burkett, now of the Du Bois Center at Harvard and editor of the *Newsletter* of the Afro-American Religious History Group of the American Academy of Religion, invited me to be its book review editor, and many of the reviews in the third section of this book are from that journal.

It has been especially rewarding in recent years to have the opportunity to be associated with the great collections and marvelous staff of The New York Public Library—the Schomburg Center, the Central Research Library, and the Performing Arts collections at Lincoln Center. To list all the individuals to whom I have become intellectually indebted over the years would take a book by itself, but I must say I am particularly grateful to Prof. Robert A. Hill of the African Studies Center at UCLA and the editor of the *Marcus Garvey Papers* for his generous willingness to write the foreword to this book.

An advantage—perhaps the only one—of growing older is the sense of having participated in some history and of developing apart from the life of the mind some historical perspective from one's own experiences. I first attended services in a black church in, I think, 1943. I made my first political speech—for Henry Wallace and the Progressive Party—in 1948. That year was also the first time I heard Adam Powell preach. In 1949 or '50 I rode in the black section of a segregated bus in Birmingham, Alabama.

That all seems—and was—a long time ago. A great deal has changed. Many of the outward forms of discrimination have been swept away. Much of what sometimes seemed impossible is now taken for granted. But now our society is racist in far more subtle and powerful ways. The deeper issues such as domestic economic injustice and contempt for the rest of the world are more real than ever, and, as far as I can see, less amenable to change than segregated buses. America in the '80s is in the grip of a neoconservative callousness toward our own people and a militaristic belligerency around the world that have gone beyond the usual American selfishness and arrogance to become actively destructive. It is not accidental that most of the victims both at home and abroad of our country's curious blend of indifference and viciousness are people of color.

But the earth does move; it will undoubtedly continue to do so. A Barthian confidence in divine providence, a Calvinist mistrust of human nature, a glimpse of the peaceable kingdom envisioned by M. K. Gandhi and Martin Luther King, Jr., a Puritan belief in redeeming the time, and a Kirkegaardian sense of paradox are not, after all, the worst equipment with which to live life. In fact, I am extraordinarily lucky to have been able to spend so many years in Afro-American studies since the material is endlessly fascinating, the ideas constantly provocative, and the people an unfailing delight.

Finally, race is and has always been America's unsolved problem. The Revolution and Constitutional Convention of the eighteenth century; Abolitionism, the Civil War, and Reconstruction in the nineteenth; and the Supreme Court decisions and the Civil Rights Movement of the twentieth have not made whole a society fragmented from the beginning by chattel slavery and marked still with the scars it left on oppressed and oppressor alike. What can one say? If the steps to understanding and healing, change and justice, are small, they are at least toward a great end.

Richard Newman
New York City
June 1, 1986

Black Power

Black Power:
A New Direction
for the Movement

The civil rights movement is over. The decade that began with the Brown decision by the Supreme Court in 1954 and the arrest of Mrs. Parks in Montgomery ended with the passage of the civil rights bills by the Congress. The enactment of those bills inaugurated nothing new since it consisted merely of enabling legislation for the Reconstruction amendments to the Constitution.

One hope of the Radical Republicans of a hundred years ago has finally been realized and the Southern Negro has now the same legal rights as any other citizen. When one thinks of the ten years just past it is heartening to realize that more has been accomplished than anyone would have predicted, and disheartening to realize that the Southern Negro now stands precisely where the Northern Negro stands. Though the southern states have been slow to comply with the new laws, history is entirely against them and pressures will force compliance in the foreseeable future. Civil rights as such, then, are no longer the issue since they will be achieved in a "mopping up" operation against the remains of southern intransigence and injustice.

This means that the civil rights movement has accomplished its immediate aims and, despite continuing southern evasion and resistance, must turn its primary focus elsewhere. The leaders of the movement know what the long-range issues are. They are the problems of education, jobs, and housing, particularly for Negroes caught in urban ghettos South and North. But they do not know how to solve these problems, and it is no consolation that nobody else knows how to solve them either.

The moral suasion so effective in the drive for civil rights loses its edge when placed against the impersonality, the bureaucracy, the financial dilemmas, and the indifference of urban centers. It is one thing to march for the right to vote in Mississippi; it is another thing to picket for decent education in a northern city where few get a decent public education, where there is insuffi-

3

cient money for schools, and where the school board reflects a general public which really doesn't want its children to go to school with Negroes any more than the white Mississippi public does. The moral case may be just as strong for education as for voting in a democracy, especially in an increasingly technological society, but ethical pressures do not build school houses as easily as they open voter registration books. Moral example may desegregate a lunch counter but it does not provide jobs for unskilled workers.

It is on the basis of this realization that some of the younger and more militant civil rights leaders have begun to talk about something called "black power." They have learned that the white majority which controls all the institutions of a complex society gives nothing away and yields ground only when it is forced to do so. These more militant leaders are unsatisfied by the slow cooperativeness of the old civil rights organizations like the Urban League and the NAACP, which they correctly assess as too often identified with the white power structure (especially the federal government) to be adequately critical of it.

Despite their respect for Martin Luther King, based in part on their realization that he commands the loyalty of the Negro masses and is acknowledged as the spokesman for the whole movement by the white world, King's doctrinaire non-violence with its overtly religious base is sometimes viewed as unduly weak and sentimental by more secular Negroes. In order to avoid trouble which could lead to violence and guided by the moderation which responsibility creates, King has sometimes complied with white directives, leaving himself open to the charge of Uncle Tomism.

Hence the emphasis on power. Other groups in society have achieved and continue to achieve places for themselves through the acquisition and use of political, economic, and social power of their own. The Negro community does not have any of these means and is anxious to discover how to obtain them. Political power exists only on the base of real or believed voting blocs and is the most easily obtainable. Few Americans believe that others should be denied the franchise, the national Administration is eager to enroll Democrats, the law is clear, and the methods of effecting the law are increasingly conducive to Negro registration and voting.

Social power is the most difficult to come by since it involves a status which is related to but finally transcendent over political and economic power. What the Negro can hope for is group cohesiveness and self-respect, but this is difficult since Negroes have no distinctive links to African culture. That is to say that Negroes are more thoroughly Americanized than other minority groups because the unique institution of slavery destroyed Negro identity and family patterns, and therefore self-esteem and stability. Since Negroes are American they have had little choice but to accept the caste barriers and prejudices against them and try to overcome the walls of caste differentiation by as much movement as possible up the class ladder. In typical American fashion this has resulted in a "black bourgeoisie" which identifies more with the white middle class than it does with the Negro lower class and its aspirations.

The more militant Negroes, then, are trying to organize and solidify as much Negro political power as they can, especially in the South. In northern Negro areas they are beginning to challenge the entrenched Negro politicians who tend to be concerned primarily with maintaining their own prestige through subservience to the dominant white political hierarchy. In terms of social power, the militants are encouraging greater interest in and identification with the new African states in order to give American Negroes a greater sense of identification, self-regard, cultural heritage, and nationalism.

But all this leaves the crux of the matter, which is economic. A hundred years ago Thaddeus Stevens realized that only by having a firm economic base on which to stand could the freed slaves hope to maintain the political liberation won for them by Reconstruction as well as begin to achieve the social equality which is supposed to characterize free men in a free society or at least the opportunity to compete for a place in a ranking system supposedly based on ability. Perhaps if Stevens had been successful and every Negro family had been granted forty acres and a mule, the Second Reconstruction would not be necessary.

But in 1966 economic problems are more complex. Education, jobs, and housing are part of a package in which education is necessary for the kind of jobs which provide money for the kind of housing and life style which provide the cultural impetus for education. How to break into that circle is the question of all those wrestling with the dilemma of poverty and the "sub-normal" value system and hopelessness which poverty creates. In short, whether they know it or not, these new leaders are trying to tackle not only the current problems of the Negro, but the current problems of all those who are poor in the midst of American abundance, a sizable percentage of whom are Negro.

It is at this point that the Negro militants ambiguously converge with the rest of the "New Left" in their idealistic hope of altering the basic structure of American society to distribute more justly the nation's wealth and to broaden the base of political participation. One can cite the ineffective Negro middle class and argue that it is naive to expect radical shifts since Negroes do not want to change the economic-class structure, they want to be able to move upward into it. On the other hand, one can make the case that only by some radical transformation can the society fully be opened to admit and include Negroes on an equal basis.

Their point is that in American society, money more than anything else means the power to achieve and is in turn the symbol of achievement. Black power illustrates the desire of poor people to participate in the greatest period of prosperity the richest country in the world has ever known. Negroes have learned from whites that in America money means power and that power is the way to get what you want, and they want to know how to get the share that has been denied them for 350 years.

Black power, then, more than anything else, is an expression of desire for full participation in the totality of American society. Whether Negroes have any real chance of obtaining power, except in a few political situations, is an open question, especially the issue of how economic power is to be obtained by a group which has no economic levers (except some purchasing power) to begin with. For the moment black power is taking the form of belligerent self-assertion, the depreciation of tokenism, and the cutting of ties with white liberals. The advocates of black power must first discover whether or not large numbers of Negroes will be willing to subordinate their idealistic American hopes for integration and become quasi-racist, and whether or not large numbers of Negroes are able to be led out of the apathy and self-hatred caused by subjugation and become militant and prideful.

Parenthetically, it might be noted that it is within this general framework that a number of civil rights leaders have joined in the protest against American involvement in Viet Nam. That is, they see the American Negro movement as part of a world-wide struggle against white imperialism and for social reform, the self-determination of peoples, and a more equitable redistribution of the world's resources.

The Negro militants are at the point where they must take some calculated risks. If they give up non-violence for a self-protection they feel is more manly, they may alienate their pacifist and religiously oriented support. If they encourage the indigenous Negro leadership which they have been chided for not producing, they may alienate sincere white liberals (and their money) who are insensitive to the inherent culture-produced condescending superiority of any white face. If they sacrifice integration as the movement's immediate goal and substitute black power (even as a device for achieving real integration in the long run) they may alienate supporters who are humanistically motivated and repelled by tough-minded practicalities.

In a sense the Negro leaders want to be able to sit down at the bargaining table and have something more substantial than white sympathy with which to bargain. They draw an analogy to the labor movement where concessions were made finally only because power was met and balanced by power.

It may be true that the Negro community must become obnoxiously nationalistic in order to wrest from the whites the things Negroes want. If that is true, then we may see the emergence of a Negro group which has the extreme self-consciousness that other minority groups had while they were still in a quasi-immigrant status. These other national and ethnic groups, having acquired power through an exaggerated self-consciousness, have only recently been able to discard their arrogance and magnified unity and begin to blend into the mainstream of American life. American Negroes may yet have to go through that process.

—*Concern* 8:15 (September 1, 1966), 4, 8, 11

White Liberals
and Black Power

The term "black power" has evoked more response from both whites and Negroes than did "civil rights." The civil rights movement focused on pressuring government to enforce rights which already legally or morally belonged to Negroes, and was centered geographically in the South where there is a long and tragic history of subjugation. The black power movement presupposes the guarantee of those rights, and is pushing forward into new and less clearly defined areas of equality, especially in urban ghettos where Negroes are free in terms of liberties but trapped at the bottom of the American class and caste structure.

Whites in this country, however anti-Negro in their personal feelings, have enough respect for law and enough regard for fundamental liberties to have gone along with the civil rights movement with a minimum of obstruction. While some fanatics opposed—and continue to oppose—voter registration and the desegregation of public schools and facilities, most white Americans saw these moves as inevitable and basically fair and did little either to advance or hinder the Negro cause.

But black power is creating a different reaction. Polls indicate a growing white reaction to Negro progress and the increasingly expressed fear that Negroes are demanding and getting too much too soon. Although there is nothing in the term itself necessarily to suggest it, whites seem to associate black power with violence or black racism or both.

This is a matter of special concern to so-called white liberals since it is they in the white world who especially identified with or actually participated in the civil rights movement; it is they who maintain some involvement in the Negro community or at least inter-racial organizations; and it is they who believe in and articulate the goal of an integrated society where men are judged on their merits and not on their color.

The white liberal prides himself on his understanding, and he does understand that black power does not imply violence. He knows that Negroes have not been violent, that whites have, and

9

that the summer disruptions in the cities are the result of hostility, frustration, resentment, and the need to dramatize the plight of the disinherited urban masses. It is the white liberal who is rebuffed when Negroes talk about and actually begin to exclude whites from previously cooperative projects and organizations, but here, too, his understanding forces him to realize the reasons behind the drive for more Negro autonomy, self-assertion, and leadership.

It is at the point where his dream of integration is challenged by some overt or covert hint of black nationalism that the white liberal feels threatened and where his real mistrust of black power begins. Although white liberals are too enlightened to identify with any popular back-lash against Negro demands and expectations, they are unwilling to sacrifice their ideal of integration either as the ultimate goal of the good society or as the means to attain that goal. And they are unsympathetic to any suggestion of black racism, since they do not see "Black is good; white is bad" as anything but the ugly reverse of the white racism they abhor and oppose. This means that the white liberal's understanding stops at Stokely Carmichael's well-publicized dictum "Integration is irrelevant."

This is a shocking statement, but it is the clue to the direction the more militant Negroes are taking. What does it mean? Because they are as much the products of a materialistic and status-conscious society as all other Americans, Negroes want more and better things for themselves and their families. They want education, they want jobs, they want housing, and they want these things with or without whites' being included or involved. They are tired of paternalism, tokenism, and condescension, and of being "given" opportunities as if there were some reason why they do not have the same inherent right to them as any other members of our incredibly rich society.

What the white liberals fail to realize, therefore, is that integration as such is not the Negroes' goal. For Negroes there is no particular virtue in working next to a white man or living next door to a white family, or having one's children enrolled in a white school. What Negroes want is to be able to work at any job they choose, to live where they like, and to have their children attend good schools. This has meant a struggle to be included in white companies, white neighborhoods, and white schools simply because it is only in the white world that quality jobs, housing, and education exist.

Negroes are entirely aware of living in a white world and of therefore being caught in a society of which they are a part and yet not a part. They are not a part because whites have never fully accepted them or allowed them fully to participate. They are a part because they have lost any vestiges of identification with African culture and have taken on all the values of a white society.

It is precisely this dual realization which is creating the present crisis. Negroes are struggling to find or create an identity which is uniquely their own, and white liberals do not understand why color should matter to Negroes if it does not matter to them. But Negroes know that color does matter in this culture and this society whether white liberals know it, admit it, like it, or not.

Since they are white, white people are not quite aware of what it means to be white. Nor are they conscious that the United States is in reality a white world. That is to say, whites are not sensitive to the fact that they are a dominant, majority group who determine all the folkways, norms, standards of our society—in short, who determine our entire culture. This is why black power means identity and self-esteem before it means anything else. Negroes have been subject to a white culture for so long that they have come to take it as much for granted and accept it as unthinkingly as whites.

The spokesmen for black power are attempting to shake Negroes out of their unconscious subservience to white values and convince them that Negro-ness has its own strengths and virtues. These leaders feel that only by emphasizing his differences can the Negro rediscover and develop the self-esteem destroyed by the imposition of whiteness as a cultural norm.

The sense of this feeling of self-esteem may be illustrated by several examples. Many Negroes use a variety of means to straighten their hair, since straight hair is the norm of a white culture. In his autobiography Malcolm X made much of the prideful acceptance of kinky hair, and the fashion among militant young Negroes now is to allow their hair to take its natural form. The very use of the terms "black" and "Afro-American" emphasizes and glorifies the difference from the American norm of white European. The recent interest in and imitation of anything African points up the search for links to a lost culture.

The groping for self-esteem, then, leads to the placing of a premium on differences, even though emphasizing differences is exactly what the white liberals have opposed. But at this point in Negro development, the militants are claiming that it is sentimental to speak of some idyllic society where race is not a factor. In the tough realities of the present world race is very much a factor and the only way for Negroes to share in the affluence of our society is to have enough self-consciousness to create a solid bloc of power that is able to force demands from the total society.

The advocates of black power hope that Negroes can develop a sense of pride and create a feeling of unity which will make it possible for them to take the education, jobs, and housing which are rightfully theirs rather than subserviently wait for them to be offered by kindly but superior white men. The drive of the black power movement is away from white benevolence and toward self-emancipation. The logical sequence is clear: create self-esteem which will lead to the emergence of a power bloc which can demand a share in the rights and opportunities and affluence of contemporary America.

It is this whole struggle for identity, which is the machine to drive Negroes forward to take what is legitimately theirs, that the white liberal has not understood. The search for self-esteem necessarily calls for an exaggerated individual and group self-consciousness. In a sense this self-consciousness can be called black nationalism, or even black racism when it takes extreme forms, because by definition it must depreciate what is white and esteem what is black. In that context it must condemn as naive and utopian the sincere but over-simplified integrationism of the white liberals.

This is not to say that the black power spokesmen and their ideas are not caught in a series of contradictions. As has already been suggested, Negroes are as much or more American than anyone else since slavery destroyed ties to the old world, ties which were indispensable to minority groups of immigrant classification in maintaining their identity. This means that any attempt to find links to African culture on the part of American Negroes must have a largely artificial basis and that Negro identity will have to be worked out within the ambiguities of an American culture which is both egalitarian and racist.

Middle-class Negroes who have become suburbanites simply will not return to the ghettoes from which they escaped in order to provide leadership or help unite the Negro community. Also, it will be difficult to sustain the kind of reverse snobbery by which Negroes who used to decry stereotypes, about musical ability for example, now glorify them as unique characteristics or cultural contributions. And whatever group-consciousness can be created will not result in enough political or economic power either to make self-improvement possible or to affect significantly the vast white power structure. The right to education, jobs, and housing will probably still have to be granted by the white majority rather than taken by the Negro minority.

The Negro masses are too much the products of white America to alter their values, especially their desire to enter the middle class and their disinclination toward any kind of real social reconstruction. And the white masses are too insecure in their own frantic pushing for social status and material goods to tolerate any competition. In the long run Negroes are finally as integrationist as the white liberals because they share the same American ideal of a society where color is not a factor. But so long as they continue to be excluded from American affluence they will claim that integration is irrelevant, and until the ideal society comes about they will attempt to solidify black power as a constant pressure on a recalcitrant society to open its doors to more full equality.

—*The Register-Leader* 149:9 (November 1966), 7–8

The Black Power Revolution

According to the newspapers, Martin Luther King has been in the Bahamas working on a book tentatively entitled *Where Do We Go from Here?* The title could hardly be more appropriate, for it reflects the current ambiguity and lack of direction of what has been known as the Civil Rights Movement. What is clear is that the civil rights movement is over—in the sense that the drive for equality before the law has been largely accomplished. In only a few recalcitrant areas is there open rebellion against the judicial decisions and legislative enactments of the past decade, and that defiance only demonstrates the anachronism of those communities.

For ten years of our recent history Negroes marched and demonstrated, sat-in and freedom-rode, prayed and loved. Whites responded with mass jailings and mayors' commissions, beatings and murders, and finally enough vocalization of public conscience (when whites were killed by whites) to make possible governmental action. Negroes thus gained the right to vote, the privilege of eating lunch next to white men, and the knowledge that segregated schools are unconstitutional.

In 1954 these accomplishments lay only somewhere in a utopian future; today they are pathetically meager, deficient, inadequate. We have made these gains—and seen how wanting they are for an unskilled people in a technical society, for an uneducated people at a time when knowledge is imperative, for an ill-housed people in a land of incredible plenty. More fundamentally, we have made these gains without changing the racist nature of our national psychology and without altering the social separation of whites and blacks which reinforces that racism.

Now we are confronted with one central set of facts: the white man in America has not yet accepted either the depth of his own racial bias or the repressive character of the society he controls. The black man has not yet accepted either his own human worth or the immense potential for social change implicit in Negro militancy.

15

The concept of Black Power focuses on precisely these issues. Like any successful slogan it is amorphous enough to provide a variety of popular interpretations. But there is a rough general agreement that Black Power is a movement to create among Negroes enough personal self-esteem and group consciousness to build a truly democratic political power bloc which can take its rightful share of our nation's economic abundance.

First of all, Black Power exposes the essentially racist and middle-class character of our society. Whether we know it or admit it or not, white people believe that Negroes as Negroes are inherently inferior. We are all products of a culture which transmits stereotyped racial myths, and none of us is finally able to escape the internalization of the norms and values of our culture. Who of the most proudly "liberal" of us is able to explore his deepest psychological recesses and understand his deepest motivations? Who dares pretend that he transcends centuries and generations of cultural conditioning? Since the time when slavery justified the economic traffic in human beings by rationalizing a myth of racial superiority, we are all tainted by the belief in white supremacy.

What white people further fail to comprehend is that ours is a white culture. Every norm, every value, every standard, every criterion, model, type, pattern, is, unconsciously, white and middle class. Simply because they are white, whites must take this for granted, and therefore cannot imagine what it means not to be white in a culture predicated on whiteness.

And Negroes are the product of the same general culture! What happens to identity, self-worth, personal autonomy when one internalizes from the beginning of childhood a value system which negates the validity of one's own existence? a value system which deprecates the essence of one's own personality? Everyone learns who he is and how he should act from his culture; in our culture whites and Negroes both learn that black is inferior to white and that Negroes live and behave in certain racially predictable ways.

The problem is compounded by the middle-class nature of white America. Most Negroes are poor, and poverty creates (and is, in turn, partially created by) its own sub-culture—a culture which necessarily affirms its own characteristics and makes virtues out of what, by middle-class standards, are vices. So poor Negroes live in a world where blackness is a psychological

burden and where cultural values contribute to a further alienation from the mainstream of society. And middle-class Negroes
frantically attempt to disguise their blackness by an exaggerated
over-acceptance of white middle-class values and behavior.
The Black Power movement begins by affirming the inherent
quality of Negritude. Stokely Carmichael tells Negro audiences,
"Go home and tell your daughters they're beautiful!" He means
that skin bleaches, hair straighteners, favoritism for light-
skinned Negroes, are all an acceptance of self-debasing, self-
denying, self-destructive white standards which help perpetuate
white superiority. He means that there are unique Negro cultural
achievements—in music, in dance, in an incredibly rich and
vibrant language. He means that the lostness in time and space
which came as a result of slavery can be overcome by a recovery of
the African heritage. He means that blacks are fully men and
women with their own folkways, their own traditions, their own
distinct qualities—and that they need not be subject to further
personal dehumanization and cultural repression by whites.

Black Power says that once Negroes can realize their psychological exploitation by whites and assert the validity of their
blackness, they will constitute a self-conscious, self-affirming,
organized force in society.

Why the notion of power? Because the white society is not
going to yield anything of its privileged position. History makes
clear over and over again in every kind of situation that unless
power is met and balanced by power, those with power take
unjust and unfair advantage of those without it. Reinhold Niebuhr writes, "The domination of one life by another is avoided
most successfully by an equilibrium of power and vitalities, so
that weakness does not invite enslavement by the strong. Without
a tolerable equilibrium no moral or social restraints ever succeeded completely in preventing injustice and enslavement."

The issues now are the dilemmas which face the Negro masses
surrounded and trapped in northern urban ghettoes: education,
jobs, housing, consumer goods and services—and white America
has made clear that it is not really interested in coming to terms
with these problems. Therefore, only organized power can take
for the black dispossessed in America what is rightfully their
portion of our abundance.

Most white Americans when pushed and pressed have demonstrated that they will concede that every man has a right to eat his

lunch where he pleases and sit where he chooses on a bus and cast a ballot for either political party. But white Americans are not willing to concede that every man has a right to be educated to the limit of his potentiality, or a right to a job based on his interest and ability, or a right to live in a decent neighborhood, or a right to a minimum standard of living. In this context Black Power is about an expansion of rights into areas which have previously been considered private responsibility, an expansion of rights which the public at large is still too insecure and too indifferent and too selfish to allow.

There is a new generation of Negroes who are no longer willing to play subservient roles in order to receive as gifts sometime in the future that which belongs to them now by right. There is a new generation of Negroes who are no longer content to wait for white sympathy or white sentimentality or condescending white generosity. Their goal is to organize the black people of America into a militant, aggressive political power bloc which can make just demands and expect to have those demands met. There is a new concern for a truly participatory democracy in which Negroes are led out of their culturally imposed apathy so that they can have a real and potent voice in the decisions which affect them.

The goal of political organization, the purpose for which Black Power is to be amassed, is economic justice. Black labor played a major part in creating American wealth, yet black people go hungry. America today is in the richest period the richest people in the whole history of the world has ever known. Yet one per cent of the American public holds 80 per cent of all corporation stock as well as between 10 and 33 per cent of all other types of property: bonds, real estate, mortgages, life insurance, unincorporated businesses, and cash. One per cent receives 40 per cent of property, income-rent, and interest dividends. There is a new generation of Negroes who are no longer willing to live on promises and pledges and hollow myths.

This is all why Black Power is a revolution: a cultural revolution which seeks to destroy the psychosis of white supremacy; a political revolution which seeks to broaden the base of representative democracy; an economic revolution which seeks to expand democracy to encompass the distribution of wealth. Black Power is not violence—unless violence is the only way the mute ghetto can communicate. Black Power is not "racism in reverse"—

unless white supremacy forces an over-statement of the legitimacy of being black. Black Power is not black nationalism—unless there is no room in America for blacks. Black Power is the next logical step from the civil rights movement. It is racist America being informed that those who have been excluded are now including themselves in.

This is all not to pretend that there are not vast problems and questions here which have to be faced. How is it possible to square an affirmation of the self-worth of the ghetto community and its sub-culture with the fact that most of us cannot in good conscience approve many of its values and practices? How is it possible to decrease poverty without strengthening the middle class and its standards? How much demanding can be done by the black minority over against a massive federal government, massive corporations, and massive political parties? Is moral suasion a better device despite the inherent justice of demands?

Can Negroes themselves break away from the middle-class American success sickness? Can they affirm their Negritude in the face of cultural pressures, or find ties to an essentially alien African civilization? Can the ghetto be made livable by its inhabitants alone, so that it is no longer necessary to depend upon the artificial integration of white suburbia? Can Negroes ignore, even as a strategy, the American ideal of an integrated society in order to create black unity? Finally, is Black Power not revolutionary at all since it seeks not an elimination or even a very radical change in American structures, but merely alterations and adjustments so that Negroes are included?

Despite these questions and despite white America's fearful retreat, Black Power continues to convince American Negroes that the time of liberation has finally and truly come—not from the hands of charitable white men, but a liberation which comes from within and by a people themselves—and is therefore authentic and complete.

—A sermon preached in Marsh Chapel, Boston University, January 15, 1967

A Third Party for Negroes

Conventional wisdom informs us that third parties don't ever win American elections, but that their ideas are often eventually absorbed by the major parties and thereby work their way into American life. Wisdom that is not so conventional is beginning to wonder if a third party for Negroes is the necessary impetus to press the demands of the lagging and divided civil rights movement.

After ten years of struggle the immediate goals of civil rights have been enacted by the Congress, decided by the courts, and are being enforced by governmental agencies. A plateau has been reached, and nobody really knows how to approach the big problems that remain. These are jobs, education, housing, and consumer goods and services, primarily for the Negro masses trapped in northern urban ghettoes. Buried beneath these problems lies their cause—the racism which makes the younger and more militant civil rights leaders impatient with petty gains and frustrated by strategy which merely reinforces white supremacy.

That impatience and frustration has led to the cry for Black Power. Whatever Black Power means, it certainly includes the notion of organizing as much political strength as possible in order for Negroes to achieve the things they want. Black Power adherents are thwarted and angered by the thread of racism which runs through all American institutions, especially the unconscious racism of the traditionally liberal political institutions. Stokely Carmichael has said that asking a Negro to join the Democratic party is like asking a Jew to join the Nazis.

The debate which has followed has centered on the question of realism and effectiveness: are Negroes better off inside a Democratic party which, though cautious and white supremacist, is powerful to effect change when it can be moved to do so? Or are Negroes better off in a party of their own which, though racist, is at least their own race, but which represents such a numerical minority that it is apparently powerless? Do Negroes have to be content with crumbs from the Democratic table, or can they get more by being an independent political force?

21

Assuming that the Negro community does not owe the Democrats any gratitude for past accomplishments, it is fair to speculate on what blacks may expect in the immediate future. Not much is in the offing. It seems clear that there will be only business as usual in the Congress, that poverty and employment programs will continue to falter, that schools will remain segregated and second-rate, and that the Democratic party will generally reflect the timidity and indifference of a middle-class America which believes that Negroes are getting too much too soon. In the face of this, Negro militants are unwilling to wait for yet a third Reconstruction, but in terms of political structures they have nowhere to go.

It can be argued, then, that Negroes can get more from the Democratic party by being an outside rather than an inside pressure group. Those who can be trusted to stay inside the party need only be placated; those who are outside must be won by greater concessions. If Negroes were to organize a national third party, it, like New York's Liberal party, obviously could not win any elections. But it could so threaten the Democrats that only at great risk could they ignore demands for real federal action in housing, education, jobs, medical care, welfare, minimum income, and all the related programs for a more democratic society.

Political predictions are always safely protected by "iffy" qualifications, but if Johnson and Humphrey run again in '68, if the GOP comes up with a moderate candidate, if George Wallace runs independently—the Democrats are already in trouble. A third party on the left would add considerably to that trouble. It might well insure a Democratic defeat. Lyndon Johnson would find it difficult to duplicate the miraculous victory of Harry Truman 20 years ago when both the right and left wings of the party defected. What greater bargaining tool could Negroes ask for?

What chances for actualization does a third party have? SNCC and CORE have not been overly successful in their attempts to organize large groups of people, probably because of the culturally imposed civic apathy of the Negro masses. But there are whites as well as blacks who are disappointed by the failure of the Great Society and who would conceivably support the Negro cause with their votes. This is particularly true if the widespread dissatisfaction with the Vietnam War could be channeled into a third party which called for an end to the war as its chief theme of foreign policy. There are a good many people who would not consider this kind of two-edged protest a wasted vote.

Rightly or wrongly, the political left is deeply disappointed in Lyndon Johnson and complains bitterly about the present administration. This complaining is the favorite indoor sport of liberals, but by election day their idealism will be pierced by a flash of realistic insight which will make it obvious that the only alternative is a Republican. If that *is* the only alternative. A new political movement could offer a meaningful option free from the ideological obscurity and pragmatic futility of the present left-of-center splinter parties.

There are not many significant group realignments in American political history, but the shift of Negroes from the party of Lincoln to the party of FDR is one of them. As Negroes moved North and as they received the benefits of New Deal legislation, the big city machines, and national Democratic liberalism, they deserted the party of their fathers and rejected Frederick Douglass' dictum, "The Republican party is the ship; all else is the sea." Negro support for Kennedy and Johnson was overwhelming, but if the Democratic party has gone as far as it will go, Negroes have demonstrated historically that they can shift political allegiance when it is to their advantage.

So far the Black Power movement has failed (except to provide something for militant Negroes to talk about) because it has not convinced middle-class Negroes that they are black and it has not organized poor Negroes. Were the Black Panther party of Lowndes County to go national, these issues would be brought into focus and a means provided for resolving them. The resulting strength, aided by white support, could create a pressure group capable of effecting real social and economic change. And the recalcitrant racism of white America would be challenged honestly and realistically.

—*Scarlet* 3:3 (March 1967), 3

Black Power,
Black Nationalism,
Black Rebellion

The cry of the American Negro has shifted from "Freedom" to "Power." The pacific philosophy of passive resistance and non-violent action has given way to a new ideology of social rebellion and cultural revolution. Long-suffering Negroes patiently praying on court house steps have been replaced by angry mobs looting ghetto stores.

To understand these dramatic changes it is necessary to see that the concept of Black Power is a bridge between the old Civil Rights Movement and the new Black Nationalism; that Black Nationalism is understood by its militant adherents as the only possible countervailing force against racism; and that urban violence is the spontaneous uprising of a suppressed people bent on liberation.

Civil Rights and Black Power

"Black Power" emerged as the watchword of the Meredith march through Mississippi in the summer of 1966. It had become clear at that point that the combination of public conscience and federal action was an inadequate tool for rapid and effective change beyond the civil rights and voting legislation already enacted by the Congress. However dramatic those advances seemed at the time, too few Negroes were affected, too many unresolved problems continued to exist, and the American public was inclined to rest rather than move forward. Hence the natural emergence of a new tack.

A combination of various definitions of Black Power indicates that it is a movement with several interrelated and mutually reinforcing goals. It is a serious attempt to create self-pride and group acceptance among Negroes whose identity has been destroyed by slavery, subjection, racism, and poverty. It is a serious

25

attempt to create political strength among previously disenfranchised Southern Negroes as well as enfranchised Northern Negroes whose political choices are usually limited to white or
colored servants of the white power structure. It is a serious
attempt to create economic security for the thousands of Negro
families whose standard of living falls below anyone's concep-
tion of subsistence.

The established leaders of the civil rights movement at first
rejected the call for Black Power. Rather than working through
tested channels, Black Power sought new forms of expression.
Rather than being cooperative and integrationist in both ends
and means, it sounded suspiciously racist. Rather than being
middle-class in style, it was uncouth and vulgar. Rather than
consolidating gains, being grateful for them, and carefully planning new strategy, it appeared at precisely the moment when the
movement's immediate goals had been achieved and demanded
even greater changes.

Upon reflection, the old civil rights leaders have come to
realize that the new militants are in the main pressing the movement into its next logical phase. That is, they are calling for new
opportunities for Negroes in education, jobs, housing, health,
and income, particularly the masses of urban Negroes trapped in
northern ghettoes. In that sense, the political and economic goals
of the Black Power movement have been recognized to be an
extension of the legally realized goals of desegregated facilities
and the right to register and vote.

But there is a substantial difference, a difference predicated on
an essential disagreement over the nature of the white community. The old leadership holds to the American dream of an
integrated society where everyone is color blind. It maintains that
Negroes can be meaningfully included by existing political structures, economic abundance, and the middle class. In short, it
believes that what we shall overcome some day is racism.

The militants, on the other hand, see racism as the decisive
and continuing factor in American social differentiation. Racism, they hold, is no more destroyed by fragmentary political
alliances and ineffectual business enterprises than it is by persua-
sion and example. They have decided, therefore, to sacrifice the
noble means and utopian ends of racelessness for a pragmatic
and realistic acceptance of white America on its own terms.

Therefore, the new militants seek to strike at the heart of racism itself by a radical reconstruction of society, a revolutionary change which requires a revolutionary ideology and revolutionary means. The failure of assimilation, they argue, has created the necessity for pluralism. This dispelling of illusions must lead to a whole new self-understanding by the Negro in America, an understanding which takes account of the persistent reality of racism and develops the only possible counter-force: Black Nationalism.

Black Is the Opposite of White

The Nationalists' presupposition is that the assimilationist-accommodationist position is made untenable by the conscious and unconscious racism of white America, an aspect of culture so deep, strong, and widespread that it can never be eliminated. The Nationalists are aware of what no white person can fully comprehend and which most Negroes have been conditioned to accept: the fact that America is a total culture constructed on whiteness.

The Negro who does achieve in any of the ways society measures and rewards success must do so by rejecting his chief social characteristic—his blackness—and by taking on the coloration (or non-coloration) of the white culture. A new generation of Negroes is dissatisfied with methods of advancement that play into the hands of white supremacy as well as being impatient with gains that are only minimal and token. In short, the price tag of self-denial, the Nationalists insist, is too high for any man to have to pay to be accepted by the society, and only partially accepted at that.

For pluralism to be an effective reality, however, Negroes must overcome the self-denial, self-hatred, and group-hatred that are the psychological results of domination by a white culture. Self-affirmation can be accomplished only by taking that factor by which the general culture defines and classifies them—their color—and turning it into a personal virtue and positive force. Hence the whole emphasis on racial consciousness, racial pride, and "the beauty of blackness."

It is revealing to note the vocabulary involved here. Negroes who are closest to white culture and white norms often use the word "colored," which indicates only a shade of difference from whiteness. "Negro," or mere racial identification, then becomes a sort of middle-ground term. And "black," the very opposite of white, is a vigorously and positively proclaimed word of the Nationalists. It is interesting, too, to see how liberals of all colors choke on the word "black," brought up as they were on the notion that color is irrelevant and that the proper approach is to pretend it doesn't exist.

But precisely what the Nationalists are saying is that color does exist, that despite our pretentions we all know and act as if it makes a crucial difference, and that the only honest solution is for the black man to stop trying to be a white man and to be himself. Just what that self is, is not entirely easy to define, given 350 years of the acculturation process. It certainly includes the accentuating of whatever distinctive elements can be found in the Negro subculture: history, heroes, music, foods, dance, as well as the affirmation of the African heritage and "natural" Negroid physical characteristics.

Nationalist extremists want, in fact, a separate Negro state, presumably where their own culture could find legitimate expression and where political power could be wielded and economic opportunities enjoyed. The notion of radical separatism is, of course, out of touch with realistic possibilities. Most Negroes are too Americanized even to consider leaving the country, and the United States government is not famous for relinquishing territory.

Nonetheless the hope, however vague, of real and independent self-determination is a powerful tool for evoking black strength and creating unity and purpose. This kind of separatism with its anti-integrationist ideology may, as a matter of fact, serve as a device for helping achieve integration in the future by giving Negroes a new sense of worth, dignity, and power now and thereby forcing the white community into greater concessions.

At this point, however, Black Nationalism, if nothing else, is a state of mind. Like Zionism it is the self-consciousness and group-identity of a nation without a state, or the conviction that participation in one community is not incompatible with ties of sentiment and support for another community where one has ethnic loyalties.

The point is that many members of America's oldest and largest minority group are psychologically withdrawing into their own nation, having been consistently denied full citizenship in the general society. They are accepting their non-acceptance and determined to go forward on the basis of that realization. The question is whether Negroes are going to work for political and economic advancement as the traditional leaders propose, by accommodating themselves to the white society, or as the Nationalists are demanding, by mounting a campaign of resistance and self-liberation.

A Natural Response to Inequity

Talk of resistance, rebellion, and revolution is partly rhetoric, partly the necessary vocabulary of creating a new psychological state, and partly related to the actual upheavals in black ghettoes across the country. It would be assigning Black Nationalist leaders too much influence to say that their incendiary words are responsible for the flames of burning slums. The ghetto resident is not moved and motivated by ideology and oratory so much as he is by anger and frustration.

The Negro masses do not need to read Fanon's *The Wretched of the Earth* or hear Stokely Carmichael's speeches to know that they are exploited, colonialized, and denied a share in America's fantastic abundance. The link between the Nationalist philosophy of independence and urban rebellion is simply that Negroes who are articulate and those who act out their aggressions are both responding to the inequities and injustices of a society where blacks are the victims of a caste-like denigration.

Black rebellion in the form of urban violence and disorder, then, is the product of two interdependent factors: poverty and humiliation. Poverty is insufferable in the midst of plenty, especially when avenues to a better standard of living are dead ends. Statistics on Negro employment, education, income, health, and housing, though they show improvement over the past, make clear that black people can expect a very great deal less from American society than white people. The Negro college graduate will earn in his lifetime only as much as the white high school graduate.

Still, job competition and class antagonisms have probably been overrated as causes of disruption. New Haven and Detroit are hardly the worst places for Negroes to live in America. The more basic explanation is that even when blacks are reasonably well off the hostility and resentment against the indignities of racism need to find an outlet.

Whites brought up on the middle-class mythology of Social Darwinism, the Protestant ethic, and American success stories find it difficult to sympathize with the Negroes' lack of opportunities. And because they themselves are the products and carriers of white supremacy, whites find it impossible to comprehend that Negroes are frustrated to the point of explosion by the secondary status assigned them by the whole social system.

All this new restlessness and militancy in both thinking and action is traceable to the fact that only the absolutely oppressed are apathetic to social improvement and change. It is those who have a taste of new possibilities who expect more and who will become active in order to realize their expectations. It is ironic, therefore, that the white society, which finally compromised and capitulated in the realm of civil rights, now finds itself threatened by violent demonstrations demanding the extension of rights into more sensitive areas.

Violence is not a new phenomenon. Herbert Aptheker chronicles at least 250 major slave revolts, a piece of history generally overlooked by a public whose view of the old South is primarily informed by *Gone With the Wind*. Revolts in the past were not unrelated to other struggles for freedom—the American, French, and San Domingo revolutions—and the present black rebellion is encouraged by the recent world-wide emergence of people from colonialism and racial exploitation. Chattel slavery itself was ended, not by the intellectual and moralistic Abolitionist movement, but by military force and the nation's greatest domestic disruption.

The danger now is that the white majority and its government, terrified of disorder, will respond to rebellion by invoking even more repressive and restrictive measures. It is rare to discover a public official like Joseph Resnick of Poughkeepsie, New York, who personally bailed out of jail the rioters arrested in the city he represents in Congress. More likely one finds white attitudes to be fearful, uncomprehending, and bitterly antagonistic to the point of suggesting the sealing off and containment of ghettoes by laser beams or the use on Negroes of gases that destroy, appropriately enough, "the will to resist."

It is easy in cool detachment to call for the alleviation of the causes of disturbance; the residents of the ghetto know that nothing substantial is going to be done. It is easy, too, to insist piously upon the maintenance of order; Negroes know that the white community's obsession with stability is what keeps them in subjection. Black rebellion will cease only when white people use their power not to repress a minority but to come to terms seriously with massive injustice of their own creation. In the meantime there are black men with literally nothing to lose whose rage at their powerlessness will continue to break out spontaneously in symbolic acts of revolution, rebellion, and self-liberation.

—*Concern* 9:16 (October 1, 1967), 5–6, 22. Reprinted as "The Black Power Revolution" in *Boston University Graduate Journal* 15:3 (Fall 1967), 3–6. Revised and reprinted as "The American Racial Crisis" in *Contemporary Review* 213 (September 1968), 121–124, 145

Blacks and the University

Black people make up 11 per cent of the national population, but constitute only 4.6 per cent of the country's college enrollment. The Admissions Office does not know how many Negroes are at Boston University, but Sylvia Fleisch's extensive study of the class of 1970 in ten of our undergraduate colleges indicates that they are only 2 per cent.

It is difficult to believe that a university which prides itself on its urbanism, its academic quality, and its liberal social tradition could be so totally oblivious to the need for providing educational opportunities for blacks. It becomes even more difficult to believe when one discovers that this indifference is a clear violation of the expressed will of the University faculty.

Several years ago the Faculty Senate created a special Committee on Opportunities for Disadvantaged Students under the leadership of Prof. Freda Rebelsky of the CLA psychology department. In the area of admissions, the committee discovered (by counting year-book pictures) that the absolute number of Negro students had remained approximately the same for the last 20 years, although the school had more than doubled in size.

The committee therefore recommended and the faculty approved that "we add high schools with largely Negro populations to our recruiting list, help such schools have college planning days, and help guidance people in these schools to see the Negro as a potential college student."

The directive was never acted upon. "Boston University has no special program for the recruitment of Negro students," according to Director of Admissions Donald Oliver.

The committee recommended and the faculty also approved a whole series of additional actions: that compensatory scholarship money be found, that a Negro staff member be added to the Admissions Office, that the University survey what other schools are doing, and that "Boston University, through its active concern, make a public and active affirmation of its long-standing policy of support for the educational and social aspirations of minority groups."

33

None of these was ever implemented. In fact, a member of the Admissions staff told me "we have to be careful what image we project . . . not catering to one ethnic group. . . . We're not a public institution which takes just anyone."

Boston University is neither more nor less bigoted than the average white middle-class institution, which is to say that it participates in and reflects all the conscious and unconscious racism of a white supremacist society. The arguments of rising academic standards and "non-discriminatory" admission requirements have their validity for certain purposes; but they work out in practice to the detriment of black students and they provide a convenient device for failing to come to terms with the question of the University's responsibility to the poor and to those who suffer discrimination.

An institution which is sensitive to individual and social needs, especially one situated in the midst of a community marked by urban crisis and black rebellion, has a unique opportunity to contribute in its own area of competence to the solution of the inequities. The final report of the Committee on Opportunities for Disadvantaged Students states that "the planned inclusion of the disadvantaged in the university population would serve to stimulate, enrich, and magnify Boston University's creative contributions to social growth."

During the Civil Rights decade from 1954 to 1965, concerned people sought to eliminate reference to race in a serious attempt to reduce discrimination. When the goals of that movement were essentially accomplished it became clear that the indifference to race was as much a perpetrator of injustice as outright acts of discrimination. Black students tend to be poor financially, poorly motivated toward educational goals, and poorly prepared by both their primary and secondary schools.

This means that in order to achieve some equilibrium, greater opportunities must be given to black people in order to compensate for the shortcomings which characterize their whole social-cultural experience. This is in part the purpose of the various black power and black nationalist movements within the Negro community itself; white sympathizers can best act now not so much in the black ghettoes, but in the white communities where they can exert influence to reduce racism in white institutions so crucial to personal development, social mobility, and increased opportunity.

It is precisely in this direction that the faculty determined that the University should move. The University has completely failed to do so. Perhaps officials believe that admissions policy is an administrative rather than a faculty matter. Perhaps in the bureaucratic labyrinths nobody knows what anybody else is doing. Perhaps most people don't care.

It ought to be embarrassing to Boston University, however, that other schools not only care but activate their concern into programs of positive action. Harvard College, for example, gives great attention, energy, and priority to the recruitment of black students. There were three Negroes in the Harvard class of 1948. The number has risen annually and there are 40 Negroes in the class of 1969. And the overall freshman class size has remained roughly the same. Interestingly enough, Harvard and BU have about the same number of Negro freshmen even though our class is nearly three times the size of theirs.

Harvard has an intensive recruitment program, and regular funds as well as designated gifts are channelled into special scholarships. Students who show promise are accepted even though they do not meet normal admission requirements. Students with obvious deficiencies in background are sent to Andover Summer School, and great personal attention is given students once they are accepted. The drop-out rate is only slightly above that for whites, but, as one admissions officer said, "We figure a year at Harvard won't ruin their lives."

It will be argued that Harvard is free to do whatever it chooses to do because it has money. That is partially true, of course, but the more relevant consideration is that Harvard in addition to other area schools has the will to be socially responsible. Once that decision is made and priorities established, available resources can be re-directed and new resources attracted by the nature of the program itself. The BU faculty has spelled out its position but seems willing to allow its resolutions to be rather ingloriously ignored.

Another local school which sees itself facing the responsibility for, in its own words, "massive reform" is MIT. It established a Committee on Educational Opportunity which proposed a series of recommendations, some of which might be borrowed for implementation by BU.

In brief these are: establish a summer and Saturday school and tutorial program for deprived Boston and Cambridge children; set up ten special undergraduate scholarships for Negro and low-income students; help organize a consortium of Boston colleges and universities to offer guidance, financial aid, and probably admission to local poverty-area students; study the relationship between technology and vocational education in general and the possibility of a new regional two-year technical institute under MIT sponsorship in particular; encourage training institutes for teachers working in poverty areas and consider establishing a one-year non-degree course for urban teachers; explore the possibility of helping to establish a school of science and technology in a strong southern Negro college.

The MIT report also surveyed various programs and projects either planned or already under way in the Boston area. Brandeis has conducted a remedial and guidance summer school for Roxbury 7th and 8th graders; Northeastern organized a pre-admission summer school for specially recruited Negroes; Harvard "adopted" Miles College, a black school, with faculty and student exchanges, administrative support, and aid in procuring staff and material.

Simmons set up a part-time day program leading to a master's degree in urban teaching; Tufts held an Institute in Teaching Disadvantaged Youth in Urban Communities for teachers and supervisors; Wellesley has brought a few Negro and low-income students to spend their junior year in college. Boston University did not appear on MIT's list.

One BU administrator has made serious though unsuccessful attempts to bring more blacks to the University. This is Dean Horatio LaFauci of the College of Basic Studies, a school ideally suited to the admission of disadvantaged Negroes since it specializes in experimental programs for students who are marginal by traditional standards. Dean LaFauci has approached the major private foundations with a proposal that promising Negroes be specially financed and so enabled to enter CBS.

The proposal has been rejected, Dean LaFauci feels, because of its immense cost. He estimates the price tag at $3,500 a year for four years times the number of students involved. This means that to admit only 25 students in a special program of this type would cost $350,000. He points out an additional problem: as BU's standards go up, so do the standards of CBS. Therefore, the definition of "marginality" is constantly changing as it is measured against the total University's admissions norms.

At least Dean LaFauci is sensitive to the need. He indicates that the programs in which the University is involved are extremely inadequate. Opening Doors Wider in Nursing

(ODWIN), for example, has a high percentage of Negroes but very few in actual number. And the Upward Bound summer program is made up largely of whites from poor academic, cultural, and financial backgrounds. BU's record, then, is one of good intentions with meagre results. Given the uniqueness of our situation, our own strengths and weaknesses, what realistic possibilities exist?

First of all, the extensive research, enthusiasm for action, and pioneering proposals of Professor Rebelsky's committee ought to be resurrected, as well as the additional proposals made by the committee's final report under the chairmanship of Prof. Richard Rapacz of SED. These already existing recommendations provide clear foundations and directions on which to build a meaningful program. (Just as a footnote, someone ought to raise the question of what wastebasket is used to file recommendations of the Faculty Senate.)

Beyond the obvious and primary responsibility to seek out black students and secure adequate scholarship support for them, there is a wide range of constructive possibilities. The inadequate academic preparation of many Negroes could be easily compensated for by special summer school instruction for students accepted either by BU or other colleges. The integrated, interdisciplinary package programs of either CBS or DGE naturally lend themselves to this purpose and in modified form might well serve in the summer as a means for preparing students for regular academic programs.

United Church Chaplain William England points out that another neglected but potentially useful arm of the University is Metropolitan College. High tuition rates make this school, at this point, relatively impotent as far as poor people in the community are concerned. England suggests opening a branch of MET in the black community on something of the "extension" style with substantially reduced tuition and a degree-granting curriculum.

SED could play an unusually crucial role, especially in the recruitment of much-needed black students as potential teachers in ghetto schools. The weakness, lack of understanding, and bourgeois nature of the typical school in a black neighborhood is obviously a major factor in the final alienation of black children who are already damaged by their pre-school environment. Afro-American teachers can be a decisive influence in salvaging ghetto children.

Even in this period of black nationalism, it is realistic to presume that most ghetto teachers are going to be white. Here, too, SED has a unique opportunity to encourage its best people to go into the inner city and provide them with special training to appreciate and work creatively with the black cultural values and behavior they will encounter.

In the whole area of race relations, the nation faces an extraordinarily difficult and complex dilemma. Constantly thwarted by discrimination, humiliation, paternalism, tokenism, and indifference, black people move steadily leftward in the direction of nationalism, rebellion, and self-liberation. Consistently blocked by overt and covert racism, they have no choice but to take what is rightfully theirs when the ruling caste denies them the opportunities and fruits of freedom and affluence.

It scarcely needs to be argued that in our increasingly technical society, education is a central key to greater social, political, and economic democracy. Black people can clear slums by burning them down and get more political power by careful organizing and begin to overcome the self-denial imposed by a white culture by affirming "the beauty of blackness." But they cannot so easily storm the exclusive and entrenched university, although the picture of Roxbury moving en masse to the BU campus and demanding its right to be educated is not an entirely unpleasant one to contemplate.

The University has the responsibility to open itself, to find money for what is important, to take calculated risks on admissions, to be aggressive in seeking out the victims of an unjust society. It is worse than naive to assume that by eliminating the question on race on application forms for admission, one has fulfilled either his social or academic responsibility.

The University administration is guilty both of providing no leadership of its own and of shelving the policy proposals of the faculty. The faculty is guilty of walking away from the issue and of allowing itself to be treated as irrelevant. Students are guilty of being too wrapped up in their own limited surroundings to care that the opportunities they enjoy through no special merit of their own are not shared.

—Appeared as "White Power at 121 BSR" in B[oston] U[niversity] News 52:5 (October 11, 1967), 1, 6-7

White Racism

White racism is the consistent subordination of black people in our society. It presupposes that white people are inherently superior and that black people are inherently inferior. That presupposition creates a whole series of cultural forms and institutions which combine to keep black people down. The result is that black people do have inferior skills, jobs, housing, etc., and that result is used by the society to reinforce its own preconceived notion of black inferiority.

What specific forms does racism take? Firstly, racism is both individual and collective, that is, there are overt individual acts of white discrimination and domination but racism primarily manifests itself in unconscious institutional ways which we all take for granted. Because he is white it is extremely difficult for any white person fully to realize that all our cultural standards and norms are predicated on whiteness. This creates in our society a cultural and psychological imperialism of which white people by definition cannot be fully aware.

No matter how much he abhors prejudice every white person is the heir and perpetrator of the values of cultural colonialism. The skin bleaching and hair straightener ads in *Ebony* magazine reveal how much black people are forced to deny themselves and to accept the values of whiteness. Black militants are engaged in psychological warfare to encourage black people to affirm themselves with a new self-consciousness and pride.

The term that has been most widely used to describe this whole situation is colonialism. White America has, in fact, domestic colonies of black people who are kept in a subservient role and whose function is to enrich the mother country. Politically this means that the national white political power structures allow into office only Negro puppets, men who serve the organizations rather than the people in their districts. Economically this means wholesale exploitation whereby food, rent, and clothing money leaves the ghetto to go into the pockets of white suburbanites. Socially, this means that a black man must become "white" in order to be admitted to the mainstream of society, to be considered well-adjusted, and to be even partially assimilated and accepted.

Thus far integration has been only another subtle form of racism. That is, admission to good jobs, schools, and neighborhoods has meant admission to white jobs, schools, and neighborhoods. This means that integration as we have understood it only enhances white superiority and further forces the denial of black identity. Integration on white terms means the continuation of white superiority.

Most white people, however well-intentioned, have been totally unaware of the deep and far-reaching nature of institutionalized racism. Well-meaning whites have been unconscious of their implication and involvement in all the aspects of a society which is racist at heart. If you buy insurance, for example, does your insurance company use your money to invest in slum housing? Do you buy products from companies that keep underpaid blacks in menial positions? Does your local school board hire black teachers, teach courses in black history, help black children affirm their own unique cultural heritage?

The Kerner Commission has pointed to racism as the basic and underlying cause of civil disorder in our cities. Racism helps continue poverty and the ugly combination of racism and poverty constitutes an evil from which black people are determined to liberate themselves. White people can participate in the black struggle for freedom, can help in the battle for black self-determination.

Firstly, white people must understand the nature of the black movement. White people must begin to comprehend that tokenism, paternalism, and condescension are over. White people must stand aside so that blacks can voice their own feelings, express their own needs, and control their own destinies. White people can listen to black voices for a change and stop believing that black people are somehow incapable of knowing or articulating their own best interests. If white people can hear, they can begin to support the self-expressed wants of the black community in their own white communities. If blacks want community control of schools in Roxbury, for instance, whites can pressure the School Committee also.

Whites can recognize their own implication in the network of white power structures and begin to extricate themselves by demanding that these institutions be responsive to black needs.

Whites can educate and organize in their own families, their own neighborhoods, their own circles of influence. Whites can realize that they themselves are part of the white establishment and begin to disestablish white domination. Money with no strings attached can still go to black organizations. While poor blacks are struggling to get into the middle class, white members of that middle class can work to transcend and transform that class's materialism, shallowness, and hypocrisy. Whites can know that massive concern, massive organization, and massive expression can change society.

—An undated [1968?] pamphlet distributed by UCOR, the Boston University Committee on Racism

Integration or Separatism?

America is a strange country. We have the ability to send men to the moon, but not the will to feed the 15 million of our people who are hungry. Born in revolution, we are the world's oldest practicing democracy yet 90 per cent of us believe that demonstrating hippies, radicals, and students ought to be put down by force. We are a society made up of people from every race, class, nation, religion, and culture on earth, and we have deliberately set ourselves to the task of holding the 11 per cent of our population which is black in perpetual political, economic, and psychological subservience.

That 11 per cent is by no means monolithic or agreed on goals or directions. It therefore constitutes a "community" in no more sense than all white people together constitute a community. There are black people so reduced and destroyed by 350 years of colonialization that they either have no idea of what's happening or like the inmates of the Nazi concentration camps identify with their guards. There are black people so committed to the Protestant ethic, Social Darwinism, American success myths, and a capitalist economy that they could ignore fourth party candidates in 1968 and vote overwhelmingly for the candidate of Daley, Connally, and Lyndon Johnson.

But just as there is a radical minority of whites who are questioning the fundamental structures of the whole society, so is there a radical minority of blacks who are free from both the marks of oppression and the subtle deceptions of a system which promises rewards to the faithful and then never pays off. These militants offer the best hope for the black man in America, not because they will achieve their revolution any more than their white counterparts will, but because only by taking an unyielding stance substantially to the left of center and providing a counterbalance to the nation's powerful and entrenched right wing is there any chance at all of moving the center to the left and therefore salvaging the society from the present crisis.

Any serious investigation of Black Power reveals that it is not really radical at all. In the wake of continuing exploitation,

43

systematic police riots, and the unconscious racism of their best white friends, black militants are at most self-defensive, charitable to the point of sainthood, and probably the country's most ardent believers in the American Dream. If there is anything wrong with Black Power, it is that it may sell out for too little too soon. So long as the national conscience retains any semblance of sensitivity and so long as power is best confronted and contained by power, black militants ought to hold out for every single thing they might possibly get.

Black radicals know that demands for their moderation come from liberals who allowed Chicago to happen, that demands for their integrity come from those who seated Dodd but not Powell, that demands for their responsibility come from those who profit from the present status quo in all its manifestations. So long as the militants can remember this they can stay relatively free from compromises which only perpetuate injustice in more refined forms. Why they do not, except occasionally in their rhetoric, consider true radicalism, which would consist in burning down everything standing, God only knows.

The most interesting thing about the whole Black Power movement is precisely that it is essentially reformist, egalitarian, evolutionary, optimistic, and that it seeks a newer world for us all. Less interesting, as well as less important, is the fact that too many white people either do not see that or want that or both. If the doctors are sick, then of what value is their diagnosis and prescription? And what does it mean then to be healthy?

—*The Razor's Edge* (February 1969), 5, 14

The Failure of Tokenism

Boston University's experiment in tokenism is a failure. A very substantial number of black students especially recruited and admitted in the Afro-American Program are receiving failing grades. They have been allowed to drift into the second semester more by lack of policy than anything else. Unless some positive and comprehensive decisions are made one can only assume that they will be dismissed from the university at the end of this term or that the whole situation will continue to degenerate into a complete shambles.

It would be shortsighted to allow a crisis to develop this spring which could have been resolved last year and which hopefully can still be resolved now. Worse, it would be ironic to fail a great many so-called disadvantaged students out of the University at precisely the time the Admissions Office is recruiting more. Worst of all would be the easy solution of merely recruiting more Negro students who meet our standard entrance requirements and thus ignore those who are more totally disenfranchised in the society. We would thereby default on our responsibilities to the real dilemmas which we as an urban university are pledged to help resolve.

There are a number of reasons for our failure. Well-defined policies were never thought out. An Afro-American "program" does not in fact exist. A typical surfeit of committees in the bureaucratic maze made everyone important but no one responsible. Most significant was and continues to be the naive assumption of white liberals that they are dealing with an academic problem rather than an essentially social and cultural issue. We must first realize that class and caste differences do exist whether or not we believe they should, and that the marks of 350 years of colonialization, degradation, and oppression are not casually eliminated by a few weeks at Boston University.

The lack of understanding is chiefly illustrated by the fact that we recruited blacks who did not meet regular admission standards but we did not alter the requirements for their survival in a system predicated on the same values and presuppositions as the usual entrance tests. Some of these students have of course "made it." But one need not be a high scorer on SAT's to figure out that the system as it is presently constituted virtually guarantees their lack of success. This means that it is the university itself which has failed. We have arrived at the point of realizing that there are no differences in capacity among races; now we must understand that there can be cultural differences. But how do we proceed? There are three possible reactions to these students' situation. We can say that the university's only obligation is to give them an opportunity to compete on its terms, that it is unfair to everyone (including the blacks themselves) to pretend they've succeeded in this real world if they haven't, and that those incapable or unworthy of the chance we've given them don't deserve to be here.

Or we can agree that our standards should not be lowered but hold that the specially admitted be given unusual opportunities for success: reduced loads, remedial courses, small classes, 5-year plans, tutoring, etc. This is undoubtedly the dominant view. A survey of over 150 students at the conclusion of a course on "The Sociology of Minority Groups" showed that nearly all took this position.

But there is a third possibility. It is that we understand that we are dealing with cultural rather than intellectual differences, with variations in students' experiences rather than brains. We can see that the university is a white and middle-class institution, a microcosm of the society, unconsciously committed to producing people equipped to perpetuate the culture, and that we have been trying to orient black people into a white racist society. It follows that it is the university itself, not black students, which must change. It follows that black students should be evaluated by standards which encompass their thought-forms and values and experiences and judged by criteria relevant to them and their situation.

This means that if we are serious in our commitment to "disadvantaged" blacks it is ourselves and our institutions which must be reevaluated and redefined. This I would like to explore in a subsequent installment in next week's *News*.

—Appeared as "Administration Must Recognize Black Culture," in *The* [*Boston University*] *News* 1:20 (February 19, 1969), 6

A Redefinition Needed Regarding Racism

Most white people have not yet recognized that the underlying theme and thrust of black militancy is psychological. Blacks are struggling to create a positive identity in the face of a dominant culture which presupposes whiteness and denigrates blackness. Only by developing a strong ego, individually and collectively, can group cohesion, political power, and economic strength emerge and with them a chance for a real share in a new society. Within this context, the university as it is presently constituted has to be seen as a culture-bound institution with standards set by white men for white men. To speak of black students "failing" is therefore only to say that they are neither white nor middle class.

The task of the university then is to transcend its implicit racism and so relate to black students that negative self-images can begin to be overcome by affirming the legitimate and authentic claims of blackness. Whites must see that curricular offerings in white history, white literature, white sociology, white art, simply cannot provide the culture-created identity and motivation for the majority of those whose class and caste is different from the culture-created "norm." Norms must be changed.

There is no question whether the university shall serve the public. We already do that. There is a question of which public we serve. We innocently believe that the university's norms and standards are somehow permanent and inviolate and absolute. We forget that standards have always been altered to meet community needs. The existence of "colleges" of agriculture or hotel management or nursing or physical therapy or secretarial science (let alone research on rockets and missiles) make clear that the definitions as well as the standards of education vary depending on who is able to exert pressure on the universities.

And we forget that the university reflects the dominant culture in that its so-called academic expectations in motivation and skills and aptitudes are not different from the experiences of the middle class which uses the university for socialization and mobility. A white Protestant boy from Winchester in business administration or a Jewish girl from Great Neck in elementary education would have to be simple-minded or disturbed to be failed out of Boston University since their backgrounds and the university's expectations are part of a continuum and cut from the same cultural cloth.

At this point the best solution seems to be the one being explored by Harvard, Yale, and other schools: a Division of Black Studies. In such a school there could be a relevant curriculum with which students could identify, a program whose standards could reflect the needs of those who participate, and norms which are not condescendingly lower but honestly different and therefore reflective of a pluralist society where there is real equality. The form such a division would take would have to be worked out by black students and faculty. Whatever its form it would be superior to the present hypocrisy of admitting students because they don't pass tests and then failing them for the same reason.

Those who oppose autonomy by blacks over their own education must face the reality that in our society the same rules do not in fact apply. A black college graduate earns in his lifetime less than a white high school dropout. The university is the white man holding up the carrot of jobs and acceptance while wielding the stick of enforced conformity to a white institution. Since there is no real correlation between performance and reward, the carrot is a deception—and the stick then becomes a lie too. Why should blacks continue faithful obedience to a system which is itself faithless? Why play by the rules when the game is fixed?

The most fundamental question at stake is the university's self-definition, particularly in terms of the role it sees itself fulfilling in the society. Is the university willing to change only if the society changes? Admittedly the process is two-way, but are we leaders, innovators, a mechanism for change, or only a reflection of the current culture? If the university waits to be restructured until the society is, then we must be reminded that directions originate in the university—or the Pentagon. A re-defined, reconstituted, de-institutionalized, and more free university can only benefit all of us, black and white alike.

—*The* [*Boston University*] *News* 1:22 (March 12, 1969), 6

"The Only Great Revolutionary Poetry": African Cultural Nationalism and Negritude

The emergence of modern Africa must be set over against one central determinative fact—colonialism—and in the context of the ambiguous acceptance and rejection of the new culture colonialism brought with it. Basically, colonialism expressed itself in two forms: British and French. Britain ruled indirectly, using traditional political systems for local administration and traditional leaders as links between the European rulers and the African masses. France ruled directly, ignoring or repressing both traditional leaders and political systems. British policy implied inherent differences between European and African, ruler and ruled, white and black. In the British colonies separatism thus forced African attention inward and made nationalism the only hope for equality.

The French, in contrast, operated on a policy of racial equality: Africans were to be "civilized" and then integrated as equals with Europeans within a Euro-African union. French assimilationism thus forced native attention outward and made it possible to hope for equality on French terms.[1] Faith in the French posture made it possible for Blaise Diagne, the black deputy from Senegal, to write to Marcus Garvey, the leader in the 1920's of the American movement for black nationalism and African redemption: "We French natives wish to remain French, since France has given us every liberty and since she has unreservedly accepted us upon the same basis as her own European children. None of us aspires to see French Africa delivered exclusively to the Africans."[2]

Colonialism includes a variety of components, of which political domination and economic exploitation are only the most obvious and overt. More powerful, more subtle, and more ambivalent is what may be called cultural, psychological, or mental colonialism: the introduction of a new culture, including both values and behavior, which simultaneously threatens the old society and offers changes which are perceived as desirable. In contrast to Diagne's acceptance of the notion of "We French Natives" is Sekou Toure's rejection of cultural colonialism: "The education that was given to us was designed to assimilate us, to depersonalize us, to Westernize us—to present our civilization, our culture, our own sociological and philosophical conceptions, even our humanism as the expression of a savage and almost unconscious primitivism—in order to create a number of complexes in us which would drive us to become more French than the French themselves."[3]

Colonialism, of course, stands in a dialectical relationship to racism. Racism is essentially a product of slavery, i.e., the concept of inherent white superiority and black inferiority which evolved as a rationalization for the enormous profitability of the slave trade and the chattel slavery system. With the end of slavery, racism continued as the justification for European (and American) expansionism and imperialism. And today it manifests itself as the basis of Western technical superiority whereby the "underdeveloped," "disadvantaged," etc., peoples are perceived and defined from the standpoint of technology. Racism, cultural domination, psychological exploitation, affected Africans under both British and French rule, but French-speaking Africans had the additional problem of freeing themselves from the "civilizing" "egalitarian" colonialism of French assimilationism which presupposed the superiority of French culture.

This additional problem is reflected in the different forms the liberation struggle took in British and French colonies. The African freedom movement consisted of two main intellectual currents. In British colonies it was political in nature, it manifested itself in the Pan-African movement, its chief spokesman was probably W.E.B. Du Bois, and it was influenced by Western democracy, Marx, Gandhi, and American black nationalism. In French colonies it was cultural in nature, it manifested itself in the poetry of Negritude, and its spokesmen were the French-speaking African poets: Leopold Senghor, Aime Cesaire, Leon Damas, Alioune Diop, David Diop. These two strains began converging in 1946 and merging in 1958. In Paris in 1956 at the First World Congress of Black Artists and Writers, Diop said, "It is important to point out here that all of us, whether we believe in God or are atheists, whether Christians, Moslems or Communists, have in common the feeling of being frustrated by Western culture."[4] Sartre called the Negritude literature "the only great revolutionary poetry of our day."[5] The term Negritude was first used by Cesaire, of Martinique, and Senghor, a Senegalese, in Paris in the '30's. In 1947 A. Diop founded in Paris *Présence Africaine* as a journal for the movement. Negritude was influenced by French intellectual circles, the Communist Party, and the American Negro literary world, especially through Richard Wright, which provided a link to Pan-Africanism. *Présence Africaine* began with a Comité de Patronage (dropped in 1955) which included Sartre, Gide, Camus, and Mounier. This milieu also provided an influence through surrealism, the attempt to liberate the imagination from the control of reason. Surrealism sought to answer the distortions of a rational, industrial society by an appeal to the senses and a renewal of the so-called primitive vision. Surrealism wanted to wrest from the unknown knowledge born of revelation, the marvelous. In Aragon's phrase, "Reality is the apparent absence of contradiction. The marvelous is the eruption of contradiction within the real."[6]

As was mentioned, the Negritude poets were also influenced by Marxism. But Cesaire, who was a member of the French National Assembly, as a Communist from Martinique, left the Party in 1956. In his letter of resignation to Maurice Thorez he wrote, "we, men of color, in this precise moment of historical evolution, have, in our consciousness, taken possession of the whole domain of our particularity and we are ready at all levels and in all matters to assume the responsibilities which devolve from this consciousness. . . . What I want is that Marxism and Communism be placed at the service of black peoples and not black peoples at the service of Marxism and Communism."[7]

What is Negritude? In the light of colonialism's cultural domination, Negritude is "a means toward the achievement of a sense of full cultural identity and a normal self-pride in the cultural context" (Samuel Allen). The French enforced assimilation, said Senghor, "and thus deepened our despair. We could assimilate mathematics or the French language, but we could never strip off our black skins or root out our black souls." Negritude is a reaction against the notion that there is one civilization with a capital C, a destruction of stereotypes, a correction of distortions, a defense against cultural genocide, a rejection of systematized imitation. Negritude is a search for a useable past, a turning to tradition for inspiration, a rediscovery of African culture, a rehabilitation of history, an awareness of a common heritage.

Negritude is self-assertion, self-esteem, a retention of dignity, self-pride, cultural identity by affirming the beauty of blackness. Negritude is a non-political nationalism, a way to assert independence, but within it is the notion that political independence is possible if cultural independence is assured. Negritude is a link between leaders (who are caught between modernization and tradition, development and democracy) and the masses (who are caught in the disorganization of urbanization and culture clash). Negritude is, functionally, the construction of a new mythology, an acceptance and an affirmation of the quality of blackness, an assertion of the collective Negro-African personality.

Negritude creates this new mythology by affirming unique Negro-African characteristics. In Senghor's words, "Negritude is the whole complex of civilized values—cultural, economic, social and political—which characterize the black peoples, or, more precisely, the Negro-African world."[8] "Negritude as we had started to conceive of it," he writes in retrospect, "was a defensive and at the same time an offensive weapon. . . . Among its values we only retained the ones that were opposed to those of Europe; to discursive, logical, instrumental reason. Negritude was intuitive Reason, reason-that-grasps and not reason-that-sees. To be precise, it was the warmth of communion, the image-symbol and cosmic rhythm which instead of sterilizing by dividing, fertilized by uniting."[9]

The essence of Negritude, then, is "intuitive reason"—a revolt against reason in the European sense. Negritude is reason which expresses itself emotionally, through self-surrender, through a coalescence of subject and object. It is the active abandon of the African toward the object. European reason is analytic through utilization; Negro reason is intuitive through participation. Negritude is softness—and a non-mechanical approach to men and things. Negritude is spirituality—and a direct but symbol-laden approach to sex. It expresses itself through primordial rhythms, synchronized with the cosmos. It is the sense of communion, the gift of myth-making, the gift of rhythm. It is humor, imagery, emotion. Negritude is, in short, soul.

The poems of Negritude[10] can be classified into a number of categories. One is the comprehension of the destructiveness of colonialism, a sensitivity to "the time of martyrdom," the realization that colonial governments built more prisons than hospitals. David Diop writes:

> The white man killed my father
> My father was proud
> The white man raped my mother
> My mother was beautiful
> The white man bent my brother under the highway
> sun
> My brother was strong
> The white man turned toward me
> His hands red with black blood
> And in the voice of a Master:
> "Hey boy! bring me a whisky, a napkin, and some
> water"

From Damas' poem "SOS":

> You will see them
> really stop at nothing
> no longer content to laugh with restless forefinger
> when they see a Negro going by
> but coldly beating up
> coldly knocking down
> coldly laying out
> coldly
> beating up
> knocking down
> laying out
> the blacks and cutting off their genitals
> to make candles for their churches

And Damas' "Limbe," in which he lists that which has been taken from him:

> Will they ever know this rancor in my heart?
> From beneath suspicion's eye that opened all too
> late

they have robbed me of the space that once was
          mine
tradition
days
life
song
rhythm
effort
pathway
water
cabin
the gray, fertilized land
wisdom
words
palavers
the aged
cadence
hands
measure
hands
footbeats
soil

From David Diop:

Africa my Africa. . . .
Your beautiful black blood spilled through the
          fields
The blood of your sweat
The sweat of your labor
The labor of your slavery
The slavery of your children
Oh tell me, Africa
Is this really you, the back bent
And laid low by the weight of your meekness
This trembling, red-striped back
Which says yes to the whip on the noonday roads

And from Senghor's "Chaka":

I saw in a dream all the lands to the far corners of
          the horizon set under the ruler, the set-
          square, the compass

Forests mowed down, hills levelled, valleys and rivers in chains.
I saw the lands to the four corners of the horizon
under the grid traced by the twofold iron
ways
I saw the people of the South like an anthill of silence
At their work, work is holy, but work is no longer
gesture.
Drum and voice no longer make rhythm for the ges-
tures of the seasons.
Peoples of the South, in the ship yards, the ports
and the mines and the mills
And at evening segregated in the kraals of misery.
And the peoples heap up mountains of black gold
and red gold—and die of hunger
I saw one morning, coming out of the mist of the
dawn, a forest of woolly heads
Arms drooping, bellies hollow, immense eyes and
lips calling to an impossible god
Could I stay deaf to such suffering, such
contempt? . . .
I did not hate the Pink Ears. We welcomed them as
messengers of the gods
With pleasant words and delicious drinks.
They wanted merchandise. We gave them every-
thing: ivory, honey, rainbow pelts
Spices and gold, precious stones, parrots and mon-
keys.
Shall I speak of their rusty presents, their tawdry
beads?
Yes, in coming to know their guns, I became a mind
Suffering became my lot, suffering of the breast and
of the spirit.

From the domination of colonialism came a sense of the
consequent loss of cultural identity. James E.K. Aggrey, the
African-born American educator visiting Africa for the Phelps-
Stokes Fund, reported African children singing for him during
his inspection of African schools. They sang "The British Gren-
adiers," "Coming Through the Rye," "Rule, Britannia." "They
laughed when their own native songs were mentioned. . . . The

children could often tell what happened in 1066, but of the history of their own country they knew nothing." "An African woman educated in a missionary school recounted learning 'A is for apple'—in a country where apples don't grow.''[11] The Negritude poets express this loss of identity through motifs of alienation and exile. From Damas:

> Paris – Exile
> My heart keeps alive
> the double regret
> For the very first awakening to the beauty of the
>   world
> And the first Negro to die on the line

> ———

> let's talk about those people
> wailing with rage and shame
> at being born in the Antilles . . .
> at being born anywhere except beside
> the Seine or Rhone. . . .
> Those people who refuse to have a soul
> those people who despise themselves. . . .
> Those people who think they can make their lips
>   thinner
> by biting them
> until they bleed. . . .
> Those people whose unchanging slavish attitude
> insults the beauteous age-old wisdom
> of their own Elders.

From Diop:

> My brother, with teeth gleaming at hypocritical com-
>   pliments
> My brother with golden spectacles
> Worn on eyes rendered blue by the Master's word.
> My poor brother in your tux with silk lapels
> Squealing and hissing and strutting around in the
>   parlors of condescension
> We pity you.

Damas ridicules his childhood "limited by the imposition of false cultural standards and stifled by unnatural social patterns":

> Hands on the table
> break your bread
> don't cut it
> don't waste it. . . .
> Bones should be eaten with measure and discretion
> a stomach should be sociable
> and all sociable stomachs
> refrain from belching
> a fork is not a toothpick . . .
> a well brought up nose
> Keeps well out of one's plate. . . .
> If you haven't learned your history lesson
> you can't go to mass. . . .
> Be quiet
> Have I told you or not that you have to speak
>   French
> the French of France
> the French of Frenchmen
> French French

> A banjo
> did you say a banjo
> what do you mean
> a banjo
> did you really say
> a banjo
> No, sir
> you must know we won't stand for any
> bon
> jos
> or gui
> tars
> *mulattoes* don't do that
> leave that for the *Negroes.*

> I feel ridiculous
> among them an accomplice

among them a pimp
among them a murderer
my hands frightfully red
with the blood of their
CI-
VI-
LI-
ZA-
TION

What Negritude makes possible is a return from exile, an abnegation of the alienation and loss through a symbolic return to authentic, natural African sources. Hence the themes: continuity, flow, timelessness, earth, nature, the rhythm of life, ritualizing the earth and life, the permanence of tribal masks, the power of the earthy black woman. Negritude explores essences, but essence and rhythm move together to bring abandon and freedom and the power to put everything into rhythmic movement, i.e., dance. Thus Negritude re-establishes the harmonious relationship of things fragmented into discontinuity by the colonialist introduction of an alien culture. These Negritude poems consciously reject Europe and Europeans in the sense of a Senegalese student's words: "But here come the 'Civilizers' with cannon and Bible aimed at the African heart." Or in Cesaire's terms: "The hour of the barbarian has arrived. The modern barbarian. The American hour. Violence, excessiveness, waste, mercantilism, bluff, gregariousness, stupidity, vulgarity, disorder." From Senghor's poem "New York":

But two weeks of the bare sidewalks of Manhattan
—At the end of the third week the fever seizes you
    with the pounce of a leopard
Two weeks without rivers or fields, all the birds of
    the air
Falling sudden and dead on the high ashes of flat
    roof tops.
No smile of a child blooms, his hand refreshed in
    my hand,
No mother's breast, but only nylon legs. Legs and
    breasts that have no sweat or smell.
No tender words for there are no lips, only artificial
    hearts paid for in hard cash

And no book where wisdom may be read. . . .
New York! I say to you: New York let black blood
flow into your blood
That it may rub the rust from your steel joints, like
an oil of life,
That it may give to your bridges the bend of but-
tocks

And Cesaire's ironic lines:

I too
Have assassinated God with my laziness
with my words with my actions with my obscene
songs . . .
I have tried the missionaries' patience
insulted the benefactors of mankind. . . .
The extent of my perversity confounds me!

Out of this rejection comes the heart of Negritude: self-accep-
tance, the affirmation of a positive identity. From Cesaire:

No, we were never horsemen for the King of Dahomey nor princes
of Ghana with 800 camels nor doctors in Timbuktu when Askia
the Great was King nor the architects of Djeune nor Mahdis nor
warriors. The pits of our arms do not itch like those of men who
used to wield the lance. And since I have sworn not to conceal
anything of our history (I who admire nothing so much as a sheep
grazing at its afternoon shadow), I want to confess that from time
immemorial we have been lousy dishwashers, shoeshine boys of
limited scope, fairly conscientious sorcerers (looking on the bright
side) and the only record we've ever beaten indisputably is that of
endurance to the whip. . . . And the whole thing added up per-
fectly to a hideous Negro, a grumbling, melancholy Negro, a
sprawling Negro, comical and ugly. . . . An unexpected and bene-
ficial inner revolution now makes me honor my repulsive ugliness.

Here is Damas:

Give my black dolls back to me that I may play
my instinct's naive games with them
my instinct kept protected by its laws
my courage recovered

and my audacity
I am myself again
a new self
from what I was yesterday
yesterday
uncomplicated
yesterday
when the hour of uprooting came.

And Diop:

Black girl my warm sound of Africa
My land of enigma and fruit of my reason
You are dance in the naked joy of your smile
By your proffered breasts and secret powers
You are dance in dizziness. . . .
By the magic of loins that start up the world again

From R.A. Armattoe:[12]

Our god is black
Black of eternal blackness
With large voluptuous lips
Matted hair and brown liquid eyes . . .
For in his image we are made
Our god is black.

And Cesaire:

Listen to the white world
horribly exhausted by its immense effort
its rebellious joints cracking under the hard
            stars. . . .
Pity for our omniscient naive conquerors!
Hurrah for those who never invented anything
for those who never explored anything
for those who never conquered anything.

And Damas again:

The white will never be Negro
For beauty is Negro
and Negro is wisdom

for endurance is Negro
and Negro is courage
for patience is Negro
and Negro is irony

A number of question marks have to be set over against the concept of Negritude. Certainly the demand "Let me be me!" can be appreciated, but there is a legitimate question as to how artificial or contrived Negritude is. The Nigerian writer Wole Soyinka asks if the tiger finds it necessary to proclaim his tigritude.[13] Obviously the tiger simply is what he is, and the fact that Negritude needs to be proclaimed reveals the fundamental ambivalence of Negritude as a solution to the problem of identity. In fact, the African is caught between tradition and modernization, tribe and city, Europe and Africa, and in this transitional clash of cultures it may be necessary for him to over-affirm his unique heritage, partly for psychological stability, partly to free himself from the game of assimilation in which white men hold all the cards.

Cesaire has said, "We shall not come empty-handed to the rendezvous of give and take." In whatever new cultural patterns are now emerging, Africa certainly has its own special traditions and values to contribute. The question here is whether Africa's unique characteristics are in any way appropriate to the technical society which is emerging all around the earth. One can argue that reason-that-feels is precisely what the rational-bureaucratic world needs, but that begs the question, which is whether there is any chance of getting it. Especially if one believes that Negritude's glorification of the non-material is a psychologically necessary defense mechanism, but a realistically impractical reaction against the inevitably encroaching domination of white Western materialistic culture.

The situation is ambiguous at best if Africa has to assert its own traditions in order to stay afloat and move toward modernization and "progress," while those same traditional characteristics are precisely the ones which make modernization and change more difficult. Now that Senghor the poet has become President of Senegal he is reported to have said that his country needs fewer poets and more engineers. The question is how realistic Negritude's romantic naturalism can be in the modern world. In 1959, under the threat of French nuclear tests in the Sahara, a member of the Nigerian parliament said, "Blackism is the answer to our problems." And Paul Moraud has remarked that "The Negroes have rendered an enormous service to America. But for them, one might have thought that men could not live without a bank account or a bathtub."

Of course, men can live without bank accounts and bathtubs, but the question is whether they choose to, whether their lack is a virtue, and what kind of society it is that forces people to make virtues out of neutral or negative circumstances or characteristics in order to survive psychologically and culturally. The issue is further complicated by the fact that it is probably impossible to pick and choose among the aspects of modernization. Achebe is quite right in having a character say, "The white man, the new religion, the soldiers, the new road—they are all part of the same thing."[14] Put another way, the issue is whether a Vermont commune is a viable alternate life style to what's wrong with our society or a naive and irresponsible illusion of freedom. It's probably both, but even if it is the former, it can be argued that saying "Hurrah for those who never invented anything" is not exactly meeting the problems of the twentieth century head-on.

A more serious question about Negritude is whether or not it is racist. The poets of Negritude were socialized into a dominant culture which rejected blackness as well as native "primitivism." Do these poets seek to destroy racist stereotypes or have they consciously or unconsciously internalized and accepted them? It appears as if the black qualities their poetry glorifies are the very characteristics a racist society uses to demean, denigrate, and control Negroes. Racism's stereotypic image portrays blacks as childlike, primitive, irrational, rhythmical, emotional, sexual, natural, closer to the earth, deficient in technical inventiveness and competence, limited to "pre-logical" minds, etc. These themes certainly run through the Negritude poems.

Senghor makes it explicit. "The Negro is quite different. American psychotechnicians have already confirmed that his reflexes are more natural, better adapted. That explains his utilization in industry and in the technical service of the armed forces in a higher percentage than that which he represents in the population of the U.S.A." St. Clair Drake, the American Negro scholar, says that blacks have heard all this before—from their enemies and patronizing white friends. This approach substitutes mysticism for science, according to Drake, who is shocked to find pseudo-scientific rationalizations for segregation and discrimination interpreted by Senghor as welcome facts. Drake further maintains that there is nothing unique about the particular traits Negritude honors; they are simply the characteristics of any folk society anywhere.[15]

Sartre recognizes the existence of this problem and refers to Negritude as anti-racist racism. That is, it is a dialectical relationship, the point and purpose of which is to destroy racism. In this sense, Negritude is a psychological and cultural self-affirmation which transforms the negative stereotypes of racism into positive and prideful qualities. The goal is the liberation of the black man from mental colonialism. The terms are the black man's own, although it is necessary to realize that the characteristics involved come from the white oppressor's defining perception of the oppressed. In this light the necessity for Negritude reveals racism's most subtle and insidious power: the ability of white supremacy to make black men see themselves in white terms, and to make the victims of the system feel responsible for their own victimization.

Perhaps Negritude is a transitional stage, at least for Africans, between colonialism and independence. Certainly for much of Africa it provided a theoretical base for the emergence of "the African Personality," "African Socialism," and "one-party democracy." These are all present attempts at ideological, economic, and political forms which are relevant both to the indigenous culture of the past and the hoped-for modernization of the future. Senghor has recently enlarged the term "Negritude" to "Africanite" in the interests of African unity,[16] and a new line added to the Senegalese national anthem reads, "The Bantu is a brother and the Arab and the white man." The self-assertion of Negritude is at least a major link between the ugliness of colonialist exploitation and the beauty of cooperative brotherhood.

—An undated [1969?] lecture delivered at Boston University

Notes

1. This analysis of British and French colonialism is taken from William J. Hanna's essay "The Politics of Freedom" in William J. Hanna, ed., *Independent Black Africa* (Chicago: Rand McNally and Co., 1964), pp. 8, 16–17, 42.
2. Quoted by Raymond L. Buell, *The Native Problem in Africa* (New York: The Macmillan Co., 1928), vol. 2, p. 81.
3. Paul E. Sigmund, ed., *The Ideologies of Developing Nations*, rev. ed. (New York: Frederick A. Praeger, 1967), p. 213.
4. These two strains and the Congress of Black Artists and Writers are discussed by Immanuel Wallerstein, *Africa: The Politics of Unity* (New York: Random House, 1967), pp. 10–15.
5. Jean-Paul Sartre, *Black Orpheus* (Paris: Présence Africaine, n.d.), p. 11.
6. Simon W. Taylor, "Liberation Then," *The New York Review of Books*, XIV, 1 and 2 (January 29, 1970), 43–45.
7. Wallerstein, p. 15.
8. Leopold Senghor, "What Is 'Negritude'?" *West Africa* (November 4, 1961).
9. Leopold Senghor, "Negritude and Marxism," *Africa in Prose*, ed. O.R. Dathorne and Willfried Feuser (Baltimore: Penguin Books, 1969).
10. The following poems unless otherwise indicated are taken from Wilfred Cartey, *Whispers from a Continent: The Literature of Contemporary Black Africa* (New York: Vintage Books, 1969), and Mercer Cook and Stephen E. Henderson, *The Militant Black Writer in Africa and the United States* (Madison: The University of Wisconsin Press, 1969).
11. Edwin W. Smith, *Aggrey of Africa* (London: SCM Press, 1929), p. 150.
12. Quoted by Colin Legum, "The Roots of Pan-Africanism," in *Africa*, ed. Colin Legum (New York: Frederick A. Praeger, 1966), p. 415.
13. G.E. Von Grunebaum, *French African Literature: Some Cultural Implications* (The Hague: Mouton and Co., 1964), p. 18.
14. Chinua Achebe, *Arrow of God* (Garden City: Anchor Books, 1969), p. 97.
15. St. Clair Drake, "Hide My Face?" *Soon, One Morning*, ed. Herbert Hill (New York: Alfred A. Knopf, 1966), pp. 88 ff.
16. Nathan Hare, "Algiers 1969: A Report on the Pan-African Cultural Festival," *The Black Scholar*, I, 1 (November 1969), 7 ff.

Washington and Du Bois: Integration and Separatism in American Negro Protest

The failure of reconstruction following the Civil War appeared to be a failure of integration. That is, citizenship for the freedmen, the ballot, and civil rights did not result in the incorporation of blacks into the society. The reason is threefold. Southern whites resolved to regain political control, which they did through terrorism, subterfuge, and legislative enactments made possible by the Compromise of 1877. Blacks were effectively disenfranchised by the turn of the century. As soon as it could, the white South legislated an elaborate system of social segregation which was designed to institutionalize not merely distinctions based on race but a qualitative differentiation. Both these enterprises could be successful only because of the indifference of the national Republican party and the federal government and the consistent complicity of the Supreme Court. The third cause underlay the other two. The freed slaves had no economic base from which to withstand the private, political, and legal onslaughts on their citizenship. The Union's post-war failure to break up the large southern plantations and institute land reform meant that in such an agricultural society most blacks were thrown into tenant farming, sharecropping, and feudal peonage not noticeably superior to chattel slavery.

In a sense, then, integration did not so much fail as, in the main, remain untried because white people would not tolerate it. This apparent inability of political action and civil rights to integrate the freedmen thus opened the way for a shift in emphasis from politics to economics, from integration to separation, and from dependence on the white community to self-reliance. This shift is most clearly discernible in the ascendency of Booker T. Washington (1856–1915), his immediate national recognition as a result of his Atlanta Exposition address of 1895, and his assignation by whites as the chief spokesman of the Negro race. Frederick Douglass remained an exponent of protest and integration until his death in, appropriately, the same year as Washington's well-known compromise speech.

Washington symbolized a trend characteristic of the 1880's and 90's. Denied social equality, political, and civil rights, Negroes began to emphasize the acquisition of property, economic self-help, moral development, racial pride and solidarity, and a separate, self-segregated group life. Industrial education became the hallmark of the new movement since it satisfied all the groups involved: worsening conditions and the bankruptcy of Reconstruction made Negroes turn to an alternate program than civil rights; southern whites saw industrial education as a means to relegate blacks to a permanently inferior position; northern whites saw in it an opportunity both for philanthropy and the creation of a semi-skilled labor force. In his program of placating whites, Washington's economic emphasis led to a new separatism and his accommodationism became a new form of nationalism. He said, as had Martin Delany, who advocated emigration to Africa in the 1850's, "We are a nation within a nation."

Washington believed that the Negroes' permanent home was not only in the United States but specifically in the South. This meant both a lack of identification with Africa and the necessity of making it possible for blacks "to live friendly and peaceably with white neighbors both socially and politically." Washington's whole philosophy, which remained consistent throughout his career, was thus geared to accepting the realities of the black man's situation, conciliating the white South (where most Negroes lived), and urging Negroes to improve themselves by accepting the Social Darwinism, laissez-faire capitalism, and Protestant work ethic ideologies common to the time. Although the self-help philosophy could be interpreted as making Negroes themselves responsible for their situation, in its positive aspects it involved racial pride, group cohesion, and hope for the future based on confidence in one's own abilities.

This new nationalism did not involve for Washington an emphasis on a unique Negro culture, although it did stress black social and institutional separation. In the "Atlanta Compromise" speech, he said, "In all things purely social we can be as separate as the fingers, yet one as the hand in all things essential to mutual progress." "Agitation of questions of social equality is the extremest folly," Washington held; if there was to be an end to racial prejudice and discrimination in "our beloved Southland" it would be some vague future and undefined form. What was clear for Washington was that black men must earn their rights and that economic achievement was the means: "No race that has anything to contribute to the markets of the world is long, in any degree, ostracized."

In the meantime Jim Crow was not to be opposed. In segregated railroad transportation, for example, Washington maintained that "what embitters the colored people . . . is not the separation, but the inadequacy of the accommodations." Segregation was not merely to be tolerated, however; racial solidarity is to be affirmed and separation positively understood as an opportunity: "Let us, in the future, spend less time talking about the part of the city that we cannot live in, and more time in making the part of the city that we can live in beautiful and attractive."

Politically, Washington manifested a separatist posture by eschewing political agitation and action. "I have always advised my race," he wrote to the Louisiana State Constitutional Convention, "to give attention to acquiring property, intelligence and character, as the necessary bases of good citizenship, rather than to mere political agitation." Believing that "too much stress has been placed upon the mere matter of voting and holding political office," it is not surprising to find Washington supporting restrictions on the franchise in terms of property and educational tests. Although he expressed hope that these limitations would be applied to the poor and ignorant of both races, their enactment meant in effect the disenfranchisement of blacks by the revision of state constitutions. Washington optimistically held that "The best course to pursue in regard to the civil rights bill in the South is to let it alone; let it alone and it will settle itself."

In the interrelationship of politics and economics, that is, of the acquisition of political and civil rights on the one hand, and financial progress and improvement on the other, Washington held economic self-advancement to be the necessary precondition. "Elevation" would bring respect, and rights would be granted to black people by white people because black people had demonstrated that they had earned them. Essentially, however, Washington's appeal was to black people, urging them to self-consciousness, solidarity, and self-improvement. The future was always tactfully unspecific and unspecified.

"We ask help for nothing that we can do for ourselves,"

Washington said of the Tuskegee Normal School, and he meant that dictum to be the motto of the whole Negro advance. Asserting that Reconstruction had forced Negroes to begin at the top rather than at the bottom of life, he admonished blacks to "Cast down your bucket where you are" since "No race can prosper till it learns that there is as much dignity in tilling a field as in writing a poem." Economic self-help was possible through applying the gospel of wealth, conciliating the white south, and racial solidarity and separation. Washington made clear that "in every wise and legitimate way our people are taught to patronize racial enterprises." Washington's emphasis, then, was the essentially nationalistic, separatist posture of self-reliance, self-pride, self-segregation, and racial cohesion.

Led by W.E.B. Du Bois, reaction set in against Booker T. Washington because of the dominating power of the "Tuskegee Machine," the conviction that a "Talented Tenth" of black intellectuals were better qualified as racial leaders than the products of mere industrial education, and the question: "Is it possible, and probable, that nine million of men can make effective progress in economic lines if they are deprived of political rights?" Du Bois openly attacked the Washingtonian program in an essay in 1904, which included a substantial critique of Washington for asking blacks to give up insistence on civil rights and accept membership in a "servile caste." Du Bois considered the period around the turn of the century, when Washington's influence was paramount, to be more critical than Reconstruction: Negroes were being lynched at the rate of nearly five a week, they were segregated into jobs as unskilled labor in industry and domestic service, they were being educated only to be tractable, and "a legal caste system based on race and color, had been openly grafted on the democratic constitution of the United States."

Perhaps no figure in American Negro history is more difficult to classify than Du Bois. He is the "epitome of the paradoxes." Through his long life (1868–1963) and extensive writing he held a variety of positions, ranging from early support of Washington to his ultimately joining the Communist party. He has been labelled a "revolutionary antagonist," a "cultural nationalist," a "cultural pluralist," a proponent of "Negro-Americanism," etc. Crucial to an understanding of Du Bois is his perception of the inherent duality of the American black situation, the "inner psychological paradox" of being a black citizen in a racist society. "In the folds of this European civilization," he wrote, "I was born and shall die, imprisoned, conditioned, depressed, exalted, and inspired. Integrally a part of it and yet, much more significant, one of its rejected parts." Experiencing within himself the ambivalence of "two-ness"—being both an American and a Negro—Du Bois' whole career was an attempt to reconcile that paradox, the contradiction of identity.

Although his different stances reflect the complexity and evolution of his thought and involvement, Du Bois is most consistently, and therefore best understood as, a pluralist-integrationist. That is, he worked for full citizenship rights for Negroes, whom he defined as Americans in limited and restricted ways, and at the same time he worked to strengthen the black community as such. This latter effort he understood as partially an end in itself, and partially as the only means for achieving the eventual destruction of prejudice and discrimination. It had, also, a larger purpose, via Pan-Negroism and Pan-Africanism, in providing black American leadership on behalf of submerged, but rising people of color everywhere. This, in turn, would generate inspiration for continuing the struggle at home.

Given his own intellectual abilities and unusual academic opportunities and accomplishments, it is easy to see why Du Bois would oppose Washington's industrial education with the notion that an intellectual elite was the best hope for the race, and why he could believe that "Eventually with them and in mass assault, led by culture, we were going to break down the boundaries of race." With his own leadership gifts, it is easy to see why he would resent Washington's virtually unchallenged and dictatorial role as the chief spokesman for all black Americans. Du Bois' earliest commitments were to racial solidarity, economic development, and the cultivation of the middle-class virtues, but he believed that political agitation and action was the best course to pursue. Du Bois' early intellectual approach was broadened by his realization that "one could not be a calm, cool, and detached scientist while Negroes were lynched, murdered, and starved." His political approach was modified by his realization that economic realities underlay political realities: "Politics and economics became but two aspects of a united body of action and effort."

The economic emphasis of the times which had found expression in the Washingtonian movement thus influenced Du Bois as well as his later discovery of Marx, and he sought to find a balance between political action and economic advancement. Tied to this was his perception that culturally Negroes are, despite segregation, "brought up like other Americans" yet at the same time have a unique and distinct culture of their own: "There is without doubt a certain group expression of art which can be called American Negro." Du Bois thus saw the necessity for an equilibrium of economic, political, and cultural components both to define the black man's situation in America and to construct a coherent ideology and consistent program of action for social change.

Du Bois' goal for American Negroes was neither permanent subordination nor amalgamation. It was to make a positive use of the frustration which came from the impossibilities both of being accepted by the dominant society and of merely being victims of that rejection. Therefore, Du Bois both affirmed and denied integration. He affirmed it in maintaining that constant demands for equality on all fronts are the only way to change the demeaning environment in which black people actually live. He denied it in his realization that Negroes are the "subjects" of the nation, that no direct action on the part of blacks themselves is going to alter their situation, and that the integrationist approach—"hammering at the doors of the larger group"—is a long "campaign of work and wait" until the folkways of the white society grant equality.

At the same time Du Bois also affirmed and denied separatism. Migration appeals to "prouder and more independent Negroes, tired of begging" for integration, but unskilled, uneducated blacks are "unfit for pioneers." European colonialism made Africa "the last place for freedom" and Negroes, as Americans, "have no Zion" anyway. The separatism advocated by Washington, although designed to evoke sympathy and justice from whites, ran the danger of hopelessness unless the dominant group saw its own best interests tied up with the progress of Negroes. Self-segregation could create cities of refuge, but it could also spawn centers of resentment and submission to oppression. Yet either from external pressure or internal desire, American Negroes lived, in fact, a separate group life including institutions and other cultural forms, and group affirmation necessarily involved the affirmation of that reality.

Laying out these contradictions, Du Bois proposed a third alternative. Believing economic discrimination to be fundamental, capitalism to be collapsing, and continuing segregation to be inevitable, Du Bois advanced the notion of a cooperative commonwealth. By controlling the already segregated Negro economy, blacks could use their power as consumers in a kind of group socialism eventually to influence production, particularly to encourage production by Negroes. He was careful to point out that his plan was neither segregation nor nationalism. The ultimate objective was still full Negro rights and equality: "This is our country. . . . our wrongs are still wrong." Du Bois wanted to use the realities of segregation in a positive and constructive way for economic self-support and progress, believing that this would ultimately erase the color line. Self-segregation could be an opportunity to make Negroes "spiritually free for initiative and creation in other and wider fields, and for eventually breaking down all segregation."

Essentially the scheme is a combination of Washingtonian self-help, N.A.A.C.P.-type agitation, a Marxist interpretation of economics and history, and tribal African communalism. Despite its weaknesses, it is the most carefully thought out, inclusive, and comprehensive doctrine ever constructed for a black program in America. But no popular movement followed Du Bois' attempts at synthesis and not that much critical attention was paid to his proposal, perhaps because it was spelled out immediately prior to the Second World War. It is true that Du Bois swung back and forth between the ideological poles of integration and nationalism. But what this means is that Du Bois himself tended to focus, as different circumstances arose, on the different components of his schema rather than on the whole. Thus politically he continued his battle for greater justice, equality, and civil rights both inside and outside the N.A.A.C.P.; culturally, he strengthened ties with Africa and eventually moved to Ghana; economically, his Marxism led him finally into the Communist party after he had been, at various times, a Republican, a Democrat, and a Socialist.

Du Bois began as a scholar because he believed that facts spoke for themselves and that with correct information the world could be changed. He discovered that not to be so. Reacting against Washington's accommodationism, which he regarded as capitulation to racism, he nevertheless retained the Washingtonian doctrines of economic self-help and racial solidarity. Through his role in the founding of the militant Niagara Movement and the N.A.A.C.P., for which he is of course popularly best known, he moved to integrationist legal and political agitation to demand civic rights, although he knew that blacks could never wrest equality from whites. His acceptance of socialism led him to define economics as basic, although he knew that white workers rejected black workers because of racism and that the Marxist analysis was, at least in this crucial area, inadequate. An international worldview as well as the need to re-create prideful roots and inspiration led him to emphasize the African heritage and culture, although he knew that black Americans were not Africans.

The fundamental issue, then, remained the unique "two-ness" of the black American experience and identity. Du Bois' emphasis on the Negro's Americanism made him push for integrationist equality as if race made no difference; his emphasis on the black American's negritude forced him toward deeper racial consciousness and even to operate on the same presupposition as the "enveloping" society where social differentiation is racially determined. As has been shown, Du Bois' ideological solution was a synthesis of the two: integration and pluralism. He believed that Negroes were too American to be "a nation within a nation," yet separation existed in reality and blacks had the opportunity to advance themselves through creative self-segregation at the same time as they fought for full admission to the dominant society. Thus the ambivalences which Du Bois recognized as implicit in the American Negro's situation were necessarily carried over into his synthesis. "Illogical trends and irreconcilable tendencies" were inevitably inherent in Du Bois' solution because they were inherent in the problem.

It is curious that Washington's pleasant accommodationism should be, in reality, a form of separatism and nationalism and that Du Bois' assorted Marxism, Pan-Africanism, and abrasive militancy should be essentially integrationist in nature. Through the motifs of self-liberation and self-determination which currently characterize the black movement, Negroes are again wrestling with the questions of identity, emphasis, goals, and means. The issues of separation and integration, accommodation and pluralism—what these concepts mean and how they do and should interrelate—are again very much alive.

—*Boston University Journal* 18:2 (Spring 1970), 43–48

Black Religion

Kimbanguism:
An Indigenous Church

"I beg to direct your attention to Africa." This sentence introduced the last paragraph of one of the most sensational addresses
ever made to a university audience—David Livingstone's talk at
Senate House, Cambridge, on the morning of December 4, 1857.
Professor Adam Sedgwick, the geologist, said that no speech had
ever aroused more intense excitement.

Livingstone had of course recently returned triumphant to
Britain after his first extraordinary four-year journey to Africa,
tracing the Zambezi River and, in a twenty-month trek, crossing
the continent from the Atlantic Coast to the Indian Ocean. The
popular hero concluded his Cambridge address: "I know that in
a few years I shall be cut off again in that country, which is now
open; do not let it be shut again! I go back to Africa to try to make
an open path for commerce and Christianity; do you carry out
the work which I have begun. I leave it with you."

The phrase "commerce and Christianity" immediately strikes
us as Victorianism at its worst. What Livingstone meant, however, was his belief that the introduction of "legitimate" economic exchange was the only way to defeat the Arab slave trade, a
cause more vital to him than his roles of explorer and missionary,
although he never separated the three enterprises.

Apparently, Livingstone's appeal was in his day that of Peace
Corps, VISTA, and New Politics all rolled into one. At any rate,
and whatever his intention, Africa was indeed open—open to
missionaries, explorers, economic entrepreneurs, and those who
sought political and civil control. By the time the European
scramble for Africa was over, the slave trade was technically
abolished, but a whole continent and a whole race lay in the
chains of colonialism. By 1914 only two African nations, Liberia
and Abyssinia, had retained their autonomy, and the most massive political, social, economic, and psychological exploitation
in human history was an established reality. The African struggle for independence is one of the great chapters in the story of
man's quest for freedom, a struggle which is not sufficiently

known or appreciated in this country and a struggle which is not yet completed.

I, too, "beg to direct your attention to Africa," at least to a portion of that struggle for freedom from white, European, Western domination. The Christian missionaries introduced an alien religion, but one which has taken such powerful popular hold that African Christianity may well represent, as Henry Pitney Van Dusen has suggested, "the day after tomorrow" in the ongoing history of the Christian Church.

Native religious groups began to "break away" in Africa in the latter part of the last century for a variety of reasons. Whatever the positive contributions of the missionaries, some Africans found inconsistencies between missionary belief and practice and the Christian faith and life they discovered in Scripture; missionaries too often sided with their fellow white colonial exploiters against native interests; missionaries too often confused their European and American culture with their religious message and consequently denigrated African customs and institutions; perhaps most important, Africans sought "to be free in their own house," as one expressed it, that is, to have their own churches under their own leadership.

As a result, a whole phenomenon of religious independency, known first as Ethiopianism, came into existence until now there are 6,000 native African Christian movements. These have been studied, analyzed, and classified as sectarianism, syncretism, messianism, prophetism, Zionism, separatism, culture-clash, renewal, dissidence, what-have-you. Let us examine one of these movements in more detail and obtain for ourselves some view of an indigenous African Church.

Simon Kimbangu, born about 1889, was a member of an English Baptist mission in the village of Nkamba in the lower Congo. Although there is uncertainty about his early life, he was probably a catechist for the mission, and possibly a carpenter by trade. In a series of dreams and visions, he heard himself summoned by God to preach and teach, but he felt unworthy and inadequate and resisted his call. In March 1921 the voices became more intense and evasion more difficult. Finally a stranger ordered Kimbangu to visit and pray for a sick child in a neighboring village. When he refused the stranger threatened to take Kimbangu's own soul. He yielded, found the child and placed his hands on him. Kimbangu was seized with violent convulsions, but the child was healed. In the next weeks—the month of April—word about the healing spread through the villages. As the sick flocked to Nkamba, Kimbangu emerged as a prophet. His healing services consisted of prayer, singing, Bible reading, and preaching. Kimbangu's preaching apparently evoked his power and he received the sick in an enclosure outside his house. Carrying a red flag and accompanied by the exuberant singing of his followers, Kimbangu would tremble in ecstasy and say, "In the name of Jesus I will cure you, be whole again." To those more seriously ill he directed the question, "Have you been converted?" If the response was affirmative, Kimbangu said, "Hold fast to Jesus Christ." If he received a negative reply he said, "Change your mind, believe in Jesus Christ and he will save you." There is little factual evidence that healings actually took place, although, as one might imagine, there were extensive unsubstantiated rumors of miraculous cures.

Although faith-healing was the spectacular and popular aspect of Kimbangu's ministry, it is clear that he preached as well. His preaching advocated monogamy and resulted in a large-scale destruction of animistic fetishes and the equipment of magic and witchcraft. His ecstatic convulsions and trances, however, took the same form as those of the native prophets—that is, those who were understood to be intermediaries between the people and supernatural powers.

But it was not only the substance of the preaching and the reputation for healing that brought people by the thousands to Kimbangu's enclosure at "Jerusalem," as his village began to be called. As one writer has it, "The news that the despised 'blacks' now had a prophet of their own swept over the land like a tidal wave." "Not only white people could be great and powerful, for [now] a mighty one"—perhaps even a savior—had arisen "from the ranks of the Africans whom [whites] had scorned." There are clear links, then, even at the beginning, between Kimbangu's prophetic ministry and the latent nationalism of an oppressed people.

The movement grew so rapidly and widely that Kimbangu chose additional prophets from among his followers. And, of course, many who visited Jerusalem re-enacted their experiences when they returned home and became prophets without Kimbangu's sanction. The mark of all these new prophets was Spirit-possession characterized by violent shaking. Loud and enthusiastic singing, often accompanied by dancing, was the way to induce the Spirit. The countryside was ablaze with religious fervor.

It was only days before this enthusiasm came to the attention of the colonial government, chiefly because conscripted men left their enforced work on the plantations, the railroad, and the oil company to make the pilgrimage to Kimbangu's village. On May 11 the Belgian administrator Morel went to Nkamba to investigate. He was confronted by an incredible sight: litters of sick, fifty catechists, forty singing disciples, 700 or 800 followers, and in the midst of it all Simon Kimbangu himself, in red trousers and a white shirt, carrying his staff, hysterical with ecstatic shaking. Kimbangu opened his Bible and in a loud voice read the story of David and Goliath. The point was not lost; Morel withdrew.

The anti-white nature of the movement was now intensified. The natives said, "We have found the God of the blacks." Some prophets urged that natives stop paying taxes. Work was abandoned. There was talk of establishing a native church. At the beginning of June, as might be expected, a warrant was issued for Kimbangu's arrest. An administrator and twenty soldiers entered Nkamba. Kimbangu told his followers, "If they capture me and flog me, you must not use force." He stepped out of the crowd and identified himself: "I am Simon Kimbangu." The soldiers began to beat him, a riot followed, the troops fired, and a baby was killed. The soldiers shut Kimbangu in a house and proceeded to destroy the village; the next day, as one witness recounts, "the ground was left strewn with the pages from the Bibles."

Kimbangu somehow escaped. The movement grew, the miracle stories multiplied, and the nationalistic aspect increasingly combined with a belief that the millennium was near. The notion spread that Africa would be liberated by a black messiah and the whites driven out. Although there is some evidence he was betrayed, in September Kimbangu voluntarily surrendered to arrest. The account of his last days with his disciples reads: "When he came to his village, many people came joyfully forth to meet him, but he said to them: I have only a little time to be with you, for my enemies are nigh unto me. He taught them, saying that they must now believe in God only, and not in him. He prayed for a long time and gave his soul into the hands of God, whereafter he asked the others to pray for him. He then read the 23rd Psalm."

Kimbangu was tried before a military tribunal. He was accused of saying he was the Redeemer of the Blacks, that the God he represented was mightier than the government, and that a national church would be established. He was accused of hostility to the state and among the evidence cited was the singing by his followers of "Onward, Christian Soldiers." On the charge of subversion and general insubordination, Kimbangu was condemned to death. Following the trial, the colonial government intervened with the Belgian King and the sentence was reduced to life imprisonment. Kimbangu was sent to Elizabethville where he spent nearly thirty years in prison. He died in 1950.

At Kimbangu's imprisonment the movement went underground. For security reasons 38,000 natives were deported from the lower Congo. Secret worship services were held in the jungle at night, near waterfalls to hide the sound of the singing. Followers were externally submissive to white rule, but withdrew their children from European-run schools, stopped wearing European clothing, and sought to avoid compromises with the white enemy. The third day of the week—the day Kimbangu's trial had begun—was observed as Sabbath.

Kimbangu himself was more and more viewed not merely as an ordinary human teacher, but as a messianic figure who would deliver the black race. He was expected to return and set himself on the ancient throne of the Congo. In one Kimbanguist congregation's creedal statement Kimbangu is "the one in whom lives the Lord God, the gracious father of the blacks," "the priest of the black race," "the cup with the oil of blessing for the black race," "the river with the living water for the black race," and so on, through thirteen persons. There are thirteen persons, twelve as images of Jesus' apostles, and the other for Kimbangu himself, the thirteenth apostle, who is "the way of salvation for the blacks."

In 1959, when the movement was legalized and could fully emerge from hiding, it had retained many of the characteristics of its Baptist origin: Kimbanguism is pietistic, not theologically oriented, and it rigorously and literally interprets the Bible, particularly the Ten Commandments. In addition, no sacraments are celebrated and there is no clear systematic doctrinal position. And there are distinct African characteristics: shoes are removed in church, for example; jewelry, wallets, and other worldly things are removed for worship; and the church is governed by hereditary leadership—at present by one of Kimbangu's sons.

With over one million adherents, the Church of Jesus Christ on Earth Through the Prophet Simon Kimbangu is now the largest independent African church. Last summer it was received into membership in the World Council of Churches. It is thus "the first expression of indigenous African Christianity to move into the international religious scene" and "the first young church to join the Council that was not the product of Western missionaries and Western theological thought." It joined the World Council not as Protestant or Catholic or Orthodox, but as Kimbanguist—black and African and unique!

There are questions and problems here. In an important way, an independent church like the Kimbanguist reopens the thorny issue of Christ and culture as H. Richard Niebuhr's typology articulates it. God stands over against every culture, and if he judges American Christianity and German Christianity, then he judges African Christianity as well. In addition, syncretism, secularism, and divisiveness are real perils to the Christian cause.

On the other hand, this church—and others like it—are a prophetic judgment against our white, Western Christianity. Historically, an important theme in the struggle for African redemption, in the struggle for the dignity and beauty of blackness, in the struggle for the liberation of black people, is the biblical promise that one day Ethiopia shall stretch forth her hands unto God. God can speak through Simon Kimbangu as clearly as—or more clearly than—he can speak through any of the persons past or present through whom we have heard him speaking. Jesus Christ is as authentic—or more authentic—with a black face as with a white face. God can affirm and use the cultural forms of the lower Congo as well as—or better than—he can affirm and use the cultural forms of middle-class America.

Whatever the insights of the social sciences, it is just too simple to understand a phenomenon like Kimbanguism from their perspectives alone. What the Church of Jesus Christ on Earth Through the Prophet Simon Kimbangu says to us is that God is not restricted by our prejudices or our experiences or our conventions. He can—and does—do new things. An indigenous church holds fast to Jesus Christ and connects with a particular people's life and history. Too often our churches are trivial because they do neither.

—A sermon preached in Marsh Chapel, Boston University, November 15, 1970

The Origins of the
African Orthodox Church

One of the many expressions of black consciousness and nationalism that followed the First World War, the African Orthodox Church (AOC) was associated with Marcus Garvey's Universal Negro Improvement Association (UNIA);[1] it spread to Africa, where it contributed significantly to the emergence of both religious and political independence, and it continues today as the major black denomination with a valid—though, some would add, irregular—episcopate.

The AOC's creation was essentially the work of one man, George Alexander McGuire.[2] McGuire was born on March 26, 1866, in Sweets, Antigua, British West Indies, the eldest son of Edward Henry McGuire, a planter, and his wife, Mary Elizabeth McGuire.[3] Baptized into the Anglican faith of his father, the young McGuire was graduated in 1886 from the Antigua branch of Mico College for Teachers and two years later from the Nisky Theological Seminary in St. Thomas, Virgin Islands. The seminary was operated by the Moravians, the denomination of McGuire's mother. McGuire served as pastor of the Moravian congregation at Fredrickstead, St. Croix, Virgin Islands, until 1893 when he emigrated to the United States and became an American citizen.

After working for a time with the African Methodist Episcopal Church, McGuire applied for membership in the Protestant Episcopal Church. He was confirmed in 1895 by Bishop Coleman of Delaware and enrolled as a candidate for holy orders. He studied under the Rev. Dr. Henry L. Phillips, the Jamaican-born priest of the Church of the Crucifixion in Philadelphia. McGuire was ordained a deacon in 1896, and the following year Bishop Vincent of Southern Ohio ordained him a priest.[4] He then served in a succession of brief pastorates: St. Andrew's, Cincinnati; St. Philip's, Richmond; and Philadelphia's St. Thomas's First African Church, the oldest Afro-American Episcopal parish in America, founded in 1784 by Absalom Jones.

There is no evidence that McGuire was particularly a "race man" at this time, only that he was an unusually able young clergyman. This period was, it must be recalled, what has generally been regarded as the nadir for American blacks, the time that saw the final failure of Reconstruction, the beginnings of the great black exodus from the South to the North, and even the prediction by white sociologists that the race would soon die out.

In 1905 George McGuire found himself confronted by a new situation: direct involvement with the white power structure of the Episcopal Church in the South and its determination to maintain racial supremacy. His administrative skills and preaching ability had won him the highest post in the denomination to which any resident American Negro had, until that time, been appointed, namely Archdeacon for Colored Work in the Diocese of Arkansas. The Bishop of Arkansas at that time was William Montgomery Brown, whose Arkansas Plan for Negroes in the Episcopal Church and the controversy engendered by it were to have a major impact on McGuire's subsequent thinking.[5] Brown was an uneducated man who had married a wealthy woman and had written in 1895 a successful book, *The Church for Americans.* He was consecrated Bishop of Arkansas in 1898 and served in that capacity for fourteen years. At the time Brown was made bishop, the church was still indecisive about its relationship to blacks, especially in the realm of ecclesiastical organization: on the one hand, the white Southerners believed that the church should be evangelizing blacks, but, on the other hand, they did not want to be associated with black people if association implied social equality.

This dilemma was well illustrated in Arkansas by a diocesan resolution of 1871 that declared it the church's duty to formulate a plan "for bringing the claims of the Church before the colored people of this State and the development of a native ministry among them."[6] However, when Brown's predecessor, Bishop Pierce, organized St. Philip's Mission in Little Rock and admitted it to the diocese as a parish in 1889, Christ Church, the largest and wealthiest white church in Little Rock, withdrew both its delegates and assessments from the diocesan council for seven years, ostensibly because the black delegates from St. Philip's showed a "conspicuous incapacity for the difficult task of ecclesiastical legislation and . . . susceptibility to manipulation."[7]

In the Protestant Episcopal denomination, two schemes for resolving the dilemma were debated for over sixty years following their introduction at the General Convention of 1874. One called for the consecration of black suffragans as assistants to white bishops; the other, for establishing black missionary districts under black bishops.[8] Brown proposed a third scheme, the Arkansas Plan, that suggested that blacks have their own Episcopal Church with their own bishops and clergy: "a Church which should be thoroughly autonomous but should bear somewhat the same relation to us as we then bore toward the Church of England."[9] While Brown's plan was based in part on a sincere desire to provide an avenue for black "uplift," it was also motivated by sheer prejudice, and possibly by the fresh memory of Christ Church's financial boycott.[10] The Arkansas Plan found little favorable response within the denomination. It was criticized in the South because it would put blacks and whites on an equal basis and in the North because it was interpreted as a device for segregating the church.

The person who was probably most affected by the Arkansas Plan was George McGuire, who now was brought face to face with the institutional racism of the church and the restrictions it imposed upon the dignity and development of black people, as well as the sharp limitations it set upon the future advancement of able individuals like him. Whatever his own position on Bishop Brown's scheme at the time, McGuire almost certainly carried away from Arkansas the notion of a separate, autonomous black church, and one that was episcopal in character and structure, as one option for black religious self-determination and one avenue for achieving black independence.[11]

From Arkansas McGuire moved to Cambridge, Massachusetts, accepting the invitation of Bishop Lawrence to become priest of St. Bartholomew's Church, a new congregation composed of West Indians who had been denied full participation in a white church.[12] Despite McGuire's spectacular success in his new position—the congregation became the fastest growing in the diocese—the church was not permitted self-supporting status, and McGuire resigned after two years. From 1911 to 1913 he served as Field Secretary of the American Church Institute for Negroes with headquarters in New York.[13] He left this job and returned to his native Antigua. For some five years he served as rector of St.

Paul's Church, one of the Anglican parishes in the island, but
because of personal problems with members of the congregation,
McGuire gave up this ministry and worked for a short time as a
physician in an adjoining parish before returning to the United
States in 1919.[14]

While McGuire was in Antigua, his fellow West Indian, Marcus Garvey, arrived in the United States in 1916 where he was to
inaugurate the first and largest mass movement of black Americans. McGuire, according to one source, "determined to . . . join
forces with him,"[15] though details of the original relationship
between the two men remain unknown. The available information, however, makes clear that McGuire not only identified with
Garvey's "racial vision" but that he began to translate Garvey's
ideology and program of racial independence into religious
form. His idea was to establish an Independent or African Episcopal Church "to include Negroes everywhere," which would
also function as the religious arm of Garvey's UNIA.[16]

This bold concept did not come to McGuire all at once. In
August 1919, a month after his return to the United States from
Antigua, he was licensed by the Episcopal bishop of New York to
assist at the Chapel of the Crucifixion in Harlem. In October,
however, McGuire joined the Reformed Episcopal Church[17] and
the following month organized his own Church of the Good
Shepherd, an Independent Episcopal congregation in New York
made up largely of former Protestant Episcopalians.

In August 1920, at the UNIA's first International Convention
of the Negro Peoples of the World held in New York, McGuire
emerged as a dramatic spokesman for black militancy. According
to the report in *The New York World:*

> Excitement among negro delegates to the Universal Negro Im-
> provement Association in Liberty Hall reached its highest point
> yet last night when about 1,800 gathered to hear the Rev. Dr.
> McGuire of Antigua British West Indies. . . . "The Uncle Tom
> nigger has got to go," he cried, "and his place must be taken by the
> new leader of the negro race. That man will not be a white man
> with a black heart, nor a black man with a white heart, but a black
> man with a black heart."[18]

McGuire subsequently was elected Chaplain-General of the
UNIA by the convention, after the former Chaplain-General, the

Rev. James W.H. Eason, was elected Leader of the American Negroes.[19] McGuire was also given the title of titular Archbishop of Ethiopia. It appears that he saw his election as bestowing upon him the status of the black world's chief ecclesiastical figure, as well as granting him a mandate to establish and preside over a worldwide black church that was coterminous with the membership of the UNIA. Although only recently enrolled as a priest of the Reformed Episcopal Church, McGuire attributed the independence of his Good Shepherd congregation to "an awakened Negro consciousness to the humiliating racial barriers existing in white Episcopal churches." He went on to define his new group as "the harbinger of 'The African Episcopal Church' for whom the New Negro everywhere waits."[20]

While others may have been waiting, McGuire began to act as if "The African Episcopal Church" in fact existed and he were its bishop. Interpreting his office of Chaplain-General and his new ecclesiastical title as a kind of consecration, McGuire referred to himself as "His Grace, the Most Reverend George Alexander McGuire," and went so far as actually to ordain Richard Hilton Tobitt a priest on March 22, 1921.[21] Tobitt left immediately for the West Indies with a dual commission, one from the High Executive Council of the UNIA as leader of the Eastern Province of the West Indies and the second from McGuire as "General Missionary for religious awakening among our people in the islands who desire to have their own religious teachers." This latter commission also required Tobitt to "recommend to his Grace suitable persons on the field who are able to undertake laymen's duties, or who may desire to prepare for Holy Orders."[22]

What McGuire had in mind is clear:

Last August Dr. McGuire . . . received the greatest honor of his career when he was elected Chaplain-General of the Universal Negro Improvement Association, and titular Archbishop of Ethiopia, sworn to be the spiritual guide and moral advisor of the four millions of members of the Association. . . . Archbishop McGuire feels himself fully equipped and authorized for the large work entrusted to his care and supervision, and hopes to prove himself truly an Episcopus, or overseer, of the Church for which Negroes everywhere are looking. When Dr. McGuire left the Church of England in 1919, he left behind him the fragile theory and doctrine of "Apostolic Succession." He believes that the time has come for church unity among Negroes; he believes that unity does not necessarily mean uniformity in worship, and that the coming African or Ethiopian Church will be big enough for all Negroes to enter, retaining their own worship as Methodists, Baptists, Episcopalians, etc. . . . The Negroes of the world in convention assembled made the Most Rev. Dr. G.A. McGuire the first prince of the Church Ethiopic. We understand that plans are under way for his enthronement at the coming Convention in August next.[23]

Believing himself thus authorized by the first UNIA convention to be archbishop of a coming church that would include millions of black members regardless of denomination, McGuire produced two remarkable documents for the "Church Ethiopic," a *Universal Negro Catechism* and *The Universal Negro Ritual*. In question-and-answer form, the *Catechism* was divided into four sections: religious knowledge, historical knowledge, Constitution and Laws of the UNIA, and the UNIA's Declaration of Independence. It presented a black perspective on history and religion that more than fifty years later still reads well. The *Ritual* is a collection of religious services and ceremonies based on the *Book of Common Prayer*. Composed largely of prayers and hymns, the most interesting section is the "Baptism and Dedication of Infants." In the baptismal liturgy McGuire has the priest ask the child's godparents the traditional questions with an innovative addition: "Do you . . . acknowledge the obligation . . . that this child . . . be taught the Creed, the Lord's Prayer, the Ten Commandments, and the *Catechism of the Universal Negro Association*?"[24] The child is then baptized, the flag of the UNIA placed upon him, and the priest says:

> We receive this child into the general membership of the Universal Negro Improvement Association, and lay upon him these colors, the red, the black, and the green, in token that hereafter he may fight manfully under this banner, for the freedom of his race, and the redemption of Africa unto his life's end. Amen.[25]

McGuire obviously spent a busy and productive year following his election as Chaplain-General. Unfortunately, one month before the 1921 convention, and his anticipated enthronement, McGuire's expectations for a universal black church overlapping the UNIA were to be shattered. Precisely what happened is still unknown, but it is not difficult to imagine that McGuire's notion of a universal church, let alone his design for it, did not exactly sit well with the Baptist, Methodist, and Pentecostal rank and file of the UNIA. Moreover, however much Garvey's vision of an international black nation may have been modeled on the British Empire, it did not mean that he also felt the need for an Established Church for the UNIA to correspond with the Church of England.[26] Also, Garvey was out of the country during the first half of 1921 and may not have been aware of what was happening in New York.

At any rate, on July 16, while McGuire was in Cuba on UNIA business, a meeting was held at St. Saviour's Church in Brooklyn, at which McGuire was elected bishop of a group of Independent Episcopal Churches. The same day a notice from John Dawson Gordon, Assistant President-General of the UNIA, appeared in Garvey's *Negro World* under the headline, "U.N.I.A. Favors All Churches, But Adopts None as U.N.I.A. Church." It stated:

> To the divisions of the U.N.I.A. throughout the world: there is a natural tendency on the part of the members of the U.N.I.A., when inducted into the new idealism, to come into it with the idea of a church, and there has been an effort on the part of many in different parts of the country to start a Universal Church. I want it to be distinctly understood, that the U.N.I.A. is not a church, and it does not intend to be one. So far as the present signs are, there will be no church connected with the U.N.I.A. I wish to say if anyone comes around and tells you of a church bearing the name of the U.N.I.A., repudiate it from start to finish, for it is absolutely false. There is no such church as authorized. We favor all churches, but adopt none as a U.N.I.A. Church. Let the presidents and officers of the various locals take notice and govern themselves accordingly.[27]

The message could not have been clearer. But what is not so clear is whether McGuire's episcopal election at St. Saviour's was another step toward the "Church Ethiopic." This seems unlikely, as he already considered himself a bishop. More likely, McGuire, knowing of his coming rejection by the UNIA, decided to proceed without the sanction of Garvey's organization and thus arranged for another base of legitimacy. In any event, McGuire was not enthroned during the second International Convention in August 1921.[28] Early in October *The Negro World* reported the formation of the African Orthodox Church, reiterating the UNIA's principle of not allying itself with any particular church, and announced that "Bishop McGuire resigned as Chaplain-General . . . after his election to the episcopate."[29] Apparently, the reference was to the founding synod of September 2 that officially established the AOC and confirmed McGuire's episcopal election of the previous July.

In late October, however, a dramatic story appeared in the *New York Age* under the headline, "Bishop McGuire Severs All Relations With the U.N.I.A." It stated that McGuire had given up his title at the convention in August and been named "Honorary Chaplain-General." More important, the article also reprinted an exchange of correspondence between McGuire and Garvey, both their letters curiously bearing the same date of October 25. Garvey's letter, a model of patience and restraint, chided McGuire for soliciting money from UNIA members for a "Memorial Abbey" to be built in New York, as well as for offering copies of his photograph and sermons for sale. Citing the "unreadiness among our members at this time to divide up their meagre means on race matters," Garvey admonished McGuire:

> Our members in different parts of the world have their own Liberty Halls to build and their own Organization to put into proper order, hence it is unfair for anyone to use his relationship to inflict personal obligations on our members and to have them believe that it is helping the cause for which our organization was organized.

McGuire's reply was more perfunctory: he resigned both as Honorary Chaplain-General and as a member of the UNIA.[30]

McGuire next seems to have joined the African Blood Brotherhood, a radical black group with Communist Party connections that had unsuccessfully attempted to infiltrate the UNIA. McGuire was said to have provided Cyril Briggs, the Brotherhood's founder and leader, with *The Negro World*'s subscription lists, which Briggs used in mailings of anti-Garvey circulars. Not too subtly, an editorial in *The Negro World* reminded McGuire of the usual fate of traitors.[31] McGuire's intentions—if the charges were accurate—are a puzzle. He was at the time deeply involved with the fledgling AOC, and it is unlikely either that he would stoop to seek revenge against Garvey or that he would expect support for a church from Cyril Briggs.

Again the full details are still unknown, but McGuire and Garvey were subsequently reconciled. In 1923, after Garvey was convicted and held pending bail, McGuire was mentioned as a possible successor.[32] Garvey admitted that of the original twenty-one members of the UNIA's High Executive Council, only McGuire and one other member actually earned their salaries (McGuire's was $5,000).[33] Indeed, in 1925, McGuire wrote an eloquent introduction to *Philosophy and Opinions of Marcus Garvey*, compiled by Garvey's second wife, Amy Jacques-Garvey. McGuire wrote that he was "not ashamed to acknowledge that he is an open follower of this great teacher [Garvey] . . . no man has spoken to us like this man, inculcating pride and nobility of race and pointing out to a downtrodden and discouraged people their Star of Destiny. . . ."

In August 1924 McGuire delivered a memorable address to the UNIA convention, in which he claimed that it was "the height of stupidity and self-negation" for black people to worship a Caucasian deity. Instead, he proposed that blacks should eliminate pictures of a white Christ and white Madonna from their homes, counseling: "Then let us start our negro painters getting busy and supply a black Madonna and a black Christ for the training of our children." The convention meeting at which he spoke was held with a painting of an Ethiopian Christ and black Saint Mary as a backdrop, and hymns were sung in praise of a "Black Man of Sorrows."[34] At the conclusion of the convention, six thousand people in Liberty Hall participated in an elaborate ceremony presided over by McGuire, and at which Garvey also spoke, that "canonized" a black Christ and a black Virgin Mary.[35] This was doubtless a fulfillment of McGuire's injunction: "Erase the white gods from your hearts. We must go back to our own native church to our own God."[36] The concept of a black Christ was never popularly accepted, however, even in the AOC, but it has remained a powerful symbol that reappears in the black nationalist tradition, not least of all within African churches.[37] It is certainly a theme that deserves more attention than it has so far received.

It was at the meeting of Independent Episcopal Churches held on September 2, 1921, at the Good Shepherd Church that the assembled delegates resolved themselves into the first synod of the

African Orthodox Church. McGuire "outlined his vision of a branch of the Holy Catholic Church controlled by Colored Churchmen, gathering people of African descent in all quarters of the globe, yet showing prejudice to no other racial group, nor refusing such in its membership and privileges." The synod debated a name for the new body, rejecting "African Episcopal" and "Holy Orthodox" in favor of McGuire's choice, "African Orthodox," perhaps because he had already begun negotiations for his consecration with that branch of Christendom. McGuire was careful to assert, however, that "the new church was neither schismatic nor heretical," but was rather "an expression of the spirit of racial leadership in ecclesiastical matters, in harmony with the aroused racial consciousness of the Negro people."[38] The group claimed congregations in Brooklyn, Pittsburgh, Nova Scotia, Cuba, and Santo Domingo, with expressions of interest from Bermuda, the West Indies, and Central America.

The most important concern of the new church was securing the episcopate for McGuire. His announcement barely six months earlier that he had "left behind him the fragile theory and doctrine of Apostolic Succession" was apparently a rash statement made when he believed himself already titular Archbishop of Ethiopia and when he had expected the "Church Ethiopic" to encompass all black people. Now he believed that "the time had arrived for the Negro to assume leadership in a branch of the Holy Catholic Church controlled by his race."[39] This meant, as McGuire understood that phrase, that blacks would have to "really possess the Historic Episcopate."[40] As a result, overtures were made to the Episcopal and Roman Catholic bishops of New York, but without success. The Reformed Episcopal Church may also have been contacted, and there were discussions, in addition, with the Russian Orthodox Church, which were also unsuccessful, perhaps because McGuire had no intention of the AOC's being merely a black subdivision of a white church organization. The line of apostolic succession through which McGuire and the AOC eventually found the episcopate was crucial: it changed the fundamental nature of the church.

On the fringes of those historic churches holding apostolic succession, there exists a collection of individuals, some of them with, but some without actual church organizations, who claim to be validly consecrated bishops and validly ordained priests. At their best, they can be said to be sincere people whose legitimacy is denied or ignored by the powerful established churches; at their worst, they are simply religious confidence men. Their existence is little known and their pedigrees are hopelessly tangled; as a result, they constitute something of a shadow church, or at least a shadow hierarchy, since they tend to produce more titled prelates than members. It was to this curious world of *episcopi vagantes*, or "wandering bishops," that McGuire turned for consecration, traditional and conventional avenues having been closed to him. Thus, on September 28, 1921, McGuire was consecrated by Joseph René Vilatte, Mar Timotheos, Archbishop-Metropolitan of the Old Catholic Church of America, Doctor Christiantissamus, first Primate of the American Catholic Church, etc.[41] It was as a result of entry into this milieu of *episcopi vagantes* and the consequent importance McGuire placed on the authenticity of his consecration that the AOC changed from being a church whose self-identity was explicitly black and nationalistic to one whose primary interest lay in proclaiming the validity of its apostolic succession. The original emphasis on the Black Christ was replaced by a defense of so-called Old Catholic orders.[42]

Born in Paris in 1854, Vilatte had spent his early life in and out of various religious institutions and organizations in several countries, vacillating between Roman Catholicism and Protestantism. Unlikely as it may sound, it was while serving as a Presbyterian missionary in Green Bay, Wisconsin, that he persuaded J.H. Hobart Brown, the Episcopal Bishop of Fond du Lac, to recommend him to the Old Catholic Bishop of Berne, Edward Herzog, for ordination. The result was that Vilatte was ordained in Switzerland on June 7, 1885, and commissioned to work in Wisconsin among French-speaking Belgians who had anti-Roman sympathies.

Brown was succeeded as bishop by Charles C. Grafton, a rather stiff high-churchman who was an early member of the Cowley Fathers,[43] and he persuaded Vilatte to sign over to the diocese the property of his three mission churches in exchange for financial support. To what extent Vilatte was actually under the authority of the Bishop of Fond du Lac is disputed, but when Vilatte decided that he needed to be raised to the episcopate, he was refused by Grafton as well as by the Old Catholics. Vilatte also flirted with the Roman Catholic Bishop of Green Bay as well as with Vladimir, the Russian Orthodox Bishop of the Aleutian Islands and Alaska, both to no avail.

Determined to be consecrated, Vilatte next approached a somewhat unusual ecclesiastical figure, Mar Julius I, Metropolitan of the Independent Catholic Church of Ceylon, Goa, and India.[44] Mar Julius I was a Brahmin named Antonio Francisco-Xavier Alvarez who had become a Roman Catholic priest in Goa. When a number of Catholic families on the west coast of India decided to break with Rome because of Pope Leo XIII's alteration of the traditional way by which their bishops were chosen, they went into schism for nationalistic as well as ecclesiastical reasons and elected Alvarez their bishop. Severely persecuted by the Jesuits, Alvarez sought orders from the Syro-Jacobite Church of Malabar. With the permission of Ignatius Peter III, Jacobite Patriarch of the Apostolic See of Antioch and All the East, Alvarez received consecration at the hands of Mar Paul Athanasius, Metropolitan-Archbishop and Legate of the Patriarch in Malabar. This meant that Alvarez was consecrated by the authority of the (Jacobite or Western) Syrian Church of Antioch, whose orders are undisputed and which, according to tradition, was founded by St. Peter in the year 38 A.D.[45] Antioch still considers itself the Mother Church of Christendom and claims that its line of apostolic succession antedates Rome's.

When Alvarez received Vilatte's request for consecration, he responded with enthusiasm at the discovery of other Christians who wanted freedom from "the slavery of Rome" and promised to confer the episcopate. Vilatte raised some money, though only enough to travel third class, and sailed for Ceylon. Despite a warning telegram from Grafton, Alvarez secured a special bull of permission from the Patriarch "Peter the Humble,"[46] and Vilatte was duly consecrated on December 29, 1891, in the Church of Our Lady of Good Death, Columbo, Ceylon. Alvarez was assisted by the Malabar bishops, Mar Athanasius of Kottayam and Mar Gregorios of Niranam. Vilatte emerged as Mar Timotheos, Archbishop of the Old Catholic Church of America.

Vilatte's consecration, however, was not received with universal acclaim. The House of Bishops of the Episcopal Church declared it was null and void since it came from a church that not only had been separated from the rest of Christendom since the fifth century, but also had no jurisdiction in Wisconsin.[47] Bishop Grafton deposed the new archbishop from the Episcopal priesthood, but Vilatte retaliated by saying that he had never been an Episcopal minister, and therefore the deposition had the same authority as one from the Grand Lama of Tibet. Vilatte had no sizable following and no ecclesiastical superior to whom he was responsible. During the rest of his checkered life, he ordained and consecrated a rather large number of men, so that many Old Catholic churches trace their orders to him. It was to Vilatte that George McGuire applied for consecration on behalf of the African Orthodox Church and by him that he was elevated to the episcopacy in the Church of Our Lady of Good Death in Chicago on September 28, 1921. Vilatte was assisted by Carl A. Nybladh, a deposed Episcopal priest who was now bishop of the Swedish American Church and who had also been consecrated by Vilatte.

McGuire's consecration raises the thorny issue of the authenticity of his orders and those of the autocephalous AOC. The question is a complex one, with subtle theological, ecclesiastical, and legal components. The central problem has to do with the concepts of validity and regularity, and their interrelationship.[48] Validity refers to the line of apostolic succession, i.e., whether that line is unbroken and historically traceable back to Jesus' original disciples. Some churches, like the Roman Catholic, tend to be rather mechanistic in their view. This means that providing the proper intention and form are present, those ordinations and consecrations that demonstrably stand in direct succession to the apostles are normally accepted as valid. Regularity is a more difficult notion, since it suggests that ordinations and consecrations are not only for the church but must be within the church. This immediately raises the question of what constitutes the church; those with a rather exclusivistic definition, like the Eastern Orthodox, add the test of inclusiveness to the criterion of validity. In other words, a consecration may be technically valid, but if it is outside the church, it is irregular and therefore ultimately invalid. It was on this basis that the Syrian Orthodox Patriarch in 1938 pronounced the Vilatte succession and AOC orders invalid since they were schismatic from the parent church.[49]

By all reasonable criteria, however, the Alvarez-Vilatte-McGuire line is valid. It is possible to question its regularity only if one holds such a narrow definition of the church, or rather, a particular church, as virtually to exclude by definition all others. In this context, too, the AOC has a distinct strength not shared by many other Old Catholic churches, i.e., it has all the characteristics of a real and complete church: members, congregations, services, buildings, etc. The Old Catholic churches in this country have a sorry record of schisms, lawsuits, fraudulent claims, depositions and counterdepositions, and, worst of all, the wholesale manufacture of bishops. While the AOC has had its problems, over the years it has clearly been a responsible institution under responsible leadership. From a socio-historical perspective, Alvarez, Vilatte, and McGuire (and, as we shall see, Daniel Alexander) shared a parallel experience: all were leaders of minority groups who were denied places in established religious institutions by the dominant groups of their societies. As a consequence they went outside the normative institutions in order to secure legitimacy.

After an impressive beginning and early signs of growth, the AOC came to something of a plateau. Its formal liturgy and claims to apostolic succession were limited in appeal to those West Indians and Afro-Americans who came out of an Anglican or Episcopalian tradition. The Great Depression hit the black community early and severely, and nationalistic aspirations were subsumed by a struggle for survival. McGuire died in 1934. His vision of a Church Ethiopic, however, as well as Garvey's call for the redemption of Africa, did come to a measure of fulfillment via the AOC. In 1924, a Coloured South African named Daniel William Alexander[50] wrote McGuire proposing the affiliation with the AOC of an independent separatist church of which he was head.[51]

Alexander was born in Port Elizabeth, Cape Province, in 1883. After he joined the British in the Boer War, he went on to study for the Anglican ministry and also held office in the African Political Organization, South Africa's major Coloured political association. Returning to an ecclesiastical vocation, however, Alexander became part of a religious separatist group called the African Church, under Bishop J.M. Khanyane Napo.[52] When a group of dissident clergy of this church met to secede in October 1924, Alexander was elected their leader and they decided to seek union with the AOC in America.[53] Also present at the breakaway meeting was Joseph Masoga, the local agent for Garvey's *Negro World* newspaper, further attesting to the breadth of the Garvey Movement's impact on Africa.

McGuire appointed Alexander Vicar Apostolic for South Africa, but decided to put him and his group on probation and to do some investigating before proceeding further. A sometime AOC clergyman and informer for the British Government, the Rev. Edwin Urban Lewis, reported to the British Consul-General in New York on the contents of a letter read by McGuire to a "secret conference" at UNIA headquarters. The letter was from the "Archdeacon of Pretoria" requesting admission to the AOC on behalf of himself and five hundred parishioners, and Lewis claimed to recall McGuire's written response as having been as follows:

> Yourself and congregation coming over to us will be welcome, and as Lord Primate of the African Orthodox Church, should you make it possible for Sir Marcus Garvey to get in to that country I am sure that the day will not be far off when by virtue of my high office, I will consecrate you as Bishop for South Africa.[54]

Garvey, of course, never visited Africa, but in 1927 the AOC named Alexander Bishop for the Province of South Africa. He traveled to the United States and was consecrated on September 11 by McGuire, who was assisted by Bishop William E. J. Robertson and Bishop Arthur S. Trotman, in the Church of St. Michael and All Angels in Boston. On his return to South Africa, Alexander immediately began to organize new churches and to receive into the AOC a number of Anglican priests and laymen.[55]

Alexander's most significant work, however, was his role in the founding of other independent African churches. In 1925 Reuben Mukasa Spartas, a Ugandan Anglican who had read Garvey's newspaper, founded the African Progressive Association and vowed "to go to hell, jail or die for the redemption of Africa."[56] Spartas corresponded with McGuire, who put him in touch with Alexander, after which Spartas left the Anglican Church and formed a Ugandan AOC "established for all right-thinking Africans, men who wish to be free in their own house, not always being thought of as boys."[57] He was ordained by Alexander in 1932, but becoming suspicious of Alexander's Orthodoxy, he severed the relationship and petitioned Meletios II, the Greek Orthodox Patriarch of Alexandria, for admission. Despite the question of Alexander's orders, Spartas was received in

1946 by the Pope and Patriarch of Alexandria and All Africa into full membership under his jurisdiction, Spartas renaming his church the African Greek Orthodox Church. This branch of the AOC thus became the first independent African church to place itself under European authority, the first church in the Vilatte succession to be accepted by a historic communion, and the first major contemporary expression of Greek Orthodox missionary interest.[58]

Alexander was next involved with dramatic events in Kenya that began as an expression of cultural nationalism but developed into a successful struggle for political independence. Resentment by the Kikuyu people over British land and labor policies had come to a crisis in 1929 when European missionary leaders forbade cliteridectomy (the practice of female circumcision).[59] The Africans withdrew from the missions in large numbers, taking their churches and schools with them, and eventually formed two new bodies, the Kikuyu Independent Schools Association and the Kikuyu Karing'a ("Pure") Education Association. Schools and churches were, in fact, virtually the same institutions. Separation from the missions brought educational and ecclesiastical independence, but the Kikuyu were bereft of clergy to baptize their children. Archbishop Alexander was invited to Kenya since he led a church "of the Africans, governed by the Africans and for the Africans to make daily supplications to Almighty God led by priests who have the welfare of Africans at heart."[60] Arriving in Nairobi in 1935, Alexander found the Kikuyu a proud people unshakeably committed to their independence, and so "a hard bone to chew."[61] He went about teaching, preaching, baptizing, and ordained four men.

The subsequent relationship among men, churches, and schools became complex, but "when Alexander sailed from Kenya on July 7, 1937, he left behind him an ordained African clergy functioning outside the auspices of any Kenyan mission."[62] The nationalism of the independent churches and schools became politically explosive and eventually culminated in the "Mau Mau" movement and, later still, in Kenyan independence.[63]

It is in Kenya that the AOC has taken its strongest hold in Africa, and there are now branches and splinter bodies with a total membership in the millions.[64] Archbishop Makarios, the

President of Cyprus, visited Kenya in 1971 and in the course of a single weekend personally baptized five thousand people into the African Orthodox Church.[65] In addition to Alexander's own denomination in South Africa, there is an AOC in Ghana, and innumerable other bodies throughout the African continent are, in one way or another, offshoots of his leadership. Alexander died in Kimberley May 14, 1969.

The continuing significance of the AOC in Africa, as well as its continuing links to African nationalism, is illustrated by a recent statement of Dr. Elliot M. Gabellah, vice-president of one of the factions of the African National Council in Rhodesia: "We are determined to be liberated from the yoke of oppression. We will continue to strive and struggle until we gain our liberation."[66] Dr. Gabellah is also patriarchal administrator of the African Orthodox Church for Rhodesia, South Africa, Lesotho, and Swaziland.

While the AOC in Africa, especially East Africa, has been rather well documented because of its role in political liberation and its significance for the phenomenon of African independent churches, the history of the AOC in the United States has been largely neglected. A major reason has been the unavailability of *The Negro Churchman*, the official monthly organ of the denomination, which was founded in January 1923 and edited in New York by McGuire. It is thus particularly gratifying to be able to introduce the reprinting of an extraordinarily valuable primary source. It will now be possible to trace much more carefully the developing history of the AOC, its relationship to black nationalism in general and the Garvey Movement in particular, its changing self-image in terms of the Vilatte succession, Alexander's work in South Africa, etc.

The first, and sometimes only, defensible conclusion that emerges from many recent excursions into black history, especially black church history, is that more work needs to be done. More work, and work of quality and importance, is increasingly possible, given not only the resurgence of scholarly interest in the black past but also the growing realization of the existence of great quantities of unparalleled source material in papers, records, correspondence—and living persons. *The Negro Churchman* is one such source, and it is a pleasure to be able to anticipate the new research that can now be done as a result of its republication. The church that "vowed to throw off forever the yoke of white ecclesiastical domination" deserves, at least, our knowledge, our understanding, and our respect.

—From *The Negro Churchman: The Official Organ of the African Orthodox Church*, vols. 1-9, no. 9 (Millwood, N.Y.: Kraus Reprint Co., 1977), pp. iii–xxii. Portions of this essay in an earlier form were read as "Marcus Garvey and the African Orthodox Church: Religious Nationalism in Africa and the United States," American Academy of Religion, New England Region, Brown University, April 2, 1970.

Notes

1. For some years the only book-length treatment of Garvey and the UNIA was Edmund D. Cronon's *Black Moses: Marcus Garvey and the Universal Negro Improvement Association* (Madison: University of Wisconsin Press, 1955). Now there are a number of important new studies. Among the more useful are John Henrik Clark, ed., *Marcus Garvey and the Vision of Africa* (New York: Random House, 1974) and Tony Martin, *Race First: The Ideological and Organizational Struggles of Marcus Garvey and the Universal Negro Improvement Association* (Westport, Conn.: Greenwood Press, 1976). Although it needs to be read carefully, there is a great deal of useful information in Arthur C. Terry-Thompson, *History of the African Orthodox Church* (New York: privately printed, 1956).

2. The best overall account of Bishop McGuire to date is Gavin White's "Patriarch McGuire and the Episcopal Church," *Historical Magazine of the Protestant Episcopal Church*, June 1969, pp. 109-141. See also the early biographical sketch in W.N. Hartshorn, ed., *An Era of Progress and Promise, 1863-1910* (Boston: The Priscilla Publishing Co., 1910), p. 473. J. Carleton Hayden has written a brief biography of McGuire that is forthcoming in Rayford Logan and Michael Winston, eds., *The Dictionary of American Negro Biography* (New York: Thomas Y. Crowell Co.).

3. McGuire's mother is sometimes listed as Henrietta (George) McGuire.

4. Kenneth Walter Cameron, ed., *Register of Ordinations in the Episcopal Church in the United States from 1785 through 1904—with Index* (Hartford: Transcendental Books, 1970), n.p.

5. In later life Brown was to discover Darwin and Marx, styling himself "Episcopus in partibus Bolshevikium et Infidelium," and was tried by the church and convicted of heresy. Unfortunately, a critical biography of "Bad Bishop Brown," as he liked to call himself, does not exist. See his autobiography, *My Heresy* (New York: The John Day Co., 1926); and his *The Crucial Race Question or Where and How Shall the Color Line Be Drawn* (Little Rock:

The Arkansas Churchman's Publishing Co., 1908). See also Ralph Lord Roy, *Communism and the Churches* (New York: Harcourt, Brace and Co., 1960), pp. 21–28.

6. Quoted by E. Clowes Chorley, "The Church in Arkansas and its Bishops," *Historical Magazine of the Protestant Episcopal Church,* December 1946, p. 350.

7. William Postell Witsell, *A History of Christ Episcopal Church, Little Rock, Arkansas* (Little Rock: privately printed, n.d.), n.p.

8. M. Moran Weston, *Social Policy in the Episcopal Church in the Twentieth Century* (New York: Seabury Press, 1964), pp. 140–147. See also David Reimers, "Negro Bishops and Diocesan Segregation in the P.E. Church," *Historical Magazine of the Protestant Episcopal Church,* September 1962, pp. 231–242.

9. Brown, *My Heresy,* p. 44.

10. It is still claimed in the AOC, probably originating with McGuire, that Brown was personally so biased that he even disliked putting his hands as bishop on the "woolly" heads of black children. Brown's later conversion to Communism, however, resulted in radically changed views. Speaking in Harlem in 1926, Brown called it "the most likely place in America . . . for the new order to begin" and said, "The black man is the great white hope." He even urged his listeners to march into churches, exhorting them: "I want to see them [the churches] liberated. I want you to go into them and set them free" (*New York Times,* February 23, 1926, p. 17).

11. There is some lack of consistency in the positions of both McGuire and Brown. In *The Crucial Race Question* Brown advocated an autonomous Afro-American church in contradistinction to both the suffragan and missionary schemes. In his autobiography he admits this to have been his earlier view, as he also does in "The American Race Problem," published in the first issue of his own quarterly magazine, *Heresy* (January 1930, p. 34). In both places, writing as a Communist, he repudiated his earlier views as racist and the Arkansas Plan as Jim Crowism. In McGuire's case, he was quoted by Brown as heartily approving the Arkansas Plan and stating: "What the distant future may accomplish in the way of obliterating racial lines in State, in Church or in Society, is no very grave concern of ours. The fact cannot be denied that at present there must be total cleavage—complete separation—all along the lines, if we desire peace, success, and full development for all parties" (Brown, *The Crucial Race Question,* p. 174). In the *Diocesan Journal* for 1908, however, Brown seems to have been advocating the use of missionary bishops and jurisdictions. And in McGuire's eloquent speech before the 1906 session of the Council of the Diocese, he advocated the appointment of black suffragans since he thought that it had a more realistic chance of being voted in the South, even though he admitted he believed the missionary arrangement was the "desired goal." In March 1908, McGuire's friend George F. Bragg, Jr., published in *The Church Advocate* a letter from McGuire stating his conversion from the suffragan to the missionary scheme with the explanation that, as a West Indian, he had "failed to fully appreciate at first the necessity for this movement." In the June issue of the magazine, Bragg announced that McGuire was leaving Arkansas, stating: "The 'Arkansas Plan' under which, of necessity, he must work, is radically at variance

with what the late Archdeacon [McGuire] and his brethren, believe to be fundamentally necessary for the growth and expansion of the Church among our people." Brown, on the other hand, complained that he spent $200 in sending McGuire to Boston to raise money for the Plan but that McGuire raised a mere $100 and then accepted another job: "The unkindest cut of all was the losing of the Archdeacon to Boston. That was almost more than I could bear; for Boston, you will remember, is the citadel of the opposition to the Arkansas Plan. Archdeacon McGuire has gone over soul and body to the enemies' camp" (*Diocesan Journal*, 1908, p. 56). It has been said that McGuire was offered a suffragan bishopric in Arkansas but refused it. (See Terry-Thompson, p. 49.)

12. Kenneth deP. Hughes, "The History of St. Bartholomew's," St. Bartholomew's Fiftieth Anniversary Brochure, 1958, n.p.

13. The Institute was an auxiliary organization of the Board of Missions of the Episcopal Church. It contributed financial support to Bishop Payne Divinity School, Petersburg, Va.; St. Augustine's School, Raleigh, N.C.; the St. Paul Normal and Industrial School, Lawrenceville, Va.; St. Athanasius' School, Brunswick, Ga.; St. Mark's School, Birmingham, Ala.; and the Vicksburg Industrial School, Vicksburg, Miss. As Field Secretary, McGuire raised funds and, during the summer of 1911, lectured on industrial education in Antigua and Barbados. The Institute's task, McGuire believed, was to "develop" black youth so that "ultimately by their righteousness of life, strength of character, trained usefulness for service, and increase in intellectual attainment and material prosperity the Negroes of our land shall silently, but eloquently and successfully, appeal to their fellow citizens for possession and enjoyment of all the rights and privileges of American Citizenship" (*Annual Report of the American Church Institute for Negroes, Fifth Year—1910-1911* [New York: Office of the General Agent], p. 28).

14. A useful corrective to published misstatements on the founding of the AOC is Byron Rushing, "A Note on the Origin of the African Orthodox Church," *Journal of Negro History* 57 (1972), 37-39. His implication, however, that McGuire left Antigua at this time because he had supported striking sugar-cane workers is misleading. Gavin White contends that McGuire had a worthless medical degree from the Boston College of Physicians and Surgeons. Terry-Thompson, on the other hand, states that McGuire took a medical course at Jefferson Medical College in Philadelphia and received an M.D. in 1910. Standards for medical education and licensing were then, of course, much different from those of today. At one point McGuire planned to establish a children's dispensary and sanitarium in Cambridge, Massachusetts.

15. Terry-Thompson, p. 50.

16. *The Negro World*, November 6, 1920, p. 5. Randall K. Burkett, in his unpublished dissertation, "Garveyism as a Religious Movement" (University of Southern California, 1975), spells out McGuire's early association with the UNIA and indicates the original relationship between the AOC and Garvey's UNIA. See especially Chapter 3, "Sect or Civil Religion: The Debate with George Alexander McGuire," pp. 93-146. My account draws heavily upon Burkett's work.

17. On October 9, 1919, McGuire "with the enthusiasm of a discoverer" was

received into the Reformed Episcopal Church, having found in that denomination "an answer in his heart's desire." He indicated his intention of establishing a church for West Indians in New York City. On March 21, 1920, Bishop Paul L. Rudolph of the Reformed Episcopal Church visited McGuire's flock and confirmed six people. The congregation already numbered 220 communicants and was meeting in the Rush Memorial A.M.E. Zion Church on West 138th Street. By this time McGuire had abandoned his plan to continue with the Reformed Episcopal Church, and his Church of the Good Shepherd was described as the "Independent Episcopal Church," looking to the Reformed Episcopalians for oversight only until it could secure its own bishop. On January 10, 1921, McGuire and his congregation withdrew, in good standing, from the Reformed Episcopal Church to the Independent Episcopal Church. See *Minutes of the Proceedings of the Thirty-Ninth Council of the New York and Philadelphia Synod, Reformed Episcopal Church,* pp. 18, 25–26; *Minutes of the Proceedings of the Fortieth Council,* p. 17; *Minutes of the Proceedings of the Forty-First Council,* pp. 15, 48; *Journal of the Proceedings of the Twenty-Third General Council of the Reformed Episcopal Church,* pp. 40, 41, 51. I am indebted to Bishop Theophilus J. Herter for this information. For an early history of the denomination, see Annie Darling Price, *A History of the Formation and Growth of the Reformed Episcopal Church, 1873-1902* (Philadelphia: Armstrong, 1902).

18. *The New York World,* August 17, 1920, p. 10.
19. Eason, a North Carolinian by birth, graduated from Livingstone College in 1912 and Hood Theological Seminary in 1915. He was pastor of A.M.E. Zion churches in Philadelphia until he resigned to work for the UNIA. Eason served from 1919 to 1920 as the first Chaplain-General of the Association. He retained the position of Leader of the American Negroes until 1922, when he was ousted from the UNIA. He then took up active participation in the anti-Garvey movement. Eason was assassinated in New Orleans on January 1, 1923, allegedly by Garveyites. His death was used by those opposed to Garvey to intensify the "Garvey Must Go" campaign.
20. *The Negro World,* November 6, 1920, p. 5.
21. Tobitt, an African Methodist Episcopal deacon in Bermuda, was dismissed from the ministry of that denomination and the government cut off funds for his school when he became an active member of the UNIA. *The Negro World,* October 20, 1923, p. 10. See also William F. Elkins, "Marcus Garvey, the *Negro World,* and the British West Indies: 1919-1920," *Science and Society* 36 (Spring 1972), 71.
22. *The Negro World,* April 2, 1921, pp. 1, 5. The ecclesiastical vestments required by McGuire for his new role as a bestower of ordinations were paid for by the UNIA.
23. Ibid. The article is reprinted in part in Theodore G. Vincent, ed., *Voices of a Black Nation: Political Journalism in the Harlem Renaissance* (San Francisco: Ramparts Press, 1973), pp. 367–368.
24. *The Universal Negro Ritual,* p. 23. The UNIA Constitution provides that "All persons of Negro blood and African descent" are regarded as UNIA members and seen as being born into the organization by virtue of race. See Burkett, pp. 120 ff.
25. *The Universal Negro Ritual,* pp. 24–25.

26. Although this is not the place for a lengthy treatment of Garvey and religion, it is important to underscore the fact that he did not found the AOC, a correction that is necessary because of several published statements to that effect. Garvey was never a member of the AOC, and there is no evidence he encouraged McGuire in its formation or ever took an interest in it after it had been formed. Garvey was baptized in the Wesleyan Methodist Church in Jamaica, but he was never a churchman. Several clergymen in Jamaica were helpful to him, particularly the Roman Catholic bishop John J. Collins, S.J., who shared his interest in black culture and in improving the general lot of black people. During Garvey's final illness in London, an African couple named Yousoff brought a Roman Catholic priest named Clark, who visited often and impressed Garvey with his humanness and international interests. As a result, Garvey was rebaptized and received the last rites of the Roman Catholic Church. (Most of this information is from a personal interview with Amy Jacques-Garvey in Kingston, Jamaica, December 26, 1971.) Garvey might have felt that churches were divisive within the black community, channeling interest and energy away from the economic and political aspects of African "redemption" which he believed were more important. Although Garvey probably underestimated the strength of the church in black institutional life and undervalued the role of religion in black culture, he did see the role religion plays in self-perception and used it effectively in his struggle to raise black self-affirmation: "If the white man has the idea of a white god, let him worship his god as he desires . . . since the white people have seen their god through white spectacles, we have only now started out to see god through our own spectacles . . . we shall worship him through spectacles of Ethiopia" (Amy Jacques-Garvey, ed., *Philosophy and Opinions of Marcus Garvey* [1925; reprint ed., New York: Atheneum, 1969], 1: 44). Burkett's "Garveyism as a Religious Movement" offers an extended discussion of Garvey and religion and argues that Garvey took religion and the black church very seriously. He concludes that Garvey was self-consciously working through the rituals and symbols created for the UNIA to foster, in fact, a black civil religion. Based on his analysis of the religious content of Garvey's speeches, he characterizes Garvey as "the foremost black theologian of the early twentieth century."

27. *The Negro World,* July 16, 1921.

28. *The Negro World,* August 27, 1921, p. 12.

29. *The Negro World,* October 8, 1921, p. 3. In 1930 McGuire said he had broken with Garvey because Garvey insisted that he resign as head of the Independent Episcopal Churches and serve only as Chaplain-General of the UNIA. See *The Negro Churchman,* 8, no. 1 (January 1930), 3.

30. *New York Age,* October 29, 1921.

31. *The Negro World,* December 31, 1921; January 7, 1922; January 14, 1922. For an account of the African Blood Brotherhood and its relationship with the Garvey Movement, see Theodore G. Vincent, *Black Power and the Garvey Movement* (Berkeley: The Ramparts Press, n.d.). See also Harold Cruse, *The Crisis of the Negro Intellectual* (New York: William Morrow and Co., 1967).

32. Martin, p. 72.

33. Jacques-Garvey, p. 279.

34. *New York Times,* August 6, 1924, p. 3.

35. *New York Times*, September 1, 1924, p. 24.

36. Quoted by Roi Ottley, *'New World A-Coming'* (New York: Arno Press, 1969), p. 73.

37. See Bohumil Holas, *L'Afrique noire* (Paris: Bloud and Gay, 1964); Albert B. Cleage, Jr., *The Black Messiah* (New York: Sheed and Ward, 1968). See also Efraim Andersson, *Messianic Popular Movements in the Lower Congo* (Stockholm: Almqvist and Wiksell, 1958); George Balandier, *Sociologie actuelle de l'Afrique noir* (Paris: Presses Universitaires, 1955).

38. Terry-Thompson, p. 53.

39. *New York Age*, October 8, 1921.

40. *Baltimore Afro-American*, March 9, 1923.

41. The most complete account is Peter F. Anson, *Bishops at Large* (London: Faber and Faber, 1964), pp. 91-129. See also Henry R.T. Brandreth, *Episcopi Vagantes and the Anglican Church*, 2nd ed. (London: S.P.C.K., 1961), pp. 47 ff. There are summaries in Karl Pruter, *A History of the Old Catholic Church* (Scottsdale: St. Willibrord's Press, 1973), pp. 34-39; *American Review of Eastern Orthodoxy*, 20, no. 3 (March 1974), n.p.; and Elmer T. Clark, *The Small Sects in America*, rev. ed. (New York: Abington Press, 1937), pp. 170 ff. See also George A. McGuire, "The Episcopalians and Archbishop Vilatte," *The Negro Churchman*, 1, no. 8 (August 1923): 3-5.

42. The validity of the orders of the Old Catholic Church of Europe, centered in Utrecht, is undisputed. See C.B. Moss, *The Old Catholic Movement, Its Origins and History* (London: S.P.C.K., 1948).

43. See Grafton's autobiography, *A Journey Godward* (Milwaukee: The Young Churchman Co., 1910).

44. See E.M. Philip, *The Indian Church of St. Thomas* (Nagercoil: London Mission Press, 1950), pp. 430-28—430-31.

45. Churches in the Vilatte succession make a great deal of this line of bishops since it demonstrates the authenticity of their orders. See Terry-Thompson, pp. 41-42; Bertil Persson, *A Collection of Documentations on the Apostolic Succession of Joseph René Vilatte with Brief Annotations* (Solna, Sweden: St. Ephrem's Institute, 1974), pp. 5-8; *The Apostolic Succession of the Old Catholic Episcopal Church (Anglo-Catholic)* (Glendale: the Old Catholic Order of Christ the King, n.d.). The validity of the Syrian succession is presented by Odo A. Barry, *Outline History of the American Catholic Church* (Long Beach: Office of the Exarch, American Catholic Church, 1951) and *The Apostolic Church of the Indies* (Ambur, India: Church of India, n.d.).

46. The original document seems to be unavailable, though translated copies appear frequently in the literature.

47. The Syrian Orthodox Church (and the Syrian Orthodox Church in India) is one of the Oriental Orthodox churches that were divided from the rest of Christendom following the Council of Chalcedon in 451 A.D. Sometimes referred to as Non-Chalcedonian or even "Lesser Eastern" churches, the Syrians were joined by the Ethiopian Orthodox Church, the Armenian Apostolic Church, and the Coptic Orthodox Church. For a summary, see Williston Walker, *A History of the Christian Church* (New York: Charles Scribner's Sons, 1954), pp. 143 ff. The Oriental Orthodox churches are now involved with the Eastern Orthodox churches in seeking to resolve their differences. For a contemporary presentation of these bodies, see Karekin Sarkissian, *The*

Witness of the Oriental Orthodox Churches (Antelias, Lebanon: The American Catholicosate of Cilicia, 1970).

48. This is not so esoteric an issue as it may sound. In the Eastern Orthodox, Roman Catholic, and Anglican churches it is a fundamental doctrine, and in the ecumenical movement it has proved to be the major stumbling block to reunion. It has appeared most recently in the news in connection with the priestly ordination of eleven women by Protestant Episcopal bishops in Philadelphia in 1974. See Brandreth, pp. 8–15; White, pp. 131–132; *Anglican Orders* (London: S.P.C.K., 1957).

49. Reprinted in Brandreth, pp. 118–119.

50. See my unpublished paper, "Archbishop Daniel William Alexander and the African Orthodox Church," American Academy of Religion, New England Region, Tufts University, Medford, Mass., April 17, 1972 [which appears below].

51. The best overview of the phenomenon of African independent churches is David Barrett's *Schism and Renewal in Africa: An Analysis of Six Thousand Contemporary Religious Movements* (Nairobi: Oxford University Press, 1968). See also Harold W. Turner, *Bibliography of New Religious Movements in Primal Societies, Vol. I: Black Africa* (Boston: G.K. Hall, 1977).

52. See Bengt G.M. Sundkler, *Bantu Prophets in South Africa* (London: Oxford University Press, 1961), p. 39.

53. The minutes of this meeting, which are in Alexander's own handwriting, are among his uncatalogued papers in South Africa. I read them there on July 10, 1971.

54. Public Record Office, London, F.O. 371/9633, No. 213. The fact that McGuire had earlier suspended Lewis from the AOC may have outweighed Lewis's expressed concern "for the safety of the Church of England." H.G. Armstrong, the British Consul-General, apparently shared Lewis's view that the AOC was seditious, for he reported to his embassy in Washington: "It is generally understood that the consecration of clergymen by McGuire is part of his scheme to cause dissension, together with the Marcus Garvey association, among negroes of the British Empire" (Public Record Office, London, F.O. 115/3380).

55. Ellen Hellmann, ed., *Handbook on Race Relations in South Africa* (Cape Town: Oxford University Press, 1949), p. 567.

56. Basil Moustakis, ed., *Thriskeftiki Ke Ithiki Engiklopedia* [Encyclopedia of religion and ethics] (Athens: Ath. Martinos, 1967), 11: 354–357; David Barrett, "Who's Who of African Independent Church Leaders," *Risk*, 7, no. 3 (1971): 33; David E. Apter, *The Political Kingdom in Uganda* (Princeton: Princeton University Press, 1961), pp. 248–254; Norman A. Horner, "An East African Orthodox Church," *Journal of Ecumenical Studies*, Spring 1975, pp. 221–233. This includes a helpful bibliography of Greek missionary publications.

57. Fred B. Welbourn, *East African Rebels: A Study of Some Independent Churches* (London: SCM Press, 1961), p. 81. This is a pioneering study of great usefulness.

58. Discouraged by Greek paternalism, Spartas and a segment of the church later withdrew from the jurisdiction of the Patriarch. They were then reconciled, and Spartas was elevated to the episcopacy as Bishop of Nilopolis. See D.E. Wentink, "The Reaction of the Once Independent African Orthodox Church

to the Foreign Greek Orthodox Mission It Invited In," David Barrett, ed., *Theory and Practice in Church Life and Growth* (Nairobi: Workshop in Religious Research, 1968), pp. 135–142.

59. See Jomo Kenyatta, *Facing Mt. Kenya: The Tribal Life of the Gikuyu* (New York: Vintage Books, n.d.), pp. 125–148; John Anderson, *The Struggle for the School* (London: Longman, 1970), pp. 119–122; and Jocelyn Murray, "The Kikuyu Female Circumcision Controversy" (Ph.D. diss., University of California at Los Angeles, 1974).

60. Kikuyu Independent School Association connected with the African Independent Pentecostal Church, *Report and Constitution, 1938* (Nyeri: privately printed, 1938), p. 2.

61. Bartolomeo Moriondo, "Come conobbi l'Arcivescovo Ortodosso," *Missioni Consolata*, 46, nos. 8–9 (September-October 1944), 94.

62. Carl G. Rosberg, Jr., and John Nottingham, *The Myth of "Mau Mau": Nationalism in Kenya* (New York: Frederick A. Praeger, 1966), p. 130.

63. For an unreliable but interesting account of Alexander's political influence in Kenya, see F.D. Corfield, *Historical Survey of the Origins and Growth of Mau Mau* (London: H.M.S.O., 1960), pp. 171–189.

64. See David B. Barrett, et al., eds., *Kenya Churches Handbook* (Kisumu, Kenya: Evangel Publishing House, 1973).

65. *Eastern Churches Review*, 3, no. 4 (Autumn 1971), 459.

66. *New York Times*, March 7, 1976, pp. 1, 19.

Archbishop
Daniel William Alexander
and the African Orthodox Church

The African Orthodox Church (AOC) is one of several links between black separatism in America and independence movements in Africa which remain largely unexamined. The church originated in the United States as an aspect of the Black Renaissance of the 1920s, a period of positive Negro self-consciousness, artistic flowering, and prideful identification of Diaspora blacks with their African heritage. The AOC spread to Africa where it played a part in the emergence of independent churches, the rise of cultural and political nationalism, and the interrelationships between these movements. The central figure in the spread of the African Orthodox Church within Africa was Archbishop Daniel William Alexander.

Alexander was born 25 December 1883[1] in Port Elizabeth, Cape Province, South Africa, the second eldest child of Henry David and Elizabeth Alexander. His Roman Catholic father was a native of St. Pierre, Martinique, who immigrated to Port Elizabeth. His mother's maiden name was Garcia and she was the child of a Cuban father and Javanese mother.[2]

The Corfield Report, which excoriates Alexander for his role in the Mau Mau rising in Kenya, charges him with first claiming Mauritian ancestry[3] to prove his parentage to the French authorities. At this point, according to Corfield, he assumed British nationality.[4]

Alexander was educated at St. Peter's Primary and Secondary schools in Port Elizabeth and the school of the Roman Catholic Sisters of Mercy. He became a boatbuilder by trade. Joining the British in the Boer War, he was captured at Colenso and sent to Pretoria.[5] After the fall of Pretoria to the British in 1900, Alexander joined the Anglican Church and was appointed chaplain at the Old Prison. He studied for the ministry under Canon E. Farmer, the Revs. H. Mtobi and W.A. Goodwin, and, later, Fathers Herbert Bennett and Latimer Fuller of the Community of the Resurrection.[6] In 1901 in Pretoria he married Elizabeth Koster.

Involving himself in South Africa's major Coloured political association, Alexander was elected secretary of the A.P.O., Pretoria Branch. The African Political Organization—later the African People's Organization—had been founded in 1902 and was led from 1905 by the Cape Malay physician A.E. Abdurahman. Although its membership was primarily Coloured (that is, people of mixed African and European blood), the A.P.O. sought to be a united movement of all non-Europeans. It advocated extending the franchise to Coloureds outside the Cape, it identified with the British as opposed to the Boers, and, politically, it supported the South African Party.[7] Alexander also was elected secretary of the committee for purchasing the Lady Selbourne Township, Pretoria. Under the Hercules municipality, Lady Selbourne Township became one of the few areas where Africans could obtain freehold tenure and build their own houses.[8]

We do not know why, but Alexander resigned from the Anglican Church and moved from Pretoria to Johannesburg, where he became an agent in the industrial branch of the African Life Assurance Society. He subsequently left this position, however, to become Grand True Secretary of the Independent Order of True Templars, Northern Grand Lodge. Re-elected to that office in 1920–1921, he refused nomination in 1922. The I.O.T.T., although basically a temperance organization, fulfilled the additional welfare, recreational, and economic functions of a lodge. Lodges play a significant role in Coloured life, especially among skilled artisans and the commercial bourgeoisie. Unlike most Coloured fraternal groups, however, the I.O.T.T. included women, Africans, and even whites in its membership.[9]

For reasons we do not know, Alexander left these socially and politically liberal and racially inclusive organizations and returned to an ecclesiastical vocation. He became affiliated with an independent religious body known as the African Church. On 15 September 1924, a group of dissident clergy of this church, including Alexander, met and passed a resolution which viewed with alarm the "retrogression" of their denomination. Calling it the oldest separatist church in the Union,[10] they said it had become controlled by an "uneducated clique" under its founder Bishop J.M. Kanyane Napo, a former Anglican. Also, its finances were in difficulty and there were problems with legal permission to officiate at marriages. Napo had founded the African Church in 1889. He had been a colleague of Mangena M. Mokone who opposed racial segregation in the churches, sought African religious self-government, and founded the Ethiopian Church in 1892.[11] The dissidents determined to seek affiliation with the African Orthodox Church, a new Negro denomination in the United States related to the Garvey Movement.[12]

In a subsequent meeting in Beaconsfield on 6 October 1924, the group made a formal break with the African Church and elected Alexander its head.[13] Present at this meeting was Joseph Masoga, the local agent for Marcus Garvey's newspaper, *The Negro World*, and the organizer of the Afro-Construction Church of the House of Athlyi.[14] It is reasonable to assume that Alexander knew about the African Orthodox Church from Garvey's paper.[15] The Afro-Construction Church of the House of Athlyi is an example of unusually strong African nationalism. Like the Rastafari cult in Jamaica, it also illustrates religious veneration of Marcus Garvey. The church still exists in the Kimberley area. Its remarkable literature (*The Holy Piby, The Royal Parchment Scroll of Black Supremacy,* and *The Promised Key*) has recently been discovered by Robert A. Hill who is preparing it for republication. These extraordinary documents dramatically link American, Jamaican, and South African religious nationalist movements.

The African Orthodox Church had been founded in New York City on 2 September 1921, by George Alexander McGuire, a native of Antigua, a sometime Anglican priest, and one of the leading Negro clergymen of the Protestant Episcopal Church.[16] Although it has always welcomed white participation, the purpose of the new denomination was "to cast off forever the yoke of white Ecclesiastical dominance" and to express "the spirit of racial leadership . . . in harmony with the aroused racial consciousness of the Negro people,"[17] that is, the black nationalism of the Garvey Movement.

Constituted primarily of West Indians of Anglican background, the church was—and continues to be—deeply committed to formal liturgy, a hierarchical priesthood, and defending the validity of its episcopal orders. McGuire received consecration at the hands of Joseph René Vilatte, Metropolitan of the American Catholic Church in the U.S.A.[18] Vilatte's own consecration was derived from the Syro-Jacobite Patriarch of Antioch via Archbishop Francisco F.X. Alvarez, Mar Julius I, Metropolitan of the Independent Catholic Church of Ceylon, Goa, and India.[19] The display of "valid" ecclesiastical pedigrees in order to justify the legitimacy of their ordinations assumed great importance to the AOC both in the United States and Africa. In part, this was the case because its clergy tended to define themselves in relation to the Church of England where this legitimacy is taken for granted. It can certainly be argued that their lack of preferment in established denominations led both Africans and American blacks to seek alternative avenues for advancement and self-rule. For churchmen brought up on the doctrine of apostolic succession, it was only natural to seek legitimacy from the Eastern and Oriental Orthodox churches whose historical authenticity is universally recognized and even more ancient than that of Anglicanism.

The African Orthodox Church was tied to the Garvey Movement particularly through the person of Archbishop McGuire, who served as chaplain-general of the Universal Negro Improvement Association and was one of Garvey's most able lieutenants.[20] McGuire was aligned with Garvey in advocating prideful black self-consciousness, a rediscovery of the African cultural heritage, and black control over black institutions. Despite strong ties to Garvey and Garveyism, however, McGuire was always a churchman before he was a Negro nationalist or political activist, and the AOC perceived itself as a church rather than as a vehicle for social protest. Even so, the very creation of the church as a separate Negro institution made it an expression and manifestation of the black nationalism of the period.

In a petition to McGuire dated 24 September 1924, Alexander on behalf of himself and four other priests and their congregations asked to affiliate with the AOC. The Rev. Edwin Urban Lewis reported to the British government that McGuire read a letter on 29 October 1924[21] to a "secret conference" at U.N.I.A. headquarters from the "Archdeacon of Pretoria" requesting admission for himself and 500 parishioners. Lewis recalls McGuire's response to have been: "Yourself and congregation coming over to us will be welcome, and as Lord Primate of the African Orthodox Church, should you make it possible for Sir Marcus Garvey to get in to that country I am sure that the day will not be far off when by virtue of my high office, I will consecrate you as bishop for South Africa."[22]

Lewis believed the AOC to be a "gang of religious fanatics who were seditious against the government of Great Britain," and so kept the British consul general in New York informed of its activities. The fact that Lewis himself was a one-time AOC priest who had been expelled by the Fourth General Synod for laxity of duty may have outweighed his expressed concern "for the safety of the Church of England." H.G. Armstrong, the British consul, apparently took Lewis seriously, however, for he later reported to his embassy: "It is generally understood that the consecration of clergymen by McGuire is part of his scheme to cause dissension, together with the Marcus Garvey association, among negroes of the British Empire."

McGuire proceeded to authorize Alexander to act as his vicar apostolic "for the purpose of organizing an independent and local branch" of the AOC. "The various groups of our people in Africa and elsewhere must be given, when prepared, their own self-governing churches within the Communion of the Holy African Orthodox Church," McGuire stated. Presumably on the basis of McGuire's authorization Alexander was styled "the Venerable Daniel William Alexander, Archdeacon and Vicar-General of the Diocese and Vicariates of the Cape of Good Hope and Rector of the Church of St. Augustine of Hippo."[23]

A provisional synod was held in Beaconsfield on October 6, attended by 400 people, at which the AOC of South Africa was officially organized. Perhaps McGuire requested, or required, more formal proceedings than the September petition. On the motion of the Rev. Ezekiel Leagise, the Synod voted to elect Alexander bishop, to seek affiliation with the AOC in America, and to ask McGuire for credentials authorizing Alexander to administer the diocese and to deal with the South African government on behalf of the church. The expectation was that Alexander would be consecrated at the next (the fifth) AOC General Synod in New York in 1925. Alexander reported on the "disabilities confronting natives" in the Church of England in South Africa, including the low education standards for black clergy. It was clear that both McGuire and Alexander saw the new church's mission to be "to arouse people of African descent in the Anglican Communion to declare for freedom by declining the crumbs which fall from the tables of their religious overlords, and to maintain and control their own ecclesiastical institutions."[24]

Alexander suggested he had severed connections with the

Church of England, although it was the African Church of Bishop J.M. Kanyane Napo where he had been dean and vicar general and from which he had resigned. McGuire was highly enthusiastic at the whole turn of events. "The East and the West have met each other in the African Orthodox Church," he said, and without any missionary activity except through the news column of *The Negro World*, to which he expressed his thanks. McGuire used the occasion to ask rhetorically when Negro Churchmen (that is, Anglicans in America and the West Indies) would follow the example of brethren in the motherland, declare themselves free and "have the scales fall from their eyes." And, not least, "The remarkable thing about it all is that there is no appeal for funds."[25]

Events in South Africa evoked a poem from Rev. Sister Angelina Theresa, an AOC deaconess:

There's a Cry

There's a Cry from Pretoria!
"Come over and help us
In our efforts as men to be free."
How it sounds in the ear,
'Tis glad tidings we hear
From our Brothers at Home o'er the sea.
They have caught the bright Vision,
They have seen the new light
Which appeared to our Primate
As he gazed into night,—
"This change shalt thou keep,
Go gather thy sheep
From their Spiritual bondage and sleep."[26]

Alexander himself composed a poem:

Work and Wait

Up brothers! 'Tis a mighty deed
Angels would covet to begin,
Clapping their wings in eager speed
A Universe to win.

Toil on! It is your Master's will;
His own bright world in chaos stood
Waiting the labors of His skill,
Ere he pronounced it "good."

Union is Strength! A phalanx stand
Breasting the world's contempt and scorn,
E'en should not palm-branch weigh your hand,
No crown your brow adorn.

Truth,—holy truth, deathless, divine
Engraven on the immortal scroll;
With God's eternal throne for shrine,
Empire from pole to pole.

Does this demand your reverend care,
A martyrdom of faith and zeal?
Armed for the battle, boldly dare
The issue, woe or weal.

Duty is ours, and high-souled trust
In Him no mortal can defy:
Work! For His law is good and just;
Wait! Truth can never die.[27]

Alexander soon travelled to the Transvaal where he received two Anglican priests into the AOC, D.F. Brown and Fred Hugels. They joined his original clergy: Michael Moncho, Ezekiel Leagise, and James Monare.[28] Both Alexander and McGuire saw their labors as part of the new black spirit of the times. McGuire pointed out that Alexander, whose parents came from Martinique, illustrated "an instance of African forbears brought to the West in slavery contributing to the spiritual emancipation of their people in supplying them with their first independent native bishop." In the South African context, it is interesting that the AOC under Alexander, a Coloured, attracted African, Coloured, and white clergy, although most of its membership was African. This cooperation is, again, probably due to the fact that the church offered legitimacy, autonomy, and personal opportunity. Alexander wrote: "If the Black Race could only digest what is now being taught for our upliftment we would make all nations respect us. We need Race pride, respect for each other, and the ambition to achieve for ourselves that which is constructive and substantial. . . ."[29]

When the South African church's Deed of Election, dated 6 October 1924, and signed by the Provisional Synod, reached McGuire it announced that Alexander had been named not merely bishop, but archbishop and primate. McGuire explained to his own followers in America that the Africans, as former clergy and laity of the Church of England, had organized a Province of the AOC and thus required the office of primate and archbishop; these were, of course, the same titles McGuire had evolved for his own position.[30]

The African AOC first Provincial Synod was held 1 January 1925, in Alexander's Beaconsfield church. Alexander celebrated mass, omitting for the first time the filioque clause from the Nicene Creed in accordance with Orthodox usage. Three clerical and six lay deputies were present as well as members of the church and "friends of our cause" including P. Jampies, "an influential citizen of Kimberley." John Balston was elected secretary and Charles Sweetwater treasurer. The decisions of the Provisional Synod were ratified changing the title of the bishop-elect to archbishop-elect since the AOC in South Africa would be a full church in its own right but in communion with the AOC in America. Perhaps this change grew out of Alexander's visit to various governmental agencies when he went to the capital to register the denomination.[31]

Each congregation was requested to contribute £7 toward Alexander's proposed visit to the U.S. to receive the episcopate. This was described as a particular burden under "the new Hertzog Government whose policy is to oust the Black man from his job to make way for the poor White." It was expected that "the Negroes of America" would pay Alexander's return fare.

The Provincial Synod of the new church was to meet quadrennially, with annual Diocesan synods. The Rev. Ezekiel Leagise was commissioned as archdeacon of Barkly West, and the Rev. Michael Moncho, archdeacon of Douglas and Hope Town. The Synod expressed hope that the American church would establish a Pan-African Church Synod to meet every four years to be attended by delegates from both provinces and patterned after the Pan-Anglican Synod. The purposes would be to discuss worldwide expansion, promote missionary endeavor, stimulate racial welfare and uplift movements, liberate black men from the influence of white missionaries, establish a central seminary and college, and seek full communion with the "Ancient African Church of Abyssinia."[32]

Alexander sent a message to his "Fellow Churchmen in America," announcing that his receiving a valid consecration would "prove the key to our ecclesiastical freedom here in Africa." He suggested putting away selfishness, pride, and petty jealousies—

perhaps because he sensed these existed for McGuire at his request for an archbishopric and primacy—and urged making common cause for the AOC by quoting the late President Kruger's motto "Unity Makes Strength." "Pray for all Negro clergymen," he advised, "who are still in ecclesiastical bondage, hankering after the few dollars they receive. Pray that they may come out of Egypt, and following our Moses, enter with us the Promised Land of spiritual liberty."[33] He announced that he had celebrated sung masses on Christmas eve and Christmas day with procession and incense. His work was complicated, he pointed out, by the necessity of preaching in English, Dutch, Sixosa, Sesuto, and Lechuana. He planned to translate *The Divine Liturgy* so "all may understand our Catholic worship."

With no explanation, McGuire soon announced that he had appointed Isaiah Palmerston Samuels of Cape Town his commissary in the Union of South Africa "to gather such information as may be required of him." Samuel was McGuire's half-brother who had gone to Africa as an educator specializing in music.[34]

The same issue of *The Negro Churchman* carried a strongly worded statement on the new situation for blacks in South Africa at the defeat of the Smuts government. Entitled "This is Africa!," the byline gave the source as "From a Lay Contributor" but was most probably Alexander. The article pointed out that the new Nationalist government was "absolutely anti-native" and cited: the requirement that native women carry passes, the fact that lands were being taken and the Africans driven to barren tracts of "locations" to die from thirst and starvation, the selling of kaffir beer, and the lack of legislative representation, education, hospitals, and housing.

McGuire was now openly hesitant about giving Alexander the episcopate, undoubtedly because the South African Orthodox Church saw itself as independent of the American church; "except in the matter of communion," McGuire noted, "we would have no other relations with them." Also, Samuels advised caution. "We shall deal justly with our brethren in Africa," said McGuire, "but must think prayerfully, carefully and patiently before entrusting to these natives the precious gift they seek."[35]

When the Synod met in September, it countered the desire of Alexander and his church to be autonomous and autocephalous by offering to receive them on probation as a "Mission Territory" under the control of an American bishop, with Alexander confirmed only as vicar apostolic, and with a grant of financial aid, "should our terms be acceptable."[36] Alexander accepted the terms: "because we have left the white man's church, and if we have boasted of our connection with you, should we today be too proud to undergo a two year's probation. . . ?" but he did hint at an alternative affiliation—with the AME Church—if their request were not granted at the end of the period. Alexander also mentioned that he had already been consecrated "at the hands of certain native bishops (not of the Catholic episcopate)." With some annoyance, McGuire pointed out that Alexander was using an episcopal seal and mitre on his stationery and signing himself the "Right Reverend."[37]

Alexander then furnished the AOC with a copy of his report to the government on churches and membership which showed considerable progress after eighteen months of work:

S. Augustine, Beaconsfield, Very Rev. D.W. Alexander, 210 members
S. Barnabas, Greenpoint, Very Rev. D.W. Alexander
S. James, Waldecks Plant, Ven. M. Moncho, 80
S. Peter's, Good Hope, Rev. Fr. M.J. Dithebe, 30
Good Shepherd, Home Station, Rev. Fr. G. Daniels
Railway Mission, Dronfield, Rev. Fr. G. Daniels, 198
Home Station, Warrenton, Rev. Fr. G. Daniels
S. Monica's, Kimberley, Rev. Fr. J. Monare, 29
S. Paul's, Veryu, Rev. D.W. Alexander, 20
S. Monica's, Johannesburg, Ven. D.F. Brown, 50
S. Bartalomew's, Johannesburg, Rev. Fr. J. Mamane, 106
S. Peter's, South Johannesburg, Rev. Fr. D.P. Morgan, 25
S. Cyprian, Fustonburg, Reader K.P. Hagano, 400

"God is working mightily for us," said Alexander, "And all under black leadership." Four of the clergy were new: a Roman Catholic, a Swedenborgian, an Anglican, and a Wesleyan.[38]

Whatever doubts McGuire held either about "these natives" or Alexander's claim to equal him in ecclesiastical title and rank seem to have been dispelled by the time of the AOC's seventh General Synod in 1927. The happy solution was to be two provinces of the same church, one African and headed by a bishop consecrated by "Bishops of his own Race, whose ancestors were forcibly removed from their Motherland," the other American headed by another archbishop and primate—but both presided over by McGuire with the new title of patriarch or head of the entire church, now defined as a Pan-African Orthodox Conclave.[39]

Alexander arrived in New York 23 August 1927. On Labor Day he was confirmed and received minor orders from Bishop William E.J. Robertson. The same day he was ordained by McGuire. On Sunday, 11 September 1927, in the Church of St. Michael and All Angels in Boston, he was consecrated archbishop and primate of the African Province by McGuire, assisted by Bishops Robertson and Arthur S. Trotman. He was also awarded the honorary degree Doctor of Divinity by McGuire, a prerogative of Orthodox hierarchs.

At the consecration of an African for an African church by men of African descent, the congregation was visibly moved by the Gospel for the day: "Blessed are the eyes that see the things that ye see; for I tell you, that many prophets and kings have desired to see them, and have not seen them; and to hear those things which ye hear, and have not heard them."[40] Even more dramatic, at the very moment of consecration—the laying on of hands and the statement "Receive ye the Holy Ghost"—there was a peal of thunder followed by a copious shower which fell in direct vertical sheets to the earth.[41]

After his return to Africa, Alexander began to organize new churches throughout the southern part of the continent and to receive into the African Orthodox Church a number of Anglican priests and laymen. The secessions from Anglicanism apparently aroused considerable interest and discussion.[42] Apart from establishing a new denomination, Alexander's most significant work was his role in the founding of other independent churches. The beginnings of the African Orthodox Churches in Uganda and Kenya have been well documented by F.B. Welbourn's study and need be treated here only in outline.[43]

In 1925 Reuben Mukasa Spartas, a Ugandan Anglican, read *The Negro World*, founded the African Progressive Association, and vowed "to go to hell, jail or die for the redemption of Africa."[44] He corresponded with McGuire who put him in touch with Alexander in 1928. Alexander appointed Spartas a layreader. In 1929 Spartas announced his break with Anglicanism and the formation of the African Orthodox Church in Uganda: "a church established for all right-thinking Africans, men who wish to be free in their own house, not always being thought of as boys."[45]

At Spartas's request, Alexander came to Uganda in 1931 and on Trinity Sunday, 1932, ordained as priests Spartas and his brother-in-law Obadiah Basajjakitalo. Later that same year Spartas was put in touch with Nicodemus Sarikas, the Greek Orthodox Archimandrite in Tanganyika. Suspicious of Alexander's Orthodoxy, Spartas severed the relationship in order to petition Meletios II, the Greek Patriarch of Alexandria, for admission. Despite the question of Alexander's orders, in 1946 the Patriarchate received Spartas and the re-named African Greek Orthodox Church into full membership under its jurisdiction. This branch of the AOC thus became the first independent African church to place itself under European authority, the first church in the Vilatte succession to be accepted by a historic communion, and the first major contemporary expression of Greek Orthodox missionary interest.

Returning to South Africa from Uganda in late 1932, Alexander met James Beauttah, the Kikuyu nationalist leader, in Mombasa. Kikuyu resentment over British land and labor policies had come to a crisis in 1929 when the Church of Scotland Missions forbade clitoridectomy—the practice of female circumcision which was both the central rite of passage whereby girls were inducted into Kikuyu culture and society and the unifying symbol of the whole tribal system.[46] The Kikuyu had withdrawn from the Scottish, Anglican, and other missions in large numbers, taking their churches and schools with them and eventually forming two new bodies: the Kikuyu Independent Schools Association (K.I.S.A.) and the Kikuyu Karing'a ("Pure") Education Association.

Schools and churches were closely intertwined institutions. Separation from the missions brought educational independence, but the Kikuyu were bereft of clergy to baptize their children. They appealed to the Anglican bishop of Mombasa who insisted on the abandoning of clitoridectomy as a prerequisite to future baptisms. The Kikuyu argued eloquently, basing their case on Scripture, but to no avail. Hoping that political autonomy might also mean religious autonomy, they then appealed to the bishop of Liberia, but he would not intrude into the ecclesiastical territory of the bishop of Mombasa.

Alexander had kept in touch with Kikuyu spokesmen[47] and

was invited to Kenya since he led a church "of the Africans, governed by the Africans and for the Africans to make daily supplications to Almighty God led by priests who have the welfare of Africans at heart."[48] Arriving in Nairobi in November 1935, Alexander was contracted by the Kikuyu for a period of eighteen months, within which he was to ordain African priests and to baptize.[49] Provided with an automobile, Alexander travelled widely throughout the area baptizing large numbers, preaching, and teaching.

The Kikuyu then began to criticize him for profiting too much from baptismal fees, for not setting apart a native clergy, and for baptizing so many people that his clerical successors would have difficulties maintaining themselves economically. Alexander found the Kikuyu a proud people unshakably committed to their independence and so "a hard bone to chew."[50] He ordained four men[51] and was forced to give them his vestments and his automobile. Ordaining two "high priests" and two "low priests," Alexander created an immediate schism. Although all parties looked to him as their spiritual father, two churches emerged: the African Orthodox Church related to Karing'a and the African Independent Pentecostal Church[52] related to the K.I.S.A.

Although the subsequent relationships among men, churches, and schools became highly complex, the point is that when Alexander sailed from Kenya on 7 July 1937, he left behind him "an ordained African clergy functioning outside the auspices of any Kenyan mission."[53] The cultural nationalism expressed in the independent churches and schools, with their leadership legitimized by Alexander, developed into increasingly overt forms of political nationalism. The culmination was the Mau Mau movement and, ultimately, Kenyan independence.[54] Also, as in Uganda, Alexander's Orthodoxy added a unique direction to the independent church movement by introducing "high church" elements such as the sign of the cross, the crucifix, the mass, and sacraments celebrated in a mixture of Anglican and Roman rites.[55]

Alexander had relatively less involvement with the small branch of the African Orthodox Church which developed in the Gold Coast in the 1930s. Unlike the churches in Kenya and Uganda, however, it was for some time under his episcopal jurisdiction. Six black American missionaries formerly associated with the Garvey Movement went to West Africa in 1931 under the auspices of the African Universal Church. When support from that body failed, the Rev. Carey Harold Jones—the one missionary who continued—returned to the United States in 1945 to visit Archbishop Robertson, Alexander's co-consecrator and McGuire's successor as patriarch of the AOC. Robertson referred Jones to Alexander who received him into the African Province in 1955. Financial difficulties kept Alexander from ever visiting the Gold Coast, but six mission stations there remained under his authority until 1960.

That year—1960—saw the end of the loose affiliation between Alexander's churches in South Africa and the African Orthodox Church in America. Alexander provided for proper succession to his episcopacy by selecting two South Africans, Surgeon Lionel Motsepe and Ice Walter Mbina, for consecration. In June Patriarch Robertson and Archbishop Richard Robinson travelled to South Africa and, assisted by Alexander, consecrated Motsepe and Mbina in the Anglican Church of All Saints, Kimberley. Although we do not know the issues, Alexander and the Americans quarreled, and the patriarch excommunicated him; Robertson put Mbina in Alexander's place as administrator of the South African church. Further, Robertson declared Jones in the Gold Coast independent of Alexander's authority and raised Jones to the bishopric of a newly-created Province of West Africa.

Of the two new bishops, Motsepe soon died and in Natal Mbina seceded to form the Holy Orthodox Church, taking a substantial number of members with him. Alexander proceeded to rename his group the African Orthodox Church in the Republic of South Africa and to elevate his church building in Kimberley—named for St. Augustine of Hippo—from pro-cathedral to cathedral status. Alexander died in Kimberley Hospital on 14 May 1970, leaving a South African church of 20 congregations, 50 ordained clergy, and 4 bishops-elect.

Independent churches serve as entrees into white European Christianity and culture and also as conservers of black African civilization and leadership. This amalgam is particularly true of the African Orthodox Church. A constitutional statement affiliating AOC groups in Kenya and Uganda in 1943 specifically declares that a primary purpose of the church is "to preserve African customs and traditions in relation with spiritual and educational matters."[56] Sociological studies make clear that the AOC has in fact been a bridge between the new religion and old values. In Larteh, Ghana, the African Orthodox Church is the only one of the twelve local churches where menstruating women sit in the back of the church and are not permitted to receive Holy Communion. With the Larteh Salvation Army from which it split off, the AOC—unlike the other churches—allows polygamy, allows converts to keep all their wives, and allows any chief who is a member to perform traditional rites.[57] In Tiriki, Kenya, the AOC, in contrast to the other local separatist churches, permits polygamy and social and ritual beer-drinking and encourages its youth to participate in the traditional circumcision and initiation ceremonies.[58]

Archbishop Alexander, of course, was not directly responsible for these African characteristics in churches not under his jurisdiction. In fact, churches and church life under his control were consciously and intentionally Western. But by his very existence he personified for nearly fifty years Africanization in church leadership, and not only in the denomination he founded. He legitimized the authority of a large number of independent denominations by ordaining their clergy. Alexander's appeal was that he symbolized an external power with apostolic claims combined with the racial and national identity of a native African.

It is of course this claim to valid apostolic succession which sets Alexander apart from the charismatic leadership of other independent churches and which places him and the African Orthodox Church in a unique position vis-a-vis the traditional churches.[59]

The most significant recent implication of Alexander's episcopacy has to do with recent divisions among the Orthodox of East Africa. A small Westernized group remained loyal to the Greek Patriarchate of Alexandria, but, dissatisfied with Greek rule and still striving for an autocephalous national church, Father Spartas returned to independency. He led a large,[60] loose confederation of bodies which identified itself with the Coptic Church of Egypt. There was no formal affiliation, but the Copts admitted students from Spartas's group into their seminary in Cairo and, if reasonable conditions were met, considered consecrating a bishop. In the meantime this loose confederation referred to itself as Coptic—and justified the identification by its descent from Alexander. The history is now unknown or forgotten. Alexander is remembered as "a Negro from U.S.A. who came to East Africa through Ethiopia," and it is believed that he was himself consecrated by the Syrian Jacobite patriarch who sent him to East Africa. This consecration by a non-Chalcedonian Oriental patriarch is therefore perceived as tieing to Coptic Orthodoxy those who derive their orders from Alexander: "so in this case we are Originated with the Coptic Patriarchate of Alexandria."[61] More recently, Spartas has been received back into the Greek Church and consecrated a bishop.

Alexander was undoubtedly honest in denying both direct links to the Garvey Movement[62] and any political motivation in his ecclesiastical work.[63] Yet by establishing African churches with African characteristics, Alexander manifested the cultural nationalism of Garveyism and encouraged the realization among Africans—learned long before by Europeans—that if they could control their own churches they could control other institutions of their own as well. Alexander found inspiration for independence in Garvey's newspaper and a vehicle for independence in the denomination related to the Universal Negro Improvement Association. Independent churches were the first achievement in the long struggle toward the realization of Garvey's goal of self-determination, "Africa for the Africans." Of course this was a goal articulated and worked for by others as well, but Alexander's biography supports Hodgkin's claim that it was the Garvey Movement "in which the strands of Ethiopianism and Pan-Africanism were closely interwoven."[64]

While Alexander's debt to the African patriotism and nationalism of Garveyite ideology should not be neglected, Alexander—like McGuire—was a churchman before he was a social critic or political activist, despite the fact that the origin of the African Orthodox Church in both Africa and the United States was a reaction against societies built on racism. The accomplishment of political independence has not lessened the growth of independent churches, and David Barrett emphasizes the fact that for these churches "independency is basically a religious phenomenon arising out of a religious need and now that the anti-colonial struggle has been won in most territories, it is free to turn its attention to religious issues."[65] From this perspective Alexander's role as churchman comes into clearer focus and informs a better understanding of his life, his significance, and the need for independent black churches to have their own identity, integrity, and authenticity. As that need is fulfilled, the ecumenical importance[66] of the African Orthodox Church, the place of Archbishop Alexander as its chief African founder, and the historical place of the church in the development of Pan-Africanism can only become more widely appreciated.

> —*International Journal of African Historical Studies* 16:4 (1983), 615–630. Portions of this essay in an earlier form were read at the American Academy of Religion, New England Region, Tufts University, April 17, 1972; and at a conference on "Afro-American Interaction with Southern Africa," Howard University, May 28, 1979

Notes

1. T.D. Mweli Skota, editor of *The African Yearly Register: Being an Illustrated National Biographical Dictionary (Who's Who) of Black Folks in Africa* (Johannesburg, 1932?), p. 129, says Alexander was born in 1880.
2. There is an incomplete, unpublished, handwritten autobiography among Alexander's papers from which this information is taken. Alexander's papers are now on deposit in the Pitts Theological Library, Emory University, Atlanta, Georgia. I was able to examine them briefly in South Africa in July 1971. Arthur C. Terry-Thompson, *The History of the African Orthodox Church* (New York, 1956), p. 82, says Alexander's mother was Isabella Martini and that he was the "second son" of his parents. The informant of Frank H. Hulme in *Blackwall to Bloemfontein: An Unconventional Autobiography* (Durban, 1950?), p. 328, claims Alexander was the child of "a coloured American father and a coloured mother from Durban." This is repeated by Peter F. Anson, *Bishops at Large* (London, 1964), p. 267.

   For Javanese in South Africa, see Izak D. duPlessis, *The Cape Malays* (Cape Town, 1944?), passim.
3. Mauritians were often legally categorized as Europeans in South Africa.
4. F.D. Corfield, *Historical Survey of the Origins and Growth of Mau Mau* (London, 1960), p. 173. Government references for this document are Cmd. 1030, 1960, and Kenya Sessional Paper No. 5, 1959/60 (Nairobi, 1960). At Alexander's visit to the United States in 1929 the British consul in New York informed his embassy that Alexander was travelling on a French passport, No. 16, issued by the French consul in Johannesburg on 14 March 1927. The report further states that Alexander "was unable to get a British passport, but has always looked upon himself as a British subject and claims to be loyal to the British government." I am indebted to Robert Hill for this reference: FO 115/3380 (1929).

   Corfield further alleges that Alexander was convicted of theft in Johannesburg in 1912 and classified as an agitator in 1929. The Veiligheid (Security Branch) of the South African Police is unable to furnish information on the first allegation and categorically denies the second. Fred B. Welbourn, *East*

African Rebels: A Study of Some Independent Churches (London, 1961), p. 252, rightly draws attention to the questionable factual value of Corfield's source material.

5. The battle of Colenso on 15 December 1899 was a major British defeat.
6. One of the first projects of the Community of the Resurrection in South Africa was the establishment of a college for training catechists at Doornfontein in Johannesburg. According to the Rev. K.U. Davie, C.R., "I think Daniel William Alexander was probably under training as a catechist in our college and may possibly have got to the permanent diaconate." Letter to the writer, 20 November 1974.
7. Sheila Patterson, *Colour and Culture in South Africa* (London, 1953), p. 159. See also J.S. Marais, *The Cape Coloured People 1652-1937* (London, 1939), pp. 274-280.

    The Rev. John S. Likhing, Alexander's later colleague as general secretary of the African Orthodox Church, was also provisional president of the African National Congress in Bechuanaland and Griqualand West Province as well as assistant chaplain to the A.N.C. See Skota, *The African Yearly Register*, p. 172; see also Peter Walshe, *The Rise of African Nationalism in South Africa: The African National Congress 1912-1952* (Berkeley, 1971), pp. 226-227.
8. Ellen Hellman, ed., *Handbook on Race Relations in South Africa* (Cape Town, 1949), p. 252. See also "Land Tenure by Asiatics and South African Coloured in the Transvaal," *Race Relations*, II, 5 (November 1935), 42-46.
9. Patterson, *Colour and Culture*, pp. 157, 310. Olive Schreiner's brother, W.P. Schreiner, prime minister of Cape Colony, was one prominent white member. For Schreiner's views on temperance, see Eric A. Walker, *W.P. Schreiner: A South African* (London, 1969), pp. 52-53.
10. They said it had been founded thirty-six years previously. In fact, the oldest independent church is the Tembu, founded in 1884 by Nehemiah Tile, an ex-Wesleyan. See C.C. Saunders, "Tile and the Thembu Church: Politics and Independency on the Cape Eastern Frontier in the Late Nineteenth Century," *Journal of African History*, XI, 4 (1970), 553-570.
11. Bengt G.M. Sundkler, *Bantu Prophets in South Africa* (London, 1961), p. 39. For Tile's influence on Mokone, see W.M. Cameron, "The Ethiopian Movement and the Order of Ethiopia," *The East and the West*, II (1904), 376. There are biographies of Tile and Mokone in Skota, *The African Yearly Register*. For a fascinating account by Alexander himself, see "The Separatist Church Movement in South Africa," *The Negro Churchman*, V, 11 (December 1927), 3-4; VI, 1 (January 1928), 7-8.
12. See Richard Newman, "The Origins of the African Orthodox Church," *The Negro Churchman: The Official Organ of the African Orthodox Church* (Millwood, 1977), pp. iii–xxii [see above].
13. The minutes of both these meetings, in Alexander's handwriting, are among his papers.
14. Sundkler, *Bantu Prophets*, p. 58.
15. Alexander confirmed this in his address to the seventh General Synod of the AOC. Garvey's impact on Africa has always been underestimated. For the influence of *The Negro World*, see George Shepperson and Thomas Price, *Independent African: John Chilembwe and the Origins, Setting and Signifi-*

Archbishop Daniel William Alexander 127

cance of the Nyasaland Native Rising of 1915 (Edinburgh, 1958), p. 494; George Padmore, Pan-Africanism or Communism? (London, 1956), p. 349; Amy Jacques Garvey, Garvey and Garveyism (Kingston, 1963), p. 285; Robert H. Brisbane, Jr., "Some New Light on the Garvey Movement," The Journal of Negro History, XXXVI, 1 (January 1951), 59; in "His Excellency: The Provincial [sic] President of Africa," Phylon, X, 3 (Third Quarter 1949), 262, Brisbane says the newspaper was even translated into drumcode and sent into the interior.

16. Gavin White, "Patriarch McGuire and the Episcopal Church," Historical Magazine of the Protestant Episcopal Church, 38, 2 (June 1969), 109–141.

17. Terry-Thompson, History, pp. 50, 53.

18. Vilatte is generally considered an ecclesiastical adventurer whose orders may have been technically valid but were certainly irregular. See Anson, Bishops at Large, pp. 91–129. For a discussion of validity and regularity, see H.R.T. Brandreth, Episcopi Vagantes and the Anglican Church, 2nd ed. (London, 1961), pp. 8–15.

19. There is an account of Alvarez in E.M. Philip, The Indian Church of St. Thomas (Nagercoil, 1950), pp. 420–428, 430–431. While schismatic, his church had suffered from Roman Catholic, particularly Jesuit, persecution. It is fashionable to regard Alvarez and Vilatte as mere episcopi vagantes (i.e., wandering bishops without responsibility to any particular jurisdiction), or worse, although their consecrations were expressly commanded by Ignatius Peter III, Syrian Orthodox patriarch of Antioch and All the East. Admittedly, the patriarchate has since repudiated the claims of the Vilatte succession.

20. Wilson Record, "The Negro Intellectual and Negro Nationalism," Social Forces, 33, 1 (October 1954), 17. For the case that Garvey himself was the theologian of a civil religion, see Randall K. Burkett, Garveyism as a Religious Movement (Metuchen, N.J., 1978).

21. According to Alexander's Die Kategismus vir die wat leer vir Doop en Aanneming van de Afrikaanse Ortodoks Kerk (Kimberley, 1951), p. 15, the church was founded in South Africa on 6 October 1924.

22. FO 371/9633, No. 213. See also FO 115/3380. I am indebted to Robert A. Hill for this reference.

23. "The Very Latest," The Negro Churchman, II, 11 (November 1924), 1.

24. "The African Orthodox Church Links East with West," The Negro Churchman, II, 12 (December 1924), 1–2.

25. Ibid.

26. The Negro Churchman, II, 12 (December 1924).

27. Ibid., III, 1 (January 1925), 4.

28. "Our Church in South Africa," The Negro Churchman, III, 1 (January 1925), 4.

29. Ibid.

30. "The South African Church," The Negro Churchman, III, 2 (February 1925), 6.

31. "The First Provincial Synod of South Africa," The Negro Churchman, III, 3 (March 1925), 2.

32. Ibid., p. 3.

33. "A Message from Africa," The Negro Churchman, III, 3 (March 1925), 3.

34. "Commissary in South Africa," The Negro Churchman, III, 4 (April 1925), 2.

35. "The Fifth General Synod," *The Negro Churchman*, III, 7 (July 1925), 1-2.

36. "The Fifth General Synod a Great Success," *The Negro Churchman*, III, 9 (October 1925), 3.

37. "The South African Church," *The Negro Churchman*, IV, 1 (January 1926), 5. It was the Ethiopian Catholic Church where Alexander first received consecration.

38. "The South African Work," *The Negro Churchman*, IV, 7 (July 1926), 5.

39. "The Seventh General Synod," *The Negro Churchman*, V, 9 (October 1927), 3-4.

40. Luke 10:23-24.

41. Terry-Thompson, *History*, p. 75. The service is described in "Consecration Service," *The Negro Churchman*, V, 9 (October 1927), 7.

42. Hellman, *Handbook*, p. 567. Alexander later received the African United Church of some 1000 members along with its founder, the Rev. Joel Davids, who had seceded from the Anglican Church after being the first African ordained to the priesthood in the Transvaal. See "The African United Church Affiliates with the African Orthodox Church," *The Negro Churchman*, VII, 8 (October 1929), 6-7.

43. *East African Rebels*, pp. 77-100, 135-162.

44. Quoted by Welbourn, *East African Rebels*, p. 81. An early nationalist, Spartas continued to have an active and controversial political career as a leader of the Sons of Kintu and the Bataka Party which grew out of it. See David E. Apter, *The Political Kingdom in Uganda* (Princeton, 1961), pp. 248-254. It is interesting that the motto of the Sons of Kintu—"One God, one aim, one destiny"—was that of Garvey's U.N.I.A. Spartas also wanted the patriarchal see of the AOC located in Africa. See *The Negro Churchman*, VI, 11 (December 1928), 3; VII, 1 (January 1929), 4; VII, 6 (July 1929), 3-4.

45. Quoted by Welbourn, *East African Rebels*, p. 81. This and the following information was confirmed in a personal interview with Spartas in Kampala on 25 July 1971.

46. Jomo Kenyatta, *Facing Mt. Kenya: The Tribal Life of the Gikuyu* (New York, n.d.), pp. 125-148.

47. Parmenas Mukeri, the Kikuyu Central Association leader who accompanied Kenyatta to London in 1931, was publicly welcomed by Alexander in South Africa on Mukeri's journey back to Kenya.

48. Kikuyu Independent Schools Association connected with the African Independent Pentecostal Church, *Report and Constitution, 1938* (Nyeri, 1938), p. 2.

49. Negly Farson, *Last Chance in Africa* (London, 1949), p. 129, mistakenly divided Alexander in two: "To get their own priests, the Kikuyus brought up a black Bishop from South Africa—from the Orthodox Church, which is almost like the Greek Church—and a Negro pastor from the U.S.A. named William Alexander. . . ."

50. Bartolomeo Moriondo, "Come conobbi l'Arcivescovo Ortodosso," *Missioni Consolata*, 46, 8-9 (September-October 1944), 94.

51. Harrison Gacokia, Arthur Gatung'u, Philip Kiandi, and Daudi Maina.

52. Pentecostal here means apostolic rather than any of the charismatic characteristics usually associated with "Pentecostalism."

53. Carl G. Rosberg, Jr., and John Nottingham, *The Myth of "Mau Mau": Nationalism in Kenya* (Nairobi, 1966), p. 130.

54. Corfield, *Historical Survey*, p. 174, takes a somewhat contradictory view of Alexander's political influence. On the one hand, he reports the opinion of the district commissioner at Fort Hall that Alexander's presence contributed to the peace of the area; on the other, he asserts that Alexander's choice of ministers sowed "the seeds of future dissension." Kikuyu Central Association leaders he links to Alexander include Arthur Gathuma, Jesse Kariuki, Daudi Maina, Wambugu Maina, Job Muchuchu, and George Ndegwa. See also *The International Review of Missions*, 26 (1937), 67.

55. On the basis of his experiences in Kenya, Alexander served as the model for a character in Elspeth Huxley's novel *Red Strangers* (London, 1939), pp. 400–402. The story deals with three generations of a Kikuyu family and tells how their traditional life is altered by the coming of Europeans. The independent church movement, as Huxley describes it, provided an alternative way to the missions for the Kikuyu to become Christians—a way without sacrificing all their customs, especially polygamy, and a way to construct "a true Kikuyu Church, unpolluted by European prejudices." Huxley sketches a fictional character based on Alexander who is perceived as "a dignitary second to no one in importance, unless it might be King George" and is enthusiastically received by the Kikuyu. She mentions the South African base of the church and accurately reproduces details, such as the famous automobile by which Alexander travelled from Nairobi, but she takes liberties with his appearance, mentioning his "big beard." She pictures a large baptismal ceremony at the conclusion of which she has the archbishop's attendants extract a ten shilling fee from each new Christian.

56. Corfield, *Historical Survey*, p. 175.

57. David Brokensha, *Social Change at Larteh, Ghana* (London, 1966), pp. 26–31, 165–166.

58. Walter H. Sangree, *Age, Prayer and Politics in Tiriki, Kenya* (London, 1966), pp. 190, 211–215.

59. To my knowledge the only other African prelate with a similar kind of claim was His Beatitude Mar Kwamin I, Prince-Patriarch of Apam, also known as Kwamin Nsetse Bresi-Ando or Ebenezer Johnson Anderson. A comparison is unfair since Alexander was a serious churchman while Bresi-Ando appears to have been a fraud. At one time associated with Jones in the Gold Coast, Bresi-Ando set out for the United States to meet the directors of the African Universal Church. He stopped in London, however, and on 6 March 1935 was elevated to the episcopate by the Most Rev. John Churchill Sibley, metropolitan of the (virtually non-existent) Orthodox Catholic Church in England and chancellor of the Inter-collegiate University, a notorious degree mill. Sibley had been consecrated by Frederick Ebenezer Lloyd, Vilatte's successor as primate of the American Catholic Church. Unlike these *episcopi vagantes*, many of whom were little more than, in Anson's phrase, "religious confidence men," Alexander did not traffic in bogus ecclesiastical titles and academic degrees; he actually had priests and congregations under his charge, and, most important, he never consecrated other bishops. Bresi-Ando's curious career is described by Anson, *Bishops at Large*, pp. 278–279. Information

on Bresi-Ando's relationship with Jones was furnished by the archbishop in an interview with the writer in Accra on 1 July 1971. See also David Kimble, *A Political History of Ghana: The Rise of Gold Coast Nationalism, 1850–1928* (Oxford, 1963), p. 544. Appreciation for Alexander's restraint in ordaining is noted by Hulme, *Blackwall to Bloemfontein*, p. 328.

60. Perhaps of several million adherents, although accurate statistics are difficult to obtain and verify.
61. Correspondence dated 18 March 1972, from Dr. Robert Makodawa, Secretary General, The United Orthodox Independent Churches of East Africa—Coptic Patriarchate of All Africa.
62. Brandreth, *Episcopi Vagantes*, p. 57.
63. Corfield, *Historical Survey*, p. 174.
64. Thomas Hodgkin, *Nationalism in Colonial Africa* (New York, 1957), p. 101.
65. David B. Barrett, *Schism and Renewal in Africa: An Analysis of Six Thousand Contemporary Religious Movements* (Nairobi, 1968), p. 247.
66. J.E. Goldthorpe, *Outlines of East African Society* (Kampala, 1958), p. 223, draws attention to the "important departure" of a separatist church united with a major world church and points to the "double advantage" of the AOC in Uganda after 1946 when Spartas was recognized by the Greek patriarch of Alexandria: "local independence from mission control, but at the same time the full status of membership of a recognized major division of Christianity."

"Warrior Mother of Africa's Warriors of the Most High God": Laura Adorkor Kofey and the African Universal Church[1]

At 9 P.M. on Thursday, March 8, 1928, Laura Adorkor Kofey[2] was shot and killed by an unknown assassin as she addressed a large crowd in Liberty Hall, Miami, Florida. According to her followers she was, as she had claimed, an African princess; a prophetess of black pride, self-help, and African repatriation; and the divinely appointed "Warrior Mother of Africa's Warriors of the Most High God." According to her critics she was merely a fraud: an American Negro named Laura Champion from Athens, Georgia, who betrayed the black community either by luring people from the established churches, or by subverting the nationalist goals of Marcus Garvey's Universal Negro Improvement Association (UNIA) with the divisive nature of her leadership, her unauthorized collection of funds, and the religious character of her message.

Laura Kofey first appeared in the South in 1927, the last year Garvey served in Atlanta Penitentiary before his release and deportation. According to local residents, she "came up out of nowhere,"[3] although, in fact, she seems to have entered the United States from Canada and became active in the Detroit branch of the UNIA. Amy Jacques-Garvey remembers her as a particularly effective organizer.[4] Appealing to the Miami branch of the UNIA, which was vulnerable because of the imprisonment of the President-General,[5] she claimed to be a friend of Garvey's and said she had his approval for carrying on his work. She later announced that she had been sent to the United States by her father, King Knesipi of the Gold Coast, to organize Negroes and take them back to Africa.

An eloquent orator whose appeals to racial pride, the African heritage, and community self-reliance both reflected and spoke to the black nationalism of the period, Laura Kofey soon gathered dedicated disciples. Her mission, however, began to cause serious divisions within the black community. In Miami, her popular Sunday evening addresses emptied the black churches, thereby alienating the powerful Ministerial Alliance. The UNIA at first opened their doors to her, but became doubtful of her alleged alliance with Garvey. On August 1, 1927, she visited Garvey in federal prison in Atlanta in the company of several Miami UNIA members who had recommended the Princess to Garvey as "worthwhile." In the following months, however, there were complaints of her money-raising to buy a sawmill and ships for an African exodus. Garvey pointed out that he had given her no authority to collect funds; he assumed she was involved in a scheme using his name to extract money from a "dense" public, and he advised that she be reported to the police. In October, Garvey revoked the charter of Division 286 which was entertaining her and inserted a warning notice in the *Negro World*.[6]

In their investigations, Garveyites claimed to discover Laura Kofey to be, in reality, a native of Athens, Georgia, who had worked for the American Red Cross, travelled to New York, England, and Africa, and who had taught school in New Orleans before her advent in Florida.[7] Garvey's followers were further alienated when she claimed to be responsible for the commutation of Garvey's sentence late in 1927. The denunciation by the UNIA led to Laura Kofey's establishing a rival organization, the African Universal Church, under whose auspices she then began to organize and speak.[8] Details of the founding of the church are not clear, although it seems to have been legally established in Jacksonville in 1928 by Clarence C. Addison and others. One tradition has it that Laura Kofey first began a church in 1924 in Asofa, ten miles from Accra, where she lived with her husband.[9]

Pressured both by the UNIA and the Ministerial Alliance, Laura Kofey withdrew for a time to Jacksonville, but returned to Miami early in 1928. She spoke at a series of evening meetings, drawing large and enthusiastic audiences, but there were disturbances caused by Garveyite hecklers. In one struggle between friends and enemies of the Princess over the use of a hall, both sides asked for police protection, and the authorities finally padlocked the building.[10] On a subsequent evening, March 8, while preaching in Liberty Hall at N.W. 15th Street and Fifth Avenue, someone fired a pistol through a crack in the door in the direction of the pulpit, a distance of about fifty feet. Two shots struck Laura Kofey in the head. She died instantly.

Pandemonium broke loose among the two hundred people in the hall. The Princess's enraged followers seized Maxwell Cook, a Jamaican who was a captain in the uniformed branch of the local UNIA, and beat him to death on the spot. A squad of detectives, motorcycle policemen, and deputy sheriffs armed with sawed-off shotguns halted the riot.[11] The police gathered thirteen suspects, but arrested only Claude Green, president of the Miami UNIA, and James Nimmo, the Colonel of Legions (military head of the branch).[12] Nimmo recalls that only the fact that he was in custody and handcuffed to the steering wheel of a police car kept him from being attacked by the crowd. Both Green and Nimmo were charged with murder in the first degree, a charge sustained by the indictment returned by the grand jury on June 28. Green was alleged to have shot and killed Laura Kofey, "alias Princess Laura Kofey," and Nimmo was held to be "then and there aiding and abetting," and therefore an accessory before the fact.[13]

At the trial, witnesses testified that Cook had signalled to Nimmo and that Nimmo was seen firing the shots. Evidence was also introduced, however, indicating that Green, a diabetic, was at home ill. In Nimmo's defense, friends stated that they had feared trouble since Nimmo had been a prominent heckler at the Princess's talk the previous evening, and therefore were in the process of escorting him away from the hall at the very moment the murder took place. On July 10, the jury found both defendants "not guilty." To protect Green and Nimmo from Laura Kofey's supporters, the judge ordered them to spend several days with Albert Stokes, a Negro who was both a member of the UNIA and on friendly terms with the white community. Nimmo subsequently returned to the Bahamas, his birthplace, and Green eventually immigrated to Canada.

Following the assassination, funeral rites for the thirty-five-year-old Laura Kofey were conducted in Miami. The body was then moved to Palm Beach where another service was held. It was said that seven thousand people followed the funeral procession between the two cities. The body was moved again, this time to Jacksonville where a fee of twenty-five cents was charged to view the corpse. The crowds were so large that they caused traffic congestion at the undertaker's parlors. Her followers first claimed that the remains were to be shipped back to the Gold

Coast,[14] but final rites, which allegedly drew more than ten thousand people, were held at Duval Cemetery in Jacksonville on August 17. Laura Kofey's body was draped in silk and linen and laid to rest in a mausoleum especially constructed by her disciples. There was some indication that her father, King Knesipi, had engaged American attorneys and planned to come to the United States to investigate the murder, but apparently his visit did not take place.[15]

Laura Kofey's preaching was essentially a blend of Garveyism and religion. She criticized the UNIA for holding dances to raise funds, and advocated prayer meetings in their place. She opposed the uniform department's drilling on Sunday. She was against the donation of funds to the Garvey movement, but allegedly collected $19,000 herself in a few months of speaking through the South. The *Negro World* claimed not only that she took money for emigration, but also that some people actually disposed of their property to await the ships she claimed would be sent by African kings to Miami and Jacksonville to transport them back to Africa.[16] Despite her criticisms of the UNIA, it is clear that the main motifs of her message were borrowed from Garveyite ideology. What she added was a rather traditional religious dimension, but one that she and her followers transformed into a religious sanction for the black nationalist themes of racial pride, African identification, and community building.

As recalled by her followers,[17] the essence of her proclamation was: "Negroes you have lost your name, you have lost your language, you have lost your heritage. My God showed me, it come [sic] a time you will wish you were as black as the ace of spades. Negroes be proud of your woolly hair and the color of your skin. Go back to yourselves, that's back to Africa and that is back to God." The message was directed against those who believed that "Negroes must think white, not black. We ain't lost nothing in Africa."

A note of authority was added by Laura Kofey's account of her own background and experience:

> I am a representative from the Gold Coast of West Africa, seeking the welfare of Africa's children everywhere. God called me out of Africa to come over here and tell you, His people, what He would have you to do. I travelled from place to place in Africa trying to keep from answering the Call. I could not get away from that All-

Seeing Eye. He prevailed with me wherever I went. He finally afflicted me with a fearful sickness unto death three times until I said Here Am I Lord sent me. . . . I have come to bring you a message of good news and glad tidings. . . . Your kings and leaders of Africa who are your fathers and your native people who are your brothers and sisters have also given me a MESSAGE to ask you: They say you have been a long time away from home, why have you not made PREPARATIONS to come home? They say, if you want to come let we [sic] know, and if you don't want to come let we know. In the Gold Coast of West Africa there is a DOOR (to all Africa) OPEN to you and a hearty welcome waiting you there.

Racial self-affirmation combined with the idea of the African diaspora led Laura Kofey to advocate both repatriation and, like the spokesmen of other black nationalist movements, economic self-sufficiency. She is reported to have said:

Negroes, learn to help yourselves, create your own jobs, build your own enterprises. Clean up your lives—love one another, patronize one another. If you don't learn to help yourselves and build industries and commerce with your Motherland Africa you are doomed and done for. Don't send preachers to Africa who don't know nothing else to do but preach. Send dedicated and God-fearing men and women skilled in the trades and qualified in the professions.

The Africa she described was "the kind of Africa the people had not been told about," one with cities and towns with modern conveniences, black mayors and legislative houses, industrial and commercial activity. In the words of her followers, "She was emphasizing that Africa is so big that the surface has not yet been scratched. She was, indeed, opening the eyes of the people urging them to participate in the economic development of their mother-land Africa for the benefit of all concerned." Taking from Garvey the notion of a commercial shipping line that would also serve as a carrier for African return, the Princess reportedly collected funds to charter Japanese ships that would sail from New Orleans to West Africa.

Laura Kofey's nationalism was built on a religious foundation intertwined with her own prophetic and charismatic personality. "Children," she stated, "my hand's in Jesus' Hand and Jesus' Hand in God's Hand and my other hand in my children's hand."

Her addresses were all based upon the reading of Scripture; she would interpret the Bible in the light of contemporary racial conditions and then announce how "my Old Man God" would have people respond. At the conclusion of her preaching services she would extend her right hand and say, "Enroll your names with your Mother, children. If you don't have but one drop of black blood in you, and know you cannot pass for white, enroll your name with your Mother."

With this "Gospel of Love and Race Redemption," Laura Kofey preached throughout the South for eighteen months. Despite the large number of followers she attracted, Miami was not the only place where she met with opposition. She was arrested in St. Petersburg at the instigation of "enemy race leaders to whom she first came 'but they received her not,'" leading the Princess to comment, "Some of my children good, some of my children bad, but your Mother loves every one of you." Arrested in Jacksonville, she was stripped while in prison to discover if she had, as her enemies claimed, "voodoo roots" on her body to account for her power.[18]

Faced with arrests, harassment, and deportation attempts, Laura Kofey is said to have stated:

> Children, now your Mother knows how St. Paul felt and how all the Apostles felt when they were put in jail for His Name's Sake. My God told me if I go back to Africa it is death and if I stay here it is death, but if I die in His Program over here, then I can be in HIS SPIRIT and be able to take care of my Africa's children everywhere. If God deem me worthy to suffer and die in His Program for His people, then I tell Him "thankee." No man taketh my life, I give up my life that I might take it up again. All I've asked my Old Man God is to take me in the presence of my children that they may be witnesses I went down for them.

Following her death, Laura Kofey's adherents continued the African Universal Church, but now with the added purpose of perpetuating her memory as well as to carry out her ideology and program. The title "Universal" was chosen to signify the nondenominational character of the church. The church's motto is Garvey's "One God, One Aim, One Destiny." In the early period there were local churches in Miami, Jacksonville, St. Petersburg, and Tampa, Florida; Mobile and Belforest–Daphne City, Alabama; Atlanta, Georgia; and New York City, but these have now decreased in number. The first leadership was African—not men who had known or been associated with Laura Kofey, but African students in the United States who were attracted to the church because of its African interests. DeWitt Martin-Dow of Gambia was the Church's first Supreme Elder. E.B. Nyombolo from Central Africa was the first Managing Director, followed by a Reverend Ajaye from Sierra Leone. A Nigerian named Idowu was also an early leader.[19]

With the denomination's decline and the elimination of a central administration, the local churches are now essentially autonomous although there is some voluntary cooperation. One governmental characteristic is that each congregation has both a pastor (often ordained in another denomination) and a lay chairman who is in effect overseer of the church. Services are in the free church tradition. Infant baptism and Holy Communion are celebrated as sacraments. Perhaps the most unique feature is that March 8, the anniversary of Laura Kofey's death, is kept as a memorial to her and every fourth Sunday is celebrated as Mother's Day. The church in Liberia, a black section of Dania, Florida, is called St. Adorkor's African Universal Church. The church in Carver Ranches, a black neighborhood of West Hollywood, Florida, has a large framed portrait of the Princess over the chancel and a banner on the central pulpit which reads "In Memory of Princess Mother Laura Adorkor Koffey of Gold Coast West Africa, Assassinated in Miami, Florida, March 8, 1928, May She Rest in Peace."

The church's hymnal consists of gospel songs and Negro spirituals, but also of some African group songs in the Xhosa language as well as American black nationalist lyrics by Rabbi Arnold J. Ford and others. A number of hymns are original or adaptations that have been rewritten to incorporate references to Africa and Laura Kofey. Two examples:

> How bright our mighty hosts of Light
> With blest Adorkor by Thy Grace,
> Our Mother whose body united
> Africa's remnants in Thy Name.[20]
>
> O Africa my zion!
> My paradise serene
> Land of my Leader Jesus,
> Home of my hopes and dreams;

> I know now, yes, I know now,
> Since Mother set me free;
> That thou art God's anointed
> And shelter for oppressed.[21]

An adaptation of "Were You There?":

> Were you there
> When Adorkor brought the Light?
> When she preached in Jesus' Name?
> When my Mother shed Her tears?
> When they stripped Her in the Jail?
> On that day She prayed all day?
> On that night She paid the price?
> When the bullet pierced Her Head?
> When She fell in Jesus' Name?
> When this righteous blood was shed?[22]

The African Universal Church's creed summarizes its articles of belief:

I believe in God, the Father Almighty, Maker of heaven and earth, Father of all races of mankind; and in His holy Word as set down by His Prophets and Apostles, in the Old and New Testaments.

I believe in the fulfillment of God's Word and the destiny of my race, that the scattered sons and daughters of Africa shall again be redeemed in the name of Jesus of Nazareth who glorified the Cross a sacrifice for the salvation of the hearts of men.

I believe in St. Adorkor the saintly Messenger of God who so nobly emulated the life and teachings of our Blessed Lord and Savior Jesus Christ and suffered martyrdom for the Cause of her race of people.

I believe in God's Words, that before the end of time, the second coming of Christ, we shall have worked our way back to the homeland.

I believe in the Christ way of life and life more abundantly here on earth, and in the brotherhood of all men.

I believe in the Universal Church for African people at home and abroad with Jesus Christ as the Chief Corner Stone and Laura Adorker as the Sainted Mother of the race at home and abroad.

I believe in the forgiveness of sins, eternal salvation, the power of the Holy Ghost, and life everlasting. Amen.[23]

This is a remarkable document, synthesizing as it does conventional Christian teachings, an underlying belief in brotherhood, a race with a destiny to fulfil, and a homeland to which believers must "work our way back," and a sainted martyr who is "Mother of the race at home and abroad."

The African Universal Church thus obviously constitutes a cult of Laura Kofey who became "Mother Kofi," the "Patron Saint for African-American Relations," and whose motto was "I'll Take Care of Mine." She is also referred to as "Remnants Gatherer—Soul of Africa By Precept, Example, and Martyrdom" and "Warrior Mother of Africa's Warriors of the Most High God." The church distributed free copies of "Mother's Sacred Album" which contained her picture, a picture of the mausoleum, and "The Holy Fan on which Her Blood was Spilled." In addition, it advertised "7 Days' Free Closet Prayer Treatment" in the form of "Mother's Closet Prayer Book" which promised "No Matter How Bad Your Condition, Divine Help in Your Affairs." These objects elicited testimonials such as the following from Oklahoma City, Oklahoma:

> I was having such a hard time, it seemed like everything was working against me. I sure appreciate Mother's Sacred Album and the Closet Prayer Treatments you sent me. I have also been very sick but much better.

The church emphasized, however, the nationalist themes Laura Kofey had articulated. It announced, "A people who are a people, are people who pride themselves in their own." The church encouraged the use of African language by distributing free lessons in Xhosa-Zulu. E.B. Nyombolo wrote a "Sentence Maker" as well as primer and vocabulary books for "conversation and Scripture passages." "Miracle blessings" were claimed by "growing numbers of her [the Princess's] children in Alabama, Florida and elsewhere" who prayed in Banta, which was advanced as "among [the] best known of original African languages." Tshaka, or the Reverend Eugene Preston McCarroll, the A.U.C.'s Territorial Director, wrote a *Biblical Key* "chock full of Biblical research tracing our Lord Jesus to both Houses of Shem and Ham." The Church also offered free copies of *How to Read and Understand Drawings of the Land of Ham.*

In 1931 the African Universal Church sent six missionaries to
Africa, three to the Gold Coast and three to Nigeria. There was
insufficient financial support from the directors in the United
States, however, and the project failed. The three missionaries in
Nigeria returned home and two of the missionaries in the Gold
Coast secured employment in Accra from a West Indian baker
named Shackelford. The one missionary who remained, Carey
Harold Jones, was a Floridian who had been active in the Garvey
movement and was ordained in the A.U.C. in Jacksonville by
Martin-Dow. He began a mission in Apam where he cooperated
with Ebenezer Bresi-Ando, a Ghanaian who was, at the time,
Bishop of The Primitive Church.[24] Jones split from Bresi-Ando,
tried unsuccessfully to carry on the A.U.C. mission alone, and
finally in 1945 returned to the United States to make contact with
the African Orthodox Church, the religious body most closely
identified with the Garvey movement.[25] He and the people of six
mission stations were received under its jurisdiction in 1955, and
he was later made Archbishop of the African Orthodox Church
Province of West Africa.[26]

The African Universal Church has also sought to combine the
nationalist characteristics of African identification and economic
self-help. Laura Kofey herself reportedly gathered goods to be
shipped to Africa for sale. Ernest Sears, chairman of the church
in Carver Ranches, joined the A.U.C. because "the black man is
looked down upon" and needs a "bread and butter program" of
racially organized industries for self-esteem and financial betterment. It is part of the church's ideology to construct a commercial program of international investment that would both contribute to African development and benefit the black community
in the United States. Sears himself has visited Ghana twice, in
1968 and 1971, looking toward the establishment of business, as
well as a church and school, in that country. The holder of an
import-export license, he was favorably received by members of
Laura Kofey's family and officials of the Ga tribe.[27]

In addition to its hopes for commercial ties to Africa, the
church did develop a rather extensive domestic program of economic self-reliance. The national denomination encouraged
"field workers" to "establish your own work" through an industrial club as well as through racially conscious clubs, such as
Africa study or Negro history, and more conventional religious
organizations, such as prayer bands and Bible study. The church

in Belforest–Daphne City, Alabama, advertised a "Thriving Community Pioneered by Mother's Children," consisting of a church edifice, educational building, Samaritan Home, guest dormitory, dining hall, and community enterprises. The most extensive program seems to have been in Jacksonville where Adorkaville, "A Self-Help, Non-Profit Church Community," was established in the early 1940s. Off U.S. Highway No. 1, on Dabula Drive, the church built and offered "homes within the means of her [Laura Kofey's] children" in a "year-round, quiet, cheerful Christian community." The church advertised Adorkaville as a "symbol of God's miraculous victories for the welfare of his people."

Under the leadership of E.B. Nyombolo, it was decided in July 1944 to establish a community. The reasons were the war-time housing shortage, the desire to improve living conditions, and a commitment to group cooperation and protection, the latter reason being particularly consistent with Laura Kofey's teachings. As a result, eleven acres on the edge of Jacksonville were purchased in August, 75 percent of the funds being provided by Nyombolo who was employed at the time at the Walker Business College. The land was cleared communally, and it was decided to construct houses and to erect a church building. There is one deed and title to the property, in the name of the African Universal Church, but the houses are owned by the dozen or so families who moved there. The selection of families to occupy the community was made by the group itself, with places going to those who were felt to be most qualified and deserving.

The aims of Adorkaville were to create (1) a law-abiding Christian community, (2) a memorial to Laura Kofey, (3) a vehicle for cooperation, (4) an opportunity to educate the group's children, (5) a means for cooperation with the political state, and (6) a way to live an African-American existence. A school was established that taught African history, languages, geography, and culture. Plans were drawn for an African International Center where there would be vocational and cultural training, all for the purpose of greater cooperation between Africa and the United States, including a dormitory for visiting Africans. In fact, no buildings besides houses were ever constructed except a temporary wooden church and the foundation for a larger cinder-block church.[28]

The commitment to repatriation continued within the group. When Senator Theodore Bilbo of Mississippi sponsored a bill to

use war debts owed to the United States to finance sending
American Negroes to Liberia, he received the following telegram
dated April 23, 1939, from the Missionary African Universal
Church, Inc., of Jacksonville:

> Your law-abiding citizens, followers of the martyred African Prin-
> cess Laura Adorkor Koffey, assassinated Miami, Fla., March 8,
> 1928, in hearty accord with your views as published under your
> name in Chicago Defender of April 22, 1939. Prayerful wishes for
> your continued interest and courageous efforts in this cause so
> thoroughly misrepresented by an element of our visionless mis-
> leaders![29]

Archbishop Addison kept up his own campaign against civil
rights, calling integration "sinful"[30] and arguing for an economic self-sufficiency, a position which was allied with the Louisiana Sovereignty Commission, the Congress of Christian States
of America, and other conservative white groups.

Since he met people who claimed to be her relatives, Ernest
Sears's trips to Ghana have settled the question of the authenticity of Laura Kofey's African origin. Also, Sears holds a letter
dated April 24, 1969, from the Ga Mantse, Paramount Chief of
the Ga (Accra) State, which says, "The late Adorkor Cofie hailed
from Sempe Division of the Ga (Accra) Traditional area."[31]
Sears's visit also disclosed that before her coming to the United
States, Laura Kofey was pastor of a church in the village of Asofa
and that she had a mission in Kumasi. Her original scheme
appears to have been to travel to America and then return to
spread her nationalist-religious-commercial program throughout Africa. It is well known that, through the role of medium,
women may have an extremely significant place in traditional
Ga religion and society.[32] Given this cultural background combined with her Christianity, her exposure to Garveyism, and her
own personal charismatic gifts, reasons exist to explain how
Laura Kofey was prepared to assume her position of leadership.

Is the phenomenon of Laura Kofey unique? On the surface, it
certainly seems unusual that an African woman of royal blood in
the 1920s left a religious career in her own country, absorbed the
philosophy of Marcus Garvey,[33] emigrated to America, led a
black nationalist movement, and had a church established in her
memory. On the other hand, the richness of black history—

African, West Indian, and American—has yet to be explored, and until that is more fully done there can be no adequate criteria to determine either norms or uniqueness. This is probably particularly true of that most continuous, influential, and neglected of institutions, the black church. In the meantime, it can be said that Laura Kofey expressed the heart of the black religious nationalist tradition with her exhortation, "Go back to yourselves, that's back to Africa and that is back to God." It is because of her articulation of that sentiment—with all its connotations for the black experience—that Laura Kofey's followers could say, "It was revealed and made manifest to her children that their Blessed Mother is the Daughter of the Most High God—that she is a living spirit in Christ Jesus for the Welfare of her children and whosoever will, everywhere."

—Portions of this essay in an earlier form were read at the American Academy of Religion, National Meeting, Chicago, Ill., November 10, 1973; American Academy of Religion, National Meeting, St. Louis, Missouri, October 29, 1976; Department of American Studies, Florida State University, February 16, 1977; Department of Special Studies, College of the Holy Cross, October 27, 1978; and the African Studies Center, UCLA, May 17, 1982

Notes

1. I am indebted to a number of people for their assistance in the preparation of this paper, particularly Robert A. Hill, Alma Marcus, Garth Reeves, and those cited in the notes who granted interviews.
2. Kofey, in any of its variant spellings—Kofi, Coffie, etc.—is a common Ghanaian surname. See H. Dwight Beers, "African Names and Naming Practices," *LC Information Bulletin* (March 25, 1977), 206. For consistency I have used Kofey unless it is spelled differently in a direct quotation.

   It is the custom on the Akan Coast to name children after the day of the week on which they were born. Kofi is the name for Friday. Plantation blacks in the New World followed the same custom. Coffee is mentioned among names of slaves of the Royal African Company in 1680. Before the nineteenth century, Cuffee, Cof, and its variants were the most common given names of African origin among male slaves in the South, among free Southern blacks, and among free Northern blacks in the Revolutionary War. In the nineteenth century, the use of African names declined significantly. See Murray Heller, ed., *Black Names in America: Origins and Usage* (Boston, 1974), passim. Prof. Marion Kilson informed me that Adorkor is a common given name among the Ga people.

3. Interview, the Rev. Leon Brown, West Hollywood, Florida, July 24, 1973.
4. Letter to the writer, January 31, 1972.
5. Interview, Jacob Dean, Miami, Florida, July 26, 1973.
6. I am indebted to Robert A. Hill for copies of the exchange of telegrams between Garvey and his followers which document this.
7. Interview, James Nimmo, Miami, Florida, July 28, 1973.
8. *Chicago Defender* (March 31, 1928).
9. *The Church; Why Mother Established the Church and What It Stands For* (N.p. [Jacksonville, Fla.?], n.d.), p. ii. The history of the church itself, both in the United States and Africa, needs very much to be explored.
10. *Miami Daily News* (March 9, 1928), 6. This report also carries an account of Laura Kofey's assassination which seems to have been the basis for the story in the Kingston, Jamaica, *Daily Gleaner* of April 3, 1928.
11. *Miami Herald* (March 9, 1928), 6.
12. Consisting of some seventy men, the uniformed rank was a paramilitary department of the Miami UNIA. It drilled in a park with wooden rifles and was prepared to confront racial enemies, particularly the Ku Klux Klan. Major Nimmo refers to the department as "a counter-revolutionary force."
13. Files no. 14 and 19, Criminal Court records, Dade County Courthouse, Miami, Florida.
14. *Miami Herald* (March 12, 1928), 2.
15. *The New York Times* (March 21, 1928), 13. For additional coverage, see the *Negro World* for July 14, 1928; July 21, 1928; and July 28, 1928.
16. April 7, 1928.
17. The following quotations are taken from *Mission Crusader* unless they are otherwise identified.
18. "Voodoo roots" probably means plant roots used as charms or fetishes worn next to the skin to allow for the most efficient transference of their power; letter to the writer from Michael E. Bell, April 6, 1978. An interesting parallel occurred in 1656 when the first two Quakers to arrive in Boston, Ann Austin and Mary Fisher, were also imprisoned, stripped, and searched for "tokens" of witchcraft on their bodies; see Charles A. Selleck, *Quakers in Boston, 1656–1964; Three Centuries of Friends in Boston and Cambridge* (Cambridge, 1976), p. 1.
19. Interview, the Rev. John Dean, Dania, Florida, July 28, 1973.
20. *African Universal Hymnal* (Jacksonville, 1961), p. 6.
21. Ibid., p. 30.
22. Ibid., p. 28.
23. Ibid., pp. 64–65.
24. After a disagreement with Jones, Bresi-Ando (who was also known as Ebenezer Johnson Anderson) was on his way to the United States to meet the A.U.C. hierarchy when he became involved with *episcopi vagantes* in London; he emerged as His Beatitude Mar Kwamin I, Prince-Patriarch of Apam. See Peter F. Anson, *Bishops at Large* (London, 1964), pp. 278–279.

25. See Richard Newman, "Archbishop Daniel William Alexander and the African Orthodox Church," *International Journal of African Historical Studies,* 16 (1983), 615-630; see also "The Origins of the African Orthodox Church," Introductory essay, *The Negro Churchman: The Official Organ of the African Orthodox Church* (Millwood, N.Y.: Kraus Reprint Co., 1977), pp. iii-xxii [and see above].

26. Interview, the Most Rev. Carey Harold Jones, Accra, Ghana, July 1, 1971.

27. Interview, Ernest Sears, Miami, Florida, July 25, 1973.

28. Interview, Robert E. Keyes, Jacksonville, Florida, December 2, 1975.

29. E. David Cronon, ed., *Marcus Garvey* (Englewood Cliffs, N.J.: Prentice-Hall, 1973). The Bilbo bill was also supported by the UNIA as well as by Garvey personally (see Robert A. Hill, ed., *The Black Man* [Millwood, N.Y.: Kraus-Thomson, 1975], Introduction, pp. 26-28, and Ethel Wolfskill, "Earnest Cox and Colonization: A White Racist's Response to Black Repatriation, 1923-1966," unpublished Ph.D. dissertation, Duke University, 1974, Ch. IV).

30. *New Orleans Times Picayune* (August 28, 1956), 16.

31. This is confirmed by a letter to the writer from Henry Adjei of Accra dated September 16, 1973. Laura Kofey's nearest living relative is Mr. Buitiful Ouaye, Chief Linguist of the Sempe Division and a personal friend of Mr. Adjei's.

32. See Marion Kilson, "Ambivalence and Power: Mediums in Ga Traditional Religion," *The Journal of Religion in Africa,* IV, 3: 171-177. For a more complete account of Ga religion, see Marion Kilson, *Kpele Lala: Ga Religious Songs and Symbols* (Cambridge, Mass., 1971), which also contains a full bibliography on the Ga people. For the role of women in the African independent church movement, see David Barrett, *Schism and Renewal in Africa: An Analysis of 6,000 Contemporary Religious Movements* (Nairobi, 1968), pp. 146-150.

33. According to Archbishop Jones, Laura Kofey read Garvey's newspaper the *Negro World* while still in Africa and was converted to his ideas and thus inspired to travel to the United States and identify herself with the Garvey movement.

Lemuel Haynes

Two hundred years ago, on November 29, 1780, a young black man was licensed to preach the gospel after he had been duly examined in languages, sciences, and "practical and experimental religion" by the ministers of the Congregational churches of Canaan, Coventry, and Worthington, Connecticut. At the occasion he preached on Ps. 96:1, "The Lord reigneth, let the earth rejoice." He was unanimously called to serve the new Congregational church at Middle Granville, Massachusetts, a town which had known him as a servant-boy all his life.

So began the ministerial career of Lemuel Haynes (1753–1833), a veteran of the American Revolution; the first black man to minister to a white congregation, and, so far as is known, the first black ordained in North America; the first black to receive a college degree (an honorary M.A. from Middlebury in 1804); and a preacher of such power and eloquence that one of his published sermons ran to some 70 editions and was said to be the most reprinted work since *Pilgrim's Progress*.

Haynes was born July 18, 1753, in West Hartford, Connecticut, of a white mother and black father, an unusual reversal of the pattern of miscegenation sanctioned by American chattel slavery. Haynes never knew his father, who was said to be of pure African blood, or his mother, a New Englander of respectable family who abandoned him in infancy. As a child, he saw her once as she was leaving a relative's house in order to avoid him. Tradition has it that Haynes wrote an autobiography in which he named his mother, but that her family destroyed all known copies.

From infancy till the age of twenty-one, Haynes was bound out in indentured servitude to David Rose of Middle Granville. Mrs. Rose accepted him as her own child, and even favored him. Rose was a farmer, a deacon in the Congregational church, and a person of exceptional spirituality. Haynes absorbed the atmosphere of this Puritan household and was apparently a sensitive, serious, and hard-working child. For all practical purposes he was self-taught, since he supplemented the irregular and meager education of the local school with his own intense study at night by the fireside. "I made it my rule," he said, "to know more every night than I knew in the morning."

Like Luther, Haynes was once moved by a thunderstorm, but it was a fearful experience of northern lights which led him to a conviction of his sinfulness. Under an apple tree, "mourning my wretched situation," he later wrote, "I hope I found the Saviour." He joined the East Granville church and was baptized. In 1774 he became a Minute Man, and two years later volunteered for the expedition to capture Ticonderoga. Over fifty years later he remembered the text of the sermon he heard at Bennington when the troops were encamped there on their march.

The occasion of Haynes' own first sermon is the subject of a well-known story. Before and after the day's farm work, he studied theology. In due time he composed a sermon on Jesus' words to Nicodemus, "Except a man be born again he cannot see the kingdom of God." It was the Rose family's custom at Saturday night worship for Haynes to read from a book of sermons. One evening he read the sermon he had written. "Whose work is that," Deacon Rose asked, "Watts's or Whitefield's?" Haynes confessed that it was his own.

Cognizant of Haynes' intelligence and piety, his neighbors urged him to prepare for the ministry. He "shrunk at the thought," he said, of attending Dartmouth, though "a door was opened" for him there. He studied Latin and Greek privately with local Congregational clergymen, supporting himself by teaching school. So he prepared himself for licensing in 1780. Haynes served the Granville church for five years. One of his parishioners, Elizabeth Babbit, a young white schoolteacher, proposed marriage. Haynes consulted the neighboring ministers, they approved, and the wedding took place September 22, 1783, in Hartford.

Two years later, the congregation testified to the quality of Haynes' character and preaching, and petitioned the Association of Ministers in Litchfield County to ordain him. He was ordained November 9, 1785, and moved to Torrington, Connecticut, where he served for two years. Among the congregation were the parents of John Brown. It was at Torrington that a racially prejudiced parishioner came to meeting wearing his hat as a sign of disrespect, and was so moved by the sermon that he later spoke of Haynes in what were, for him, the highest terms: "He was the whitest man I ever saw."

While at Torrington Haynes first expressed his interest in domestic missions and made his first tour of the state of Vermont, preaching and visiting the sick. The state was not only a rude and thinly-settled frontier, but it was under the deistic and humanistic influences of Thomas Paine and Ethan Allen. In 1788 Haynes accepted the call of the West Rutland church, where he served for thirty years. He continued missionary visits, and saw several revivals which added large numbers to his own church. "Perhaps God has yet mercy in store for poor Vermont," he wrote.

In 1805 Haynes preached a sermon which made him famous. Hosea Ballou, one of the early and leading spokesmen for Universalism, lectured in the West Rutland church, and invited Haynes to comment on his address. It is not clear whether Haynes' remarks were extemporaneous and thus a tribute to his quick mind, or prepared and thus a premeditated attack on Ballou composed before hearing his talk; Haynes' defenders claimed the former, his detractors the latter. At any rate, his short sermon called *Universal Salvation* was published and became instantly popular. It was reprinted, and reprinted again, in at least seventy editions, well into the nineteenth century.

Universal Salvation is unusual for a sermon in that its style is essentially satirical. Haynes took Gen. 3:4 as his text, "And the serpent said unto the woman, 'Ye shall not surely die.'" He described the characteristics of "the preacher"—cunning, artful, etc.—associating the serpent with the devil, and, by implication, Ballou. The doctrine of the serpent, "Ye shall not surely die," which claims that "there is no hell; and that the wages of sin is not death, but eternal life," was then equated with Ballou's Universalism.

With tongue in cheek, Haynes claimed that, since in his discourse he "has confined himself wholly to the character of Satan, he trusts no one will feel himself personally injured," but Haynes' hearers, and the thousands who read the sermon in printed form, as well as (of course) Ballou himself, knew exactly who and what he meant. A good many supposedly humorless Calvinists thoroughly understood, appreciated, and enjoyed Haynes' witty attack. Ballou was stung. "It was the most unchristianlike behaviour I ever saw," he wrote.

There were several published attempts to answer Haynes' sermon, but these are of interest now more for the racist aspect of their polemic than for the theological importance of their arguments. David Pickering, a Universalist minister, wrote *A Calm Address to the Believers and Advocates of Endless Misery Designed for the Benefit of the Youth* in which he spoke of Haynes, "between the shade of whose mind, and whose external surface, there exists such a striking similarity," and explained the joke in a footnote: "The author of the discourse in question is a coloured man." In Joseph H. Ellis' *A Reply to Haynes' Sermon*, the devil was pointedly referred to as "this black gentleman," "his complexion is as dark as ever," etc.

The satire of *Universal Salvation* is not untypical of Haynes who, despite his piety, was famous for his ready wit and sharp tongue. A staunch Federalist, he opposed all those with differing political views, and not only with his vote. A group of supporters was celebrating Andrew Jackson's election to the presidency with a banquet when Haynes accidentally walked into their hotel dining room. They insisted he join them in a glass of wine and that he propose a toast. He raised his glass, said, "Andrew Jackson, Psalm 109, verse 8," and went on his way. Only later did someone look up the passage to discover that it read, "Let his days be few, and let another take his office."

Most of Haynes' sermons consisted of exegesis of Scripture, proclamation of orthodox New England Calvinist theology, and exhortation to righteous living. There was a strong emphasis on eternal life and the human responsibility to prepare for it. Haynes was a popular preacher, often invited to speak at ordinations, funerals, and public occasions. In 1814 he preached at the Blue Church in New Haven and his sermon moved President Timothy Dwight of Yale to tears. Several of Haynes' published addresses reproduce talks to the Washington Benevolent Society, with whose views he sympathized; the Society was a pro-Federalist, anti-republican political organization which opposed Thomas Jefferson and the War of 1812, favored British trade, and even considered secession.

Recent commentators have criticized Haynes for not saying and doing more on behalf of his fellow blacks. Of course he lived his entire life among white people, and most of that in Vermont, where there was strong anti-slavery sentiment. Whatever his own self-understanding, Haynes was certainly not unaware of overt prejudice, since he experienced it. In a Fourth of July oration only twenty-five years after American independence, he expressed his views on race and slavery:

> What has reduced them [the poor Africans among us] to their present pitiful abject state? Is it any distinction that the God of nature hath made in their formation? Nay—but being subjected to slavery, by the cruel hands of oppressors they have been forced to view themselves as a rank of beings far below others, which has suppressed, in a degree, every principle of manhood, and so they become despised, ignorant, and licentious. This shows the effects of despotism, and should fill us with the utmost detestation against every attack on the rights of men.

In fact, this position is remarkably insightful psychologically, advanced sociologically, and radical politically, especially coming, as it did, a full thirty years before Garrison founded the New England Anti-Slavery Society and the *Liberator*.

Perhaps a new generation which resented a black minister, perhaps the public expression of his political views, resulted in Haynes' dismissal from the West Rutland church in 1818 when he was sixty-five years old. It was a dramatic parting. His final sermon was scathing in its criticism of the congregation for what Haynes felt was their slander and persecution. Yet the recalling of 1,500 Sabbaths and of 5,500 sermons (including 400 funeral sermons) led him to say, "I did not realize my attachment to you before the parting time came." Faithful shepherd, but clever-minded to the end, he closed his sermon and his West Rutland ministry by asking his people for their prayers, promising them his own, and reminding them that they would meet again at the day of judgment. Haynes was later to say that "he lived with the people in Rutland thirty years, and they were so sagacious that at the end of that time they found out that he was a nigger, and so turned him away."

Haynes next served the Manchester, Vermont, Congregational church for three years, and here occurred perhaps the most remarkable public event of his ministry. He befriended two brothers, Jesse and Stephen Boorn, who had been convicted of murdering their mentally-deranged brother-in-law, Russell Colvin. Colvin had disappeared some years before, but circumstances pointed to the brothers' guilt: Colvin appeared to an uncle in a dream, saying he had been murdered; a button was found which his wife testified was Colvin's; and a dog located some supposedly human bones in a tree stump. After visiting the Boorns daily in prison, however, Haynes became convinced of their innocence.

Someone else who was also convinced advertised in newspapers for the missing man's whereabouts, and Colvin turned up in New Jersey. Colvin's return to Manchester just days before the Boorns' scheduled execution was a local event of some theatre. Haynes published a factual account of what happened, *Mystery Developed*, as well as a sermon entitled *The Prisoner Released*. The case became an important one in American judicial history as an illustration of the dangers of circumstantial evidence. And Wilkie Collins used it as the basis of a short story called "John Jago's Ghost" or "The Dead Alive," an example of the "dead-alive" theme he often employed in his fiction.

Haynes' next move was his last. In 1822, aged sixty-nine, he became pastor of the Congregational church in Granville, New York, a parish which was particularly appreciative of his ministry and where he served for eleven years. The last words he wrote were the concluding sentence of a letter to one of his ten children, "Let not the fashions of the world divert your minds from eternity." Haynes died September 28, 1833. He composed his own epitaph:

> Here lies the dust of a poor hell-deserving sinner, who ventured into eternity trusting wholly on the merits of Christ for salvation. In the full belief of the great doctrines he preached while on earth, he invites his children, and all who read this, to trust their eternal interest on the same foundation.

After Haynes' death, the *Colored American* claimed that he was "the only man of *known* African descent who has ever succeeded in overpowering the system of American caste." As such, he may have been a hero to blacks since he proved that it was possible to be successful in a white world. By the same token he may have caused New England whites to believe that black people were simply white people with dark skins. In this regard, Charles E. Tuttle, Jr., has pointed out that among Haynes' personal friends were Richard Skinner, one of Vermont's strongest anti-slavery governors; Joseph Burr, who donated $5,000 to the

American Colonization Society; and Stephen Bradley, who introduced into the Senate the bill which abolished the slave trade in the United States.

While the place of Haynes the man of color will continue to be debated, the place of Haynes the man of God is clear. "His face betrayed his race and blood, and his face revealed his Lord."

—*Bulletin of the Congregational Library* 32:1 (Fall 1980), 4–8; reprinted in Richard Newman, *Lemuel Haynes: A Bio-Bibliography* (New York: Lambeth Press, 1984), pp. 11–17. Portions of this essay in an earlier form were read at the Northeast Seminar on Black Religion, Syracuse University, October 4, 1980

The Schomburg Center's Vertical File: A Resource for Black Religious Studies

(with Betty K. Gubert)

The Vertical File at the Schomburg Center for Research in Black Culture of The New York Public Library is essentially a clipping file, although it also includes typescripts, broadsides, pamphlets, programs, book reviews, and ephemera of all kinds. The file itself consists of hundreds of thousands of items organized under some 10,000 subject headings. Coverage began in 1925, although most subject headings have been added since that date and some clippings are earlier than 1925.

Most of the material in the Vertical File, which dates through 1974, is on microfiche. In addition there are 18 microfilm reels of scrapbook clippings from the 1930s and 1940s. Material dating after 1974 exists in its original form in folders either with new subject headings or with subject headings which repeat those of the pre-1975 material on microfiche. Access is via two indexes: a notebook listing the 10,000 pre-1975 subjects, and a card file for the new, post-1974 subjects.

Material which is on fiche and which can be dated is organized in chronological order. This is followed on the fiche by undated textual material grouped by sub-topic, and this in turn is followed by undated illustrative material. Post-1974 original material in folders is not organized.

For the student of Afro-American religion, the Vertical File's 10,000 subject headings offer a variety of approaches to the material itself. The major black denominations have files: National Baptist Convention, A.M.E. Church (conferences and history), C.M.E. Church, etc. There are also fiche or folders (or both) for the major white denominations: Lutherans, Presbyterians, etc. Some other groups or movements for which there are files include Mormons, Muslims, Bahai, Jehovah's Witnesses, and Moral Rearmament.

155

Some individual congregations have files: Abyssinian Baptist, St. James Presbyterian, St. Philip's Episcopal—all in New York City. Some religious organizations have files: Baptist Educational Center, Baptist Ministers Conference of Greater New York, Knights of Columbus. Some subjects are more general, however: Preaching, Religious Education, Gospel Songs and Singers, Spirituals. A number of files exist on Jews and Judaism: Black Jews, Israel, Jews and Negroes, B'nai B'rith, Falashas, for example.

Another approach of the File is geographical, that is, there is a heading for Birmingham, Alabama—Churches. Another approach is topical: Churches—Chicago; Churches—Harlem; Churches—Southern States. The same variety of approach exists for the African material. There is a folder for Africa—Religion. There are also more specific topics, such as Ethiopia—Religion. There are four sub-topics under Missions.

A considerable amount of material exists on the Roman Catholic Church. Some sub-topics for which separate files exist are: Bishops, Race Relations, Africa, Catholic Interracial Council, Catholic Schools—New York City, and Negro Catholics.

Perhaps the File's strongest feature is its coverage of individual persons. Many are well known: Adam Clayton Powell, Jr., Father Divine, St. Benedict the Moor, Shelton Hale Bishop, Alexander Crummell. Some are not so well known: Harold Salmon, Thomas Fuller, John A. Gregg, Basil Matthews. Others include Walter McCullough, Lemuel Haynes, William Lloyd Imes, Jesse Jackson, Prophet Jones, Reverend Ike, Solomon L. Micheaux, Shelby Rooks, Gardner Taylor, W.J. Walls. Eight sub-divisions exist for the extensive material on Martin Luther King, Jr.

To examine a subject heading in detail as an illustration, the file for St. Philip's Church consists of 8 fiche cards containing over 100 separate items and comprising nearly 800 frames/pages. The file includes clippings, parish newsletters, programs, form letters to members, reports. There is a typescript history of the locations of St. Philip's Church from 1810 to 1886.

A *New York Times* clipping of December 27, 1951, "Negro Church Tops City Episcopalians," indicates that St. Philip's, with some 4,000 members, is the largest Episcopal Church in New York. A flier of April 12, 1953, announces an address on South Africa by Prof. Z.K. Matthews, sponsored by the church's Guilford Group. Shelton Hale Bishop's sermon is present from Homecoming Sunday, October 7, 1956. A program and Waldorf-Astoria menu dated June 1, 1957, honor Bishop at his retirement.

A program of September 22, 1957, lists the order of service for the installation of M. Moran Weston as rector. A flier of May 13, 1960, announces the crowning of St. Philip's May Queen. An invitation of May 22, 1963, announces a Community Service Forum at which Borough President Edward Dudley and Kenneth Clark are to speak. Sheet music by William B. Cooper, St. Philip's organist, dated 1967, is an original festival liturgy of thanksgiving composed for the church's 150th anniversary.

The material on Reverend Ike (Frederick J. Eikerenkoetter) is less extensive, consisting of two fiche cards of some 150 pages/ frames. There are four issues of *Action!* the publication of his United Christian Evangelistic Association. There is a 1974 pamphlet by Reverend Ike: *How to Have $urplu$ instead of Shortage and Rev. Ike's Blessing Plan.* This literature expounds the philosophy that "the lack of money is the root of all evil," and features testimonials of financial success and physical health by purchasers of Rev. Ike's prayer cloth. There is a *Time* magazine article of December 11, 1972, "That T-Bone Religion," and an article from the *New York Post* of July 24, 1974, "The Well-Healed [sic] Rev. Ike."

The microfiche for Gardner C. Taylor, to look at another example, consists of some 20 newspaper clippings and one issue of the Concord Baptist Church, Brooklyn, N.Y., newsletter. Clippings cover Taylor's election in February 1958 as the first black president of the N.Y. Protestant Council. There is a *Post* feature of February 16, 1958, entitled "The Mississippi Still Flows Downstream," and articles from publications as varied as *Hotel*, a trade organ, and the *Daily Worker*.

These illustrations indicate something of the varied holdings of the Vertical File. There are predictable clippings from the *New York Times*, but there are also unique, unusual, and serendipitous items of many kinds. While the Vertical File should be used as an adjunct to the more conventional avenues of research, such as the Schomburg's vast book and archives holdings and its Aids File (a name and subject index of 150,000 cards), it contains material in Afro-American life and history which has probably been preserved nowhere else.

—*Newsletter* of the Afro-American Religious History Group of the American Academy of Religion 7:1 (Fall 1982), 9–10

Some Recent Bibliographic Resources for Black Religion

Ethel Williams and Clifton F. Brown's new *Howard University Bibliography of African and Afro-American Religious Studies* (Wilmington: Scholarly Resources, 1977) is a major contribution to Afro-American religious scholarship. This is a revised and expanded version of their *Afro-American Religious Studies* (Scarecrow Press, 1972). The bibliography consists of over 13,000 entries, some of which are annotated. For each item a symbol indicates at least one location in an American library. The entries are organized as follows: African Heritage, 4,256 entries; Christianity and Slavery in the New World, 2,090; The Black Man and His Religious Life in the Americas, 4,575; The Civil Rights Movement, 1954–1967, 1,158; and the Contemporary Religious Scene, 1,159. Under these large chronological sections, the subdivisions are usually by denomination, then alphabetical by author. There is an author index, but, unfortunately, not a subject index. Since the categories are broad, it is wise, and surprisingly rewarding, to read through a great many pages in search of items of particular interest. Two valuable appendices are included: Manuscript Collections and an Autobiographical and Biographical Index.

Another remarkable compilation is James Abajian's *Blacks in Selected Newspapers, Censuses and Other Sources; An Index to Names and Subjects* (Boston: G.K. Hall, 1977). Abajian, who is Library Director of the California Historical Society, went through countless periodicals, directories, books, and pamphlets, and made a card for every reference he found to a black person or institution. The result is a file of over 100,000 cards! While the *Index*'s greatest usefulness is probably for genealogical research, there is a good deal of rare material for the historian of religion, primarily culled from newspapers. There are over 200 entries, for example, under "A.M.E. Church." A sample reads: "A.M.E. Church, St. Louis, Mo., 1852. A slave-clergyman attends N.Y.C. conference. Windsor, Ont., *Voice of the Fugitive*, June 17, 1852, p. 1." Most of the entries are about persons (there are, for example, 25 cards on Henry Highland Garnet). But the real value is the references to little-known or previously unknown people; often the citation is to an obituary notice and thus to additional information.

The KTO Press, Millwood, N.Y., a division of Kraus-Thompson, is now publishing a 1964–1974 Jamaican National Bibliography cumulation as part of their larger Caribbeana program. Two related titles are the 120,000 card *Catalogue of the West India Research Library*, available in 10 volumes, and *The Complete Caribbeana, 1900–1975: A Bibliographic Guide to the Scholarly Literature*.

The first volume of a highly promising series is Harold Turner's *Bibliography of New Religious Movements in Primal Societies, vol. 1: Black Africa* (Boston: G.K. Hall, 1977). With 1,900 entries, the book is a comprehensive bibliography of the African Independent Church Movement. It replaces Turner's earlier bibliography published by Northwestern University Press and supplemented in the *Journal of Religion in Africa*. Turner, who is now at Aberdeen, Scotland, directing a Center for the Study of New Religious Movements, is working on subsequent volumes which will cover North America, Latin America–Caribbean, and Asia–Oceania.

—*Newsletter* of the Afro-American Religious History Group of the American Academy of Religion 2:1 (Fall 1977), 3

Reviews

Andrews, William L., ed. *Sisters of the Spirit: Three Black Women's Autobiographies of the Nineteenth Century.* Bloomington: Indiana University Press, 1986.

This book reprints three autobiographies: *The Life and Religious Experience of Jarena Lee, A Coloured Lady, Giving an Account of Her Call to Preach the Gospel, Revised and Corrected from the Original Manuscript, Written by Herself* (Philadelphia: Author, 1836); *Memoirs of the Life, Religious Experience, Ministerial Travels and Labours of Mrs. Zilpha Elaw, An American Female of Colour; Together with Some Account of the Great Religious Revivals in America [Written by Herself]* (London: Author, 1846); and *A Brand Plucked from the Fire: An Autobiographical Sketch by Mrs. Julia A.J. Foote* (Cleveland: Author, 1879). There is an unusually literate and insightful introduction by Professor Andrews of the University of Wisconsin, who is well known for his earlier work on Charles W. Chesnutt.

There are similarities among these three accounts, not unrelated to other religious autobiographies and not restricted to the period. All three women suffered when very young from guilt over their extreme wickedness: Lee told a lie, Elaw took the Lord's name in vain, and Foote attended a dance. In agonizing over their apparently hopeless sinfulness and the threat of hell, all received divine messages in dreams, visions, and voices, and were miraculously delivered. All were then tempted by the devil to doubt their salvation. All experienced a second "work," i.e., sanctification, and were led by the Spirit, amidst much groaning and many tears, to holiness. All were associated with the Methodist Church in the days when it was a sectarian society of class meetings, rigorous pietism, and evangelical fervor.

All three interpreted events in terms of providential signs. All were married ("surrendered in marriage," Elaw says, perhaps because her mother died in childbirth with her 22nd baby) to merely nominal believers who thought them crazy and created problems for their religious lives. Despite resistance on their own parts, all were called to be itinerant preachers, and were opposed by established church leaders. Not surprisingly, they determined they must obey God rather than men. While these experiences are common to the genre, Lee, Elaw, and Foote shared two characteristics that set them apart from other spiritual autobiographers and added to their vicissitudes: they were women and they were black.

They responded to the arguments against women preachers with Biblical texts, logic, wit, and the assurance of the authenticity of their own callings. Rebuffed by Richard Allen, Lee writes, "If a man may preach, because the Saviour died for him, why not the woman? seeing he died for her also. Is he not a whole Saviour instead of a half one?" Pointing out that the Biblical Phoebe was a deaconess "and as such was employed by the Church to manage some of their affairs," Elaw suggests, "it was strange indeed, if she was required to receive the commission of the Church in mute silence, and not allowed to utter a syllable before them." Foote says, "If it be necessary to prove one's right to preach the Gospel, I ask of my brethren to show me their credentials."

Admitting that the double curiosity of a black woman preacher brought some to hear her message, Elaw tells her British readers, "The pride of a white skin is a bauble of great value with many in some parts of the United States, who readily sacrifice their intelligence to their prejudices." Harrassed by slave-catchers, Foote writes, "We realized more and more what a terrible thing it was for one human being to have absolute control over another." Moved by what God was doing, Lee simply says, "Here by the instrumentality of a poor colored woman, the Lord poured forth his spirit among the people."

There are other touches. Foote is opposed to capital punishment, and is something of a pacifist. Elaw speaks out against the worldliness of ministers, and says true ministers "love the flock rather than the fleece." Elaw travels to Hartford where she reports preaching to prostitutes and Universalists. There is a pre-Azuza Street account of speaking in tongues.

These three women reveal the state of evangelical religion in the nineteenth century, they show the struggle required to obey what they believed to be a divine imperative to a vocation held exclusively by men, and they lived and moved in a society of racists and slaveholders. In addition, they speak for themselves and become, as Andrews points out, "foremothers of the black feminist literary tradition."

The point should be made that all three of these books are unusually rare, especially Elaw, and are not held by most libraries, nor do they turn up in dealers' catalogues. It is a real service to make them available. *Sisters of the Spirit* is historically important for what it has to teach us about religion, race, and feminism. At times, it reads like a contemporary account, since so many of the issues faced by these women are not yet resolved. Finally, it introduces us with the power and eloquence of simplicity and sincerity to the remarkable lives of three extraordinary sisters.

Austin, Allan D. *African Muslims in Antebellum America: A Sourcebook.* New York: Garland Publishing, 1984.

This is perhaps the most important Afro-American religious history book of the season. Allan Austin has recognized the existence and significance of black African Muslims brought to America in slavery, and collected their scattered narratives of life in Africa and America. He presents them here, superbly edited, introduced, annotated, and analyzed.

While some of Austin's subjects are well known, the overall impact of his compilation calls for a rethinking of several conventional assumptions. One is the premise that the black Africa from which the slaves came was a pagan and benighted place; another is that there were no literate slaves who were able to record their experiences with sophistication; a third is that black Islam is merely a twentieth-century sociological or psychological aberration.

Here to defy these presuppositions are the accounts of fifteen African Muslims plus contemporary materials written about them, and "shorter notices" of yet another fifty. Among the longer narratives are those of Job ben Solomon, Abdul Rahahman, Bilali of Georgia, Salih Bilali, Lamen Kebe, Omar Ibn Said, Mahommah Ganlo Baquaqua, and Mohammed Ali ben Said.

Austin's notes are extraordinarily full, informative, insightful, and well-written. The book has an index, a bibliography, 36 photographs (including reproductions of Arabic manuscripts left by these Africans), and six maps. *African Muslims in Antebellum America* is a major achievement which illumines a whole new dimension of Afro-American religious history.

—*Newsletter* of the Afro-American Religious History Group of the American Academy of Religion 8:2 (Spring 1984), 15

Baldwin, Lewis V. *"Invisible" Strands in African Methodism: A History of the African Union Methodist Protestant and Union American Methodist Episcopal Churches, 1805–1980.* Metuchen: The American Theological Library Association and Scarecrow Press, 1983.

The little-known "Spencer" churches originated in 1805 when Peter Spencer and William Anderson, two black lay preachers, led a black group out of the predominantly white Asbury Methodist Episcopal Church of Wilmington, Delaware, to protest discrimination in worship. This book is a historical study of the several small regional denominations that grew out of that break.

In addition to his comprehensive chronological account, Baldwin advances the controversial thesis that this movement was the first to establish black Methodism independent of white Methodism. He also sets up a "comparative context" of the Spencer churches with the larger black Methodist groups, and analyzes the Spencer churches' worship tradition. This latter is especially interesting because of the unique "Big August Quarterly," a black religious festival in Wilmington inaugurated by Peter Spencer himself which still takes place.

"Invisible" Strands is a previously unknown chapter in black religious history, an insight into the origins of black Methodism, and the documentation of denominations which have been neglected by historians. There are detailed footnotes, a useful essay on sources, an index, and forty rare photographs.

—*Newsletter* of the Afro-American Religious History Group of the American Academy of Religion 8:2 (Spring 1984), 13–14

Bischof, Phyllis. *Afro-Americana: A Research Guide to Collections at the University of California at Berkeley.* Berkeley: The General Library and the Department of Afro-American Studies, University of California at Berkeley, 1984.

This research guide fulfils several functions. While neither exhaustive nor a bibliography of holdings, it is a useful introduction to Afro-American reference sources in general and those at Berkeley in particular.

The guide describes African, Caribbean, and Afro-American collections in the various libraries of the University, complete with names, addresses, and telephone numbers of "resource persons." It explains the use of Berkeley's card, fiche, and on-line catalogs. It lists Library of Congress Afro-American subject headings. It discusses guides to periodical literature and abstracts, computer searches, and inter-library loans. It selectively lists some of Berkeley's recent Afro-American dissertations.

The second half of the guide is a selective bibliography of Afro-American reference materials within the University, arranged by form or subject, and with location symbols. Most are well-known standard sources, but there are some pleasant surprises such as Harold A. Walters' *Black Theatre in French: A Guide,* published in Quebec by Editions Naaman, and Bertie A. Cohen Stuart's *Women in the Caribbean: A Bibliography* published in Holland by the Department of Caribbean Studies at the Royal Institute of Linguistics and Anthropology.

It is nice to see listings here for some of the most valuable but least-known Afro-American reference works such as James de T. Abajian's *Blacks in Selected Newspapers, Censuses and Other Sources.* It is too bad, but inevitable, that the guide was unable to include some of the more important newer reference publications such as Deborah Willis-Thomas's *Black Photographers, 1840–1940: A Bio-Bibliography.* The guide of course also points up what does not exist as well as what does; there has been no major reference work in black religion, for example, since Ethyl Williams' and Clifton F. Brown's *The Howard University Bibliography of African and Afro-American Religious Studies.*

Reference librarians complain about the increasing lack of sophistication of their patrons. This guide goes a long way toward combatting both subject-matter illiteracy and library usage ignorance. For the Berkeley student the values of the guide are obvious. For other researchers there are many helpful clues about reference resources and library procedures and opportunities. For other institutions the guide serves as an excellent model of what they themselves might create for their own students and readers.

Afro-Americana: A Research Guide can be ordered at $5 from Afro-American Guide, The Library Associates, Room 245 Main Library, University of California, Berkeley, CA 94720.

> —*Newsletter* of the Afro-American Religious History Group of the American Academy of Religion 10:1 (Fall 1985), 13.

Blanton, Robert J. *The Story of Voorhees College from 1897 to 1982.* Denmark: Voorhees College, 1983.

Brawley, James P. *The Clark College Legacy: An Interpretative History of Relevant Education, 1869–1975.* Atlanta: Clark College, 1977.

Butler, Addie Louise Joyner. *The Distinctive Black College: Talladega, Tuskegee and Morehouse.* Metuchen: Scarecrow Press, 1977.

Carter, Wilmoth. *Shaw's Universe: A Monument to Educational Innovation.* Raleigh: Shaw University, 1973.

One of the great difficulties in keeping track of, let alone acquiring, Afro-American books is that many are locally published, not widely advertised or distributed, and generally little known. That is the case with several of these histories of black colleges, all of which have church connections, usually the result of freedmen's aid efforts during Reconstruction.

The familiar themes are here: agricultural and industrial training versus liberal arts education; the gradual secularization of church-related schools; the slow movement to black administrators; and that ever-popular quicksand which never ceases to attract faculties—curriculum reform.

Unfortunately, some of these histories are too administrative—from one president to yet another, and draw too heavily on board minutes. But the human does break through, and there is often a sense of real persons and places. And there are insights. Tuskegee, for instance, was exceptional in having an all black staff—because it was unthinkable for a white faculty member to serve under a black president.

These books have individual differences. Butler includes some sociological analysis with her history. Brawley adds information on athletics, traditions, and social life, including a list of Clark's homecoming queens. Both Brawley and Carter have very useful biographical sketches of "personalities." All but Carter include numerous photographs.

These books contain a great deal of distilled information not easily obtainable elsewhere. They remind us that while visiting black schools one should take time away from the library to drop in the college bookstore; it may be the only place to find these locally written and published historical studies.

—*Newsletter* of the Afro-American Religious History Group of the American Academy of Religion 9:1 (Fall 1984), 12-13

Bringhurst, Newell G. *Saints, Slaves, and Blacks: The Changing Place of Black People within Mormonism*. Westport: Greenwood Press, 1981.

Despite an early universalism, Mormonism's cosmology suggested that there had been Negro misbehavior during "premortal" existence, and its theology linked contemporary blacks with Ham and Cain as biblical counterfigures. So cursed, blacks were denied the priesthood and thus full participation in Mormon life in the world to come as well as Salt Lake City. Bringhurst's study traces the doctrinal and cultural causes and effects of Mormon discrimination. While somewhat lacking in analysis, it is a fair-minded and straightforward historical account which demonstrates how a uniquely American religious group institutionalized the racism of the larger society.

—*Religious Studies Review* 8:4 (October 1982), 398

Bullock, Penelope E. *The Afro-American Periodical Press, 1838–1909.* Baton Rouge: Louisiana State University Press, 1981.

In addition to chronicling a little-known but critically important dimension of Afro-American history, this book throws considerable light on the black church as a sponsor of periodical publications. Bullock reports on 97 magazines, including biographical sketches of their editors and publishers, many of whom were clergy.

Supplementing the narrative history is a detailed "Publication Date and Finding-List." For each magazine this spells out title, first issue, frequency, place of publication, editor, publisher, price, circulation, format, publication history, and, most useful of all, library locations of extant issues.

Bullock's study ranges from 1838 when the *Mirror of Liberty* was founded in New York to 1910 when the *Crisis* began a new era. It is easy to spin theories about this period, or to say that there are insufficient records adequately to understand it. For 70 years, though, blacks spoke through their own press, and Bullock does us—and them—a favor by providing access to their words.

—*Newsletter* of the Afro-American Religious History Group of the American Academy of Religion 6:1 (Fall 1981), 14

Burgess, John M. *Black Gospel, White Church.*
New York: Seabury Press, 1982.

Perhaps there is no more interesting group of ministers than the
black clergy of the Episcopal Church. On the one hand they faced
a denomination which, it could be argued, has been one of the
most racist American churches; on the other, they were often cut
off by class and culture from the larger black community. The
fact that this group existed at all is remarkable; the fact that they
tended to be both intensely loyal Episcopalians and prideful
blacks makes them extraordinary indeed.

John M. Burgess, the retired bishop of Massachusetts (and the
first black clergyman elected a diocesan bishop) has collected 19
sermons by black Episcopal ministers. Beginning with Absalom
Jones' "Thanksgiving Sermon" of 1808, he includes sermons by
such heroic figures of the past as Peter Williams, Jr., Alexander
Crummell, and James Theodore Holly. Bishop Burgess' collection is entirely up to date as he has included such contemporaries
as Nathan Wright, Jr., Walter D. Dennis, Austin R. Cooper,
Junius F. Carter, Jr., Franklin D. Turner, and Robert C. Chap-
man.

One of the more useful features of *Black Gospel, White
Church* is that there are sermons by interesting and important
persons whose lives and work are not nearly well enough known
or appreciated: H.L. Phillips, Tollie L. Caution, Sr., and Kenneth deP. Hughes, for example. Everyone will have nominations
of names which might have been included; George Freeman
Bragg comes immediately to mind, as does Shelton Hale Bishop.

One wishes that this book had done more and gone further.
Bishop Burgess does not say enough about the differences as he
perceives them between the "Black Gospel" and a "White
Church." There might well have been more biographical information on the people whose work he includes. The book very
much needs a bibliography and an index. But until the history of
blacks in the Episcopal church is written, this book fills a need,
makes a statement, and reminds us of the lives and contributions
of a group of exceptional men.

—*Newsletter* of the Afro-American Religious History Group of the American Academy of Religion 6:2 (Spring 1982), 11

Campbell, Angus. *White Attitudes Toward Black People.* Ann Arbor: Institute for Social Research, 1971.

This book reports in detail statistical data on the racial attitudes of white people gathered by the Survey Research Council between 1964 and 1970. The bulk of the material is a study based on 2,945 interviews in 15 major cities during 1968. The survey was requested by the National Advisory Committee on Civil Disorders and supported by the Ford Foundation.

Given the significance of racial issues in our society over the past 15 years and the surfeit of publications on all aspects of ethnicity, it is surprising how little hard factual information exists about what people actually think, feel, and believe. Campbell's study is a useful contribution toward filling that gap in our knowledge.

The results of Campbell's inquiry are not particularly pleasant to contemplate. In essence they reveal that the "white population is far from a general acceptance of the principle and practice of racial equality." While the interviews do show some positive attitudinal changes in the direction of egalitarianism, the chief fact which emerges is that American whites are "racist in degree" and substantially resistant to social change.

Another of the survey's more interesting results is the discovery that in the past 25 years whites have changed their explanation for the disadvantaged position of blacks. While the rationale used to be genetic inferiority, it is now motivational inadequacy. Both are, of course, classic illustrations of the victim being made responsible for his own victimization. The majority group's ability to control the definitions of the situation is an often unappreciated ingredient in social domination, just as is the fact that its culturally created rationalizations become the "objective" presuppositions upon which thought and action within the culture are based.

The real question mark, then, that can be set over against this study has to do with the relevance of white attitudes—not to the ideology which underlies the cultural environment, but to the realities of life for most black people in America. There are few white bigots who murder black babies, but black people continue to have a higher infant mortality rate than white people. While

Campbell shows us that the white "explanation" is now in terms of the "motivational inadequacy" of black parents, his study cannot tell us why those deaths really occur because the true reason lies beyond the attitudes of either white or black people. We are just beginning to understand the nature of institutional racism. This means that those who are less as well as those who are more prejudiced are caught alike in social structures which are more limiting and determining than they are reflective and expressive. Nobody believes those babies ought to die, but they do anyway. Their deaths are not a manifestation of white attitudes but of everybody's inability to control a large, impersonal, and bureaucratic society.

W.E.B. Du Bois began his career as a scholar because he believed that facts spoke for themselves and that with correct information the world could be changed. Campbell's book is an impressive collection of facts carefully gathered and intelligently analyzed which speak for themselves all too clearly. But unless our times are very different from Du Bois's the book unknowingly perpetuates the myth that personal attitudes rather than institutional norms and networks determine social reality.

—*Journal of College Science Teaching* 2:2 (December 1972), 52–53

Davis, Charles, and Henry Louis Gates, eds. *The Slave's Narrative.* New York: Oxford University Press, 1985.

This book is a virtual one-volume reference work on that singular literary and historical phenomenon, the autobiographical accounts of ex-slaves. It was Ephriam Peabody who pointed out that "America [had] the honor of adding a new department to the literature of civilization—the autobiography of escaped slaves"; and the late Charles Davis of Yale, one of the book's editors, has suggested that black literature as genre does not in fact begin until the slave narratives. So the material itself is unique, as are the perspectives it alone is able to provide on black life under chattel slavery.

The Slave's Narrative consists of a strikingly insightful introduction by Henry Louis Gates, now at Cornell, entitled "The Language of Slavery," a short compilation of contemporary reviews of slave autobiographies, and two substantive collections of essays, seven on "The Slave Narratives as History," and eight on "The Slave Narratives as Literature." There is also a highly useful chronological list of non-fictional autobiographies to 1865, and Allan Austin's list of "Narratives of African Muslims in Antebellum America." There are illustrations, chiefly portraits, and an index.

Among the historical essays are Sterling Brown's "On Dialect Usage," John Edgar Wideman on "Charles Chesnutt and the WPA Narratives," and C. Vann Woodward's "History from Slave Sources." The literature section includes Jean Fagin Yellin's "Texts and Contexts of Harriet Jacobs' 'Incidents in the Life of a Slave Girl,'" Paul Edwards' "Three West African Writers of the 1780s" (Equiano, Cugoano, and Sancho), and Robert Stepto's "I Rose and Found My Voice: Narration, Authentication, and Authorial Control in Four Slave Narratives" (Douglass, Bibb, Northup, and William Wells Brown).

Nothing can substitute for reading the powerful slave accounts themselves, but *The Slave's Narrative* provides interpretation, analysis, and, most important, sends one back to the original texts with clearer vision.

—*Newsletter* of the Afro-American Religious History Group of the American Academy of Religion 10:1 (Fall 1985), 14

Dibble, J. Birney. *The Plains Brood Alone.* Grand Rapids: Zondervan Publishing House, 1973.

This book is a popular, anecdotal account by an American physician of his time as a medical missionary in Tanzania. Dibble has an affirmative, empathetic feeling for Africans as persons and many of his stories are quite moving in their demonstration of the enormous gifts a healing practitioner can bestow and the enormous gratitude people of the Third World can express.

Dibble's gifts are essentially individualistic and personalistic and they are not to be disparaged. Nevertheless, although he is pleased at the greater Africanization of the hospital since his earlier time there, he expresses very little appreciation of the historical and economic causes which underlie large-scale poor health, and very little sympathy for the struggle to construct an indigenous and independent African socialism on the part of President Julius Nyerere.

Dibble is caught, as all of us are, between a real desire to appreciate the validity of African culture and learn from African customs on one hand, and, on the other, the conviction that our own beliefs, priorities, and ways of doing things are in fact better. The questions are: How is it possible to aid the developing countries and remain free from neo-imperialism? How is it possible to be emissaries of the Christian faith without at the same time becoming ideological and cultural colonialists and destroyers of civilizations which differ from our own?

Dibble does not address himself to these questions, but they are painfully present, for us as well as for him, even behind his own self-sacrificing concern for people in need. For Christians the answer in part lies in the African independent church movement, where the historic kerygma of the Christian gospel is being expressed in unique, new, indigenous African cultural and institutional forms.

This issue is a problem for the sociologist who must always come to terms with the fact of cultural relativism. But it is a greater problem for the theologian, since religion must embody itself in concrete cultural forms—and Christianity is culturally iconoclastic. The medical missionary is thus trapped in a double bind. As a doctor he must practice the "science" of medicine while respecting people he sees as "primitive." As a Christian he must separate his faith from his own culture while knowing that "African Christianity" ultimately runs the same risks as any other nationalization of Christian faith.

One of the disturbing things about Dibble's book is the casualness with which animals are destroyed by Europeans, i.e., whites. While such killing can be justified by danger, the need for food or the animals' own best interests, the notion of animal slaughter as "sport" shows how an African culture in harmony with its physical environment is more truly civilized than a European culture which insists on the "mastery" of nature by its destruction. The time of the idea of animal liberation clearly has not yet come.

The Plains Brood Alone is fundamentally a collection of stories, tales, personal experiences. Without sentimentality or condescension it contains insights into a vast, complex land and a great, diverse people. The book is an often poignant account of how persons can touch each other's lives because the reality of a common humanity ultimately transcends the barriers of ethnocentrism and ignorance which all persons construct around themselves.

—The Review of Books and Religion 2:10 (July-August 1973), 14

Divine, Mother. *The Peace Mission Movement.* Philadelphia: Palace Mission, 1982.

The earliest books on Father Divine are so negative and biased that they are of virtually no use to the student or researcher. Then in 1979 Kenneth Burnham published *God Comes to America*; through Burnham's extensive use of primary source materials, Father Divine spoke for himself as a charismatic religious leader and advocate of American racial democracy. In 1983 Robert Weisbrot in *Father Divine and the Struggle for Civil Rights* developed these themes; with great insight Weisbrot perceived Father as a significant civil rights leader and American reformer.

Now we have the unusual opportunity of hearing the story of Father Divine and the Peace Mission Movement from no less a person than Mother Divine herself. Her book was originally prepared as part of an updating of the *History of Montgomery County*. By following the guidelines supplied by the editor of the *History*, Mother's account reveals a great deal of information that is not generally known: characteristics of the Movement's followers, the communal living arrangements, the concepts of death and marriage, etc.

Space is devoted to a number of important issues: the meaning of Mother and Father's spiritual marriage; the significance of the Woodmont Estate (where Mother and some co-workers live);

the interpretation of Father's "sacrifice" of September 10, 1965; the relevance of the patriotic Americanism which runs through all of Father's sermons and speeches; Father's peace proposals and Righteous Government Platform; the Movement's opposition to the name "George Baker" which some writers have claimed to be Father's real identity; the unsuccessful attempt of Jim Jones to replace Father and take over the Movement.

Mother Divine's book is important not only for its historical interpretation of Father Divine and the Movement, but for its articulation of the group's present state, both theological and programmatic. Under Mother Divine's leadership, the Movement, building upon the foundation of Father's deity, is adjusting to changing times. The book thus takes on a special significance in its own right. It is indispensable for anyone who seriously wants to understand the meaning and direction of the Peace Mission Movement as it exists today under Mother's stewardship.

The Peace Mission Movement is available only through one of the Movement's organizations: A D F D Publications, Suite 104, 20 South 36th St., Philadelphia, PA 19104. Hard cover is $7 and paper cover is $5. The price includes postage. There are illustrations and an index.

—*Newsletter* of the Afro-American Religious History Group of the American Academy of Religion 8:1 (Fall 1983), 14–15

Du Bois, William E.B. *Against Racism: Unpublished Essays, Papers, Addresses, 1887–1961.* Edited by Herbert Aptheker. Amherst: University of Massachusetts Press, 1985.

W.E.B. Du Bois wrote the way Louis Armstrong played the trumpet: one is struck first by the extraordinarily pure clarity, then by the perfection of tone and rhythm, and then by the realization that this is the artistry of a master, unmistakable in style, easily moving beyond and above the sounds around it. Even though the components may be familiar, the result is something one has never quite heard before.

Herbert Aptheker, Du Bois's literary executor, has for some time been collecting and editing Du Bois's papers from the archives deposited at the University of Massachusetts, notably three volumes of correspondence. *Against Racism* is particularly interesting and important because it consists of previously unpublished material.

The papers are arranged chronologically, and each is briefly introduced by Aptheker. The earliest is a prophetic "Open Letter to the Southern People," written in 1887 when Du Bois was a student at Fisk. The last is a short note in support of Henry Winston, the Afro-American Communist convicted under the Smith Act, written in 1961, three quarters of a century later and just a month before Du Bois relinquished the United States for Africa.

Among the papers are several of especial importance. "The Art and Art Galleries of Modern Europe" is one, a lecture at Wilberforce, probably in 1896. Perhaps Du Bois's major unpublished work is "The Negro in Social Reconstruction," printed here in 54 pages, which was written in 1936 and rejected by Alain Locke for Locke's Bronze Booklet Series because it was too radical. Since the essay spells out the views that led Du Bois to leave the NAACP in 1934 it is valuable to have the text.

Readers of this journal will be interested in "The New Negro Church," dating probably from 1917, although Du Bois's position on this subject is well known. Some of the other essays are "The Spirit of Modern Europe" (1900?), "A Proposed Negro Journal" (1905), "The Future of Africa in America" (1942), "A Farewell Message to the Alumni of Atlanta University" (1944), "Colonialism, Democracy, and Peace after the War" (1944), "In Memory of Joel Elias Spingarn" (1953), and "A Petition to the Honorable John F. Kennedy" (1961).

Against Racism contains 46 essays, a general introduction by Aptheker, a very useful chronology of Du Bois's long life, and a striking collection of photographs. Aptheker chose "Against Racism" as the title, for, despite Du Bois's lifelong movement toward the left politically, his exposure of American racism and his struggle against it remained constant. These pieces are trumpet calls, in which we see again how and why William

Edward Burghardt Du Bois was the towering figure in Afro-American history for the century following emancipation.

—*Newsletter* of the Afro-American Religious History Group of the American Academy of Religion 10:1 (Fall 1985), 15–16

Du Bois, William E.B. *Prayers for Dark People.* Edited by Herbert Aptheker. Amherst: University of Massachusetts Press, 1980.

Who would have guessed that the most remarkable book of the season would be a small collection of prayers written by a non-religious sociologist 70 years ago and edited today by the country's leading Marxist? W.E.B. Du Bois composed these prayers in 1909 and 1910 when he was on the faculty of Atlanta University. Herbert Aptheker found them on scraps of paper in a manila envelope among the material Du Bois left when he moved to Africa in 1961. They have now been published in a particularly handsome edition by the University of Massachusetts Press.

The book is an absolute gem. Aptheker's introduction is insightful, informative, and sensitive, one of the best things he has written on Du Bois. Du Bois's prayers are sometimes addressed more to human than divine listeners ("Let us realize too that even we the disenfranchised have our duties"), but they are profound, inspiring, and, it must be said to those who assume Du Bois always confused himself with the deity, reverent.

The occasion for the prayers is not clear. Some refer to the beginning of school holidays and the like, so they may have been offered at college assemblies or chapel services. Several contain the word "tonight" and include references for Scripture readings. It would be interesting to know what kind of services were held at Atlanta in 1909, and what Du Bois's participation meant.

Du Bois is not the first offerer of prayers to do a bit of sermonizing. In various prayers he asks that those on whose behalf he petitions might be delivered from sloth, ignorance, drunkenness, tardiness, and he thinks it all possible since "most men are always a little better than the worst." He encourages the virtues of endurance, service, persistence, sacrifice, and above all, work: "There is no God but Love and work is His prophet." He combines a schoolmasterish judgment with as much hope as is realistic: "A school year whose December has been thrown away may be *in part* retrieved in May."

Du Bois's great social conscience finds eloquent expression: "Mighty causes are calling us—the freeing of women . . . the putting down of hate and murder and poverty." "Grant us, O God, the vision and the will to be found on the right side in the great battle for bread." "May these young people grow to despise the false ideals of conquest and empire and all the tinsel of war."

Did someone at Atlanta, a student or teacher, die and move Du Bois to words as powerful as these? "Help us to hope that the seeming Shadow of this Death is to our human blindness but the exceeding brightness of a newer greater life." Here, as Aptheker points out, is a dimension of Du Bois's life little seen and little known, the fatherly teacher in Georgia less than 50 years after Emancipation. We are fortunate to have this glimpse of it.

—*Newsletter* of the Afro-American Religious History Group of the American Academy of Religion 5:1 (Fall 1980), 10–11

Essig, James D. *The Bonds of Wickedness: American Evangelicals Against Slavery, 1770–1808.* Philadelphia: Temple University Press, 1982.

The unusual thing about James Essig's *The Bonds of Wickedness* is of course that it deals with 1770–1808, a period of religiously based anti-slavery sentiment and activity that has been little analyzed. The preachers of the Great Awakening did not denounce slavery; in fact, they held that a Christian slave was a more faithful servant. But by chastising the planter class for neglecting the slaves' spiritual welfare, Whitefield and others sowed the seeds of the later Evangelical war against slavery.

In the late eighteenth century, for several reasons, slavery came to be included in the catalogue of sins of which an unrighteous America was called to repent. Evangelical, especially Baptist and Methodist, spirituality and apostolic simplicity led to a radical unworldliness that identified compassionately with black slaves as despised outcasts. Also, it was perceived by the Evangelicals that the gentry could never achieve primitive Christianity without renouncing the slavery which made possible their worldly idleness, fashionable clothing, and intemperate living. And these notions were clearly related to the revolutionary politics of the period which linked civic virtue and an opposition to tyranny with the integrity of the new American republic.

It is this latter theme, especially, that Essig develops through biographical sketches of David Barrow, a Virginia Baptist who freed his own slaves, believing hereditary slavery incompatible with a republican government; James O'Kelly of Virginia who opposed monarchy, episcopacy, and slavery, and founded the schismatic Republican Methodist Church; David Rice, a Presbyterian who tried to keep slavery out of Kentucky and applauded the San Domingo insurrection; and Samuel Hopkins, the New England Congregationalist New Divinity man who tied anti-slavery to an anti-cultural millenarianism.

Essig examines the anti-slavery sentiment of the orthodox Calvinist establishment in Connecticut, focusing on Jedidiah Morse, Timothy Dwight, and the Connecticut Society for the Promotion of Freedom and the Relief of Persons Unlawfully Holden in Bondage. He then explores the decline and ultimate failure of the anti-slavery evangelicals: their accommodation to culture in the South, and, in the North and Border States, their diversion by the Second Great Awakening. Essig concludes with a review of those few evangelicals like Thomas Branagan who carried on the lonely work and, in the light of subsequent history, "built better than they knew."

—*Newsletter* of the Afro-American Religious History Group of the American Academy of Religion 9:2 (Spring 1985), 13

Fletcher, James A., and Carleton Mabee, eds.
*A Quaker Speaks from the Black Experience: The
Life and Selected Writings of Barrington Dunbar.*
New York: New York Yearly Meeting of the
Religious Society of Friends, 1979.

The Religious Society of Friends has a remarkable history of
anti-slavery, civil rights, and humanitarian work. It is nevertheless true that few black people have ever joined the Society and
become practicing Quakers. One who did was Barrington Dunbar, 1901–1978, a native of British Guiana who worked for various settlement houses and relief agencies, and became a Friend
after involvement with a number of mainstream Protestant
churches.

This small book is a tribute to Barrington Dunbar. It consists
of a biographical sketch by Professor Carleton Mabee of SUNY
New Paltz, and excerpts from Dunbar's letters, speeches, and
articles. All of these date from the beginning of the civil rights
movement and are primarily concerned with Dunbar's attempts
to interpret and explain to his fellow Quakers the freedom movement of his fellow blacks. It was not an easy task.

As members of the white liberal establishment, Quakers could
not understand either black nationalism or their own paternalism. Although doctrinaire pacifists, they were unable to comprehend either the violence of racist institutions or black resistance
to that violence. As a result, Dunbar became something of a
disturber of the Quaker peace. The book is an insight not only
into a particular historical period, but into every time when
blacks must struggle with those who are closest to them ideologi-
cally but blind to the realities of race.

Dunbar the person emerges clearly from his words. One hears
him explain patiently, persuasively, honestly, eloquently, always
"speaking the truth in love." One's final impression is that here
was one of those rare saintly people of exceptional integrity and
courage who gave a new meaning to the word "Friend."

—*Afro-Americans in New York Life and History*
4:1 (January 1980), 91

Foner, Philip S., ed. *Black Socialist Preacher:
The Teachings of Reverend George Washington
Woodbey and His Disciple Reverend George W.
Slater, Jr.* San Francisco: Synthesis Publications,
1983.

Philip Foner has done a great service in locating, collecting, and
reprinting George Washington Woodbey's speeches, pamphlets,
and articles on socialism. There is, in addition, "Socialism from
the Biblical Point of View" by James Theodore Holly and "The
Negro and Socialism" by Reverdy C. Ransom (both from the
AME Church Review) as well as a series of articles by George W.
Slater, Jr. This is the first time that the writings of black socialists have been gathered in book form; the result is an impressive
insight into the social and political thinking of several active
black ministers in the early years of the century.

Woodbey's longer essays are here: "What to Do and How to
Do It, or Socialism vs. Capitalism" (1903), "The Bible and Socialism" (1904), and "The Distribution of Wealth" (1910) as well
as pieces from *The Christian Socialist* and his speech (against
Oriental exclusion) at the Socialist Party Convention of 1908.
Slater's articles are primarily from the *Chicago Daily Socialist*
where he wrote a column on "Socialism and the Negro Race."

While the lives of Holly and Ransom are generally well
known, there is not much biographical information on Woodbey
and Slater. Woodbey was born a slave in Tennessee in 1854 and
ordained a Baptist minister in Kansas in 1874. He tried the
Republican, Prohibitionist, and Populist parties before he became a Socialist after reading Edward Bellamy.

Woodbey was pastor of the African Church in Omaha, Ne-
braska, and the Mt. Zion Baptist Church in San Diego. It was in
California that he flourished as street-corner orator, defender of
free speech, and socialist popularizer. Rather surprisingly, Foner
says, "We know nothing of Woodbey after 1915." In fact, Woodbey edited the *New Idea*, a black newspaper in San Diego, from
1921 to 1927, and died in 1937. Less is known of Slater, who was
pastor of Zion Tabernacle in Chicago and Bethel African Church
in Clinton, Iowa. Unfortunately, all copies of his pamphlets and
the newspaper he edited have been lost.

The Socialists had no special message for blacks whose plight, it was assumed, would be ended when socialism replaced capitalism. But blacks as the worst off of the working class had the most to gain from a socialist transformation of society and the creation of a cooperative commonwealth. Woodbey's philosophy is summed up by the self-definition at the beginning of one of his pamphlets: "By one who was once a chattel slave freed by the proclamation of Lincoln and now wishes to be free from the slavery of capitalism."

> —*Newsletter* of the Afro-American Religious History Group of the American Academy of Religion 9:2 (Spring 1985), 13–14

Gerloff, Roswith, et al. *Learning in Partnership: Third Report from the Joint Working Party Between Black-led and White Churches.* London: The British Council of Churches, 1980.

Something remarkable is going on in Britain. In this country the ecumenical movement has become a non-event, and divisions between mainstream and other churches are widening. But in England, Birmingham University, the British Council of Churches, and the Selly Oak Colleges are sponsoring a program called Project in Partnership Between Black and White.

The Project serves as a resource center where "black-led" and white churches find information about one another, and it fosters interchurch relations across racial and cultural lines. One of the more unusual aspects of the Project is theological training for the ministers of the black churches who represent African, Caribbean, and Afro-American religious heritages. As these leaders instill their own traditions into the curriculum and examinations of the University, there is a real meeting of first and third worlds in which each participates in "education for mutual salvation and liberation."

One of the leaders of the Cherubim and Seraphim Church writes, "The church of black people today is practically the only means of reviving our native cultures and beliefs, and forms the basis of our social and spiritual lives." The Project as Gerloff describes it not only strengthens and supports Britain's black churches, but creates a unique theological school which is a "turntable" between historic and charismatic Christianity.

—*Newsletter* of the Afro-American Religious History Group of the American Academy of Religion 6:1 (Fall 1981), 13-14

Gubert, Betty K. *Early Black Bibliographies, 1863-1918.* New York: Garland Publishing, 1982.

This book is a garden of bibliographic delights. Gubert, Head of Reference at the Schomburg Center, has collected 19 old, rare, and out-of-print Afro-American bibliographies which this book photographically reproduces. A short essay introduces each bibliography, explaining its historical setting and discussing its compiler. A computer-produced master index of over 3,000 names provides access to all the authors listed.

A few of these bibliographies are reasonably well known, such as Du Bois's always useful Atlanta University series, several of which Gubert includes. But most are rare indeed. Only one copy is known, for example (at the Historical Society of Pennsylvania), of the 1894 catalogue of Robert Adger, the Philadelphia bibliophile. Also little known are several bibliographies dating from the early part of the century compiled by the Library of Congress and, until now, extant only in typescript at LC. These deal with anthropology and ethnology, slavery, the Klan, etc.

The earliest bibliography here is Samuel May's 1863 *Catalogue of Anti-Slavery Publications*. The latest is Arthur Schomburg's 1918 catalogue for the first exhibition of the Negro Library Association. Others include Marion Gleason McDougall on fugitive slaves (1891), Daniel Murray's 1900 list for the Paris Exposition, the bibliography produced by the Montgomery Conference of 1900 on "Race Problems of the South," and the 1914 catalogue of William Bolivar's library (which is particularly strong in early black religion).

These bibliographies are a great deal more than lists of early books, pamphlets, and periodicals (though the inclusion of little-known nineteenth-century periodical articles is a special treat). They also reflect interesting judgments about what was included and what was left out. Lemuel Haynes, for instance, does not appear here until Arthur Schomburg's 1918 list, and the Healy family appears not at all. This selectivity shows the significance of what Clarence Holte calls "racial identity"—the fact that Haynes and the Healys did not define themselves as black or elect to live in the black world meant that other blacks did not claim them either, even though one of the primary purposes of compiling these early bibliographies was to demonstrate the abilities and accomplishments of members of a race most whites believed incapable of serious achievement.

By photographically reproducing rather than typesetting these early documents, the book dramatically captures the authenticity and flavor of the originals as well as their content. The designer has cleverly placed the book's page numbers half-way down the side of each page so as to distinguish them from the various paginations and locations of the originals. Despite the price, *Early Black Bibliographies* is an incomparable guide to the earliest Afro-Americana, and a happy hunting ground for the bibliographic detective in all of us.

—*Newsletter* of the Afro-American Religious History Group of the American Academy of Religion 7:1 (Fall 1982), 13–14

Hill, Robert A., ed. *The Marcus Garvey and Universal Negro Improvement Association Papers*, Volume I, 1820–August 1919; Volume II, 27 August 1919–31 August 1920. Berkeley: University of California Press, 1984.

The Garvey Papers, as historian John Henrik Clarke has pointed out, is "the largest research project ever undertaken on a person of African descent." Hill's work means that for the first time Marcus M. Garvey (1887–1940), the Jamaican-born black nationalist, can speak for himself, above the myths of both his friends and enemies. Garvey is the person, more than any other in this century, who articulated the themes of black pride, racial self-reliance, and African redemption. Unlike the papers of W.E.B. Du Bois, Booker T. Washington, and a few other blacks whose collections are available for study, the records of Marcus Garvey were not simply waiting to be organized, selected from, and edited. Fifteen years ago the Garvey papers as such did not exist. Perhaps the most extraordinary facet of this remarkable project is that Professor Hill literally created the Garvey archives which now consist of over 30,000 documents, letters, pamphlets, vital records, intelligence reports, speeches, diplomatic dispatches, newspaper articles, and legal records. Hill travelled all over the world to discover, collect, and compile every significant piece of paper relating to Garvey.

Garvey's Universal Negro Improvement Association was the largest mass movement in Afro-American history, and it is important to emphasize that Hill collected the papers of this preeminent black organization as well as those of its charismatic founder. Hill's achievement makes it possible for scholars and laypersons alike to see both Garvey and the UNIA whole and to begin to unravel the complexities of this unique leader and his unique organization.

The complete Garvey papers will comprise ten lengthy volumes: the first six on Garvey's life and work primarily in the United States, two on the Caribbean, and two on Africa where Garvey's role in African liberation has never been fully understood or appreciated. The first two volumes are in an unusually useful format and handsome edition.

Volume One begins with the earliest mention in 1826 of the Garvey name in Jamaican slave records, and ends with Garvey's triumphant address at Carnegie Hall in 1919. Volume Two traces the success of the UNIA to its 1920 convention when Garvey in effect established an African government in exile. A major theme here is the fear, on the part of several colonial powers, of Garvey's influence and their attempts, especially through J. Edgar Hoover and the FBI, to discredit and destroy him.

Hill's brilliant introduction to Volume One, like all masterpieces of scholarship, is full of insights and surprises. His analysis of the influence on Garvey of Irish Republicanism and the "New Thought" movement are especially provocative. One of

the most useful and impressive features of both volumes is that
every person, of the hundreds named in the texts, is fully identified in a footnote. This makes the books a virtual encyclopedia of
the black history of Garvey's era.

I first met Robert Hill in 1970 on the steps of the former
Schomburg Center building when he was organizing the UNIA
files which had recently been discovered in Harlem. I still remember our excitement and enthusiasm as we shared our knowledge about Marcus Garvey. Thanks to Hill's indefatigable work
and incomparable achievement, we can now all know a great
deal more about Marcus M. Garvey and the UNIA than anyone
then would have thought possible.

—*The Schomburg Center Journal* 3:1 (Winter
1984), 6

Hill, Robert A., ed. *The Marcus Garvey and
Universal Negro Improvement Association Papers,*
Volume III, September 1920–August 1921. Berkeley:
University of California Press, 1984.

The third volume of the Garvey Papers lives up to the high
standards set by the first two books in the projected 10-volume
series. In fact, it is even more useful and revealing because it is a
more detailed account due to heightened activity by Garvey and
the UNIA on a number of fronts in the year following the
important convention of 1920.

Here is the story of Garvey's tour of the Caribbean and Central
America, dissension among the organization's leadership, a popular surge in UNIA membership, spying by the FBI, troubles
with the Black Star Line, Cyril Briggs and the African Blood
Brotherhood, Garvey's criticism of "social equality" as opposed
to "racial purity," and the significant convention of 1921. For
drama, this is all a high moment: Garvey as leader, African
Redemption as slogan, and the UNIA as the people's organization have powerfully emerged as the major black force following
the World War. Yet the elements of crisis are clearly present, and
the signs of denouement are clear.

As a scholarly work, Volume 3 is another splendid achievement. The Editorial Board is listed, textual devices and editorial
principles and practices are explained, as are symbols and abbre-
viations. There is a historical introduction and a useful chronology. The table of contents lists the approximately 450 documents
by date. There are four appendixes and an index as well as a
marvelous collection of rare and unusual photographs. Most
useful are the encyclopedic footnotes, especially the biographical
sketches.

Everyone now realizes that there was no archive of "Garvey
papers" waiting to be edited. Robert Hill literally created the
collection over a good many years by seeking out letters,
speeches, pamphlets, newspaper articles, secret government reports, etc., in Europe, Africa, and North and South America.
This is an unparalleled achievement combining research, determination, and informed luck to a degree it is not quite possible to
comprehend even with this 800-page volume in hand.

Bringing together this extraordinary collection of materials
makes it possible to understand Garvey and Garveyism with a
breadth and depth that has not only been previously impossible,
but has been previously not even thought possible. The fact that
these documents were unearthed shows that the primary data of
much Afro-American history exists for the dedicated and skilled
researcher to discover.

—*Newsletter* of the Afro-American Religious History Group of the American Academy of Religion 10:2 (Spring 1986), 15

Jacobs, Sylvia M., ed. *Black Americans and
the Missionary Movement in Africa*. Westport:
Greenwood Press, 1982.

One cannot be interested in Afro-American religious history without realizing how crucial the "Afro-" part of the subject is, and
how, one way or another, all roads lead to Africa. While the
influence of Africa on black America is now well established, a
good deal less has been thought and written about the black

American impact on Africa. Sylvia Jacobs' ongoing work on black American missionaries to Africa is one of the important ways in which that need is being filled.

This book is a collection of essays, most of which are new. Donald Roth writes on "The Racial Background of Afro-American Missionaries," Tom Shick on Liberia, Sandy Dwayne Martin on the Baptists, Manning Marable on Tuskegee, Thomas Howard on university education in West Africa, Walter Williams on William Henry Shepherd, Carol Page on the A.M.E. Church, and Lillie Johnson on missionary-government relations in British and Portuguese colonies. Jacobs herself provides a historical overview, an article on Afro-American women in the Congo, a concluding essay, and a fine bibliography.

—*Newsletter* of the Afro-American Religious History Group of the American Academy of Religion 7:2 (Spring 1983), 8–9

Joyce, Donald Franklin. *Gatekeepers of Black Culture: Black-Owned Book Publishing in the United States, 1817–1981.* Westport: Greenwood Press, 1983.

In his autobiography, first published in London in 1789, Olaudah Equiano, also known as Gustavus Vassa, tells a moving story about his initial encounter with books. Equiano borrowed the account from the narrative of another African, James Albert Gronniosaw, but it seems likely he did so because the incident described his own experience as well:

> I had often seen my master and Dick employed in reading; and I had a great curiosity to talk to the books as I thought they did, and so to learn how all things had a beginning. For that purpose I have often taken up a book, and have talked to it, and then put my ears to it, when alone, in hopes it would answer me; and I have been very much concerned when I found it remained silent.

The fact that Equiano soon went on to create a manuscript of his own shows how quickly he was able to penetrate the mystery of the book. Other Africans—and their descendants—have fared moderately well as authors, but, it must be said, much less well as arbiters of whether and what and how written material is made available to the public, that is, as publishers. Publishing by blacks is the neglected chapter of Afro-American history Donald Joyce, formerly of the Chicago Public Library and now at Tennessee State University, addresses in this book. In an earlier form (a doctoral thesis in library science at the University of Chicago) it was more aptly titled "A Chance to Speak for Ourselves."

The first black publishing did come out of the institution which, more than any other, has historically reflected the black community's own internal characteristics and authenticity, and, not accidentally, the one most free from white influence; this is of course the black church. The African Methodist Episcopal Book Concern was founded in Philadelphia in 1817. Over the years it was joined by the A.M.E. Zion, Colored Methodist Episcopal, and National Baptist Churches, and more recently by the Nation of Islam. These groups produced various manuals of doctrine and discipline, hymnals, catechisms, Sunday School lessons, church histories, and occasional non-religious literature.

Secular black publishing, however, has its real roots in the black attempt to counter the generally accepted racist scholarship of the late nineteenth century. White sociologists perceived blacks as innately inferior racially. White psychologists were Social Darwinists. White historians painted Reconstruction, when blacks first had minimal legal freedoms, as a disaster, and created a sentimentally benign view of slavery. As a result, black intellectuals came to realize that if there were to be a more objective analysis of the black situation and a response to white supremacists, they would have to provide it themselves. A number of individuals and organizations thus sought to become "vindicators of the race," and saw publishing as a major way to communicate their message.

The first of these, established in 1897, was the American Negro Academy founded by Alexander Crummell, which included such distinguished members as W.E.B. Du Bois, Paul Laurence Dunbar, and Arthur A. Schomburg. It produced occasional papers and in 1914 John Cromwell's *The Negro in American History*.

Its successor was the Association for the Study of Negro Life and History, which, under the leadership of Carter G. Woodson, created the *Journal of Negro History* and Negro History Week as well as an important series of monographs. A number of smaller black cultural and professional organizations produced occasional books: the Blyden Society of Willis Huggins, The Associates in Negro Folk Education founded by Alain Locke, and the Communist-supported Negro Publication Society of America.

Civil Rights organizations also developed publishing arms: the N.A.A.C.P., the Urban League, and Marcus Garvey's Universal Negro Improvement Association. Several black colleges and universities issued books, most notably Du Bois's sociological studies at Atlanta University, and Monroe Work's *Negro Year Book* series, produced at Tuskegee. More interesting are the struggles and tenacity of individuals who, one way or another, found a way to publish their own fiction or philosophy or historical studies: Sutton E. Griggs, J.A. Rogers, and James Ephriam McGirt, for example.

More interesting still are the virtually unknown and unremembered authors or titles or publishing ventures which Joyce mentions in a line or two, often all the information he could uncover. One would like to know a great deal more about the Colored Cooperative Publishing Company in Boston, issuers of the *Colored American Magazine*, which in 1900 published Pauline Hopkins' novel *Contending Forces*. Or the Bi-Monthly Negro Book Club of Columbus, Ohio, which apparently published only one book, O'Wendell (Oliver Wendell) Shaw's novel *Greater Need Below*. Or A. Wendell Malliet and Co., about which Joyce could locate no information whatsoever.

The Black Revolution of the 1960s and early '70s created a new sense of black self-affirmation, a new interest in the black experience, and a new generation of commercial black publishing enterprises. Broadside Press in Chicago issued serious poetry; The Third Press of Joseph Okpaku offered a wide range of books in several fields; the Johnson Publishing Co. of Chicago, which had done well financially with *Ebony* magazine, added a division for popular books. Most of these new efforts, however, failed because of shifts of public interest and funds away from blacks, the firms' own undercapitalization and inexperience, and a problem not uncommon to a good many other publishers: the inability to get their books reviewed by establishment periodicals.

Gatekeepers of Black Culture has several problems as a book, not least of which is that the transition from thesis to monograph has not been entirely satisfactorily made. But it is the first major study of its kind, and so it is full of information literally unobtainable elsewhere. Perhaps its most valuable contribution is an appendix which profiles 68 black publishers and printers and lists their major publications. Obviously, this is an extremely useful tool for librarians, collectors, dealers, historians, and researchers. It has been 200 years since Gustavus Vassa's concern that books "remained silent." It is no longer the case that books do not speak to black people; thanks to a handful of courageous, dedicated, and purposeful publishers, they have been made to speak on behalf of black people as well.

—*Printing History* 6:2 (1984), 33–34

Kondrashov, Satinslav. *The Life and Death of Martin Luther King*. Moscow: Progress Publishers, 1981.

I was interested in reading this book for the answers to two connected questions: what new perceptions into Martin Luther King might there be in the perspective of an "Izvestia" correspondent? What parts of the King story might that same Russian reporter be likely to ignore, or distort, or simply not know? I was disappointed on both counts. There are no special insights, and the only error is the amusing one of the author's calling Abraham Lincoln a woodchopper. In short, the book is only a journalistic and impressionistic account of black America in the 1960s, with a simplistic account of King badly interwoven.

The book does have its moments of interest and drama, though. When Kondrashov, sometimes with a Tass reporter as a fellow traveller (and always accompanied, at a distance, by the FBI) toured the South in the early 1960s, he was shocked by segregation. While his reporting is superficial, what he saw was dramatic enough to carry its own message. When he describes the television news reports of King's assassination juxtaposed with the constant assault of commercials, one does not have to be a party member to see the insincerity of American society. And one senses behind the Timespeak journalese a feeling of real empathy as Kondrashov chronicles the Civil Rights movement, the rise of Black Power, the so-called ghetto rebellions, King's failed attempt to bring "The Movement" North, his Riverside Church sermon on Vietnam, the Poor People's March, and the sanitation workers' protest in Memphis.

—*Newsletter* of the Afro-American Religious History Group of the American Academy of Religion 7:2 (Spring 1983), 9

McMurry, Linda O. *Recorder of the Black Experience: A Biography of Monroe Nathan Work.* Baton Rouge: Louisiana State University Press, 1985.

No one can do research in any aspect of Afro-American studies without soon coming upon the name of Monroe Nathan Work. His *A Bibliography of the Negro in Africa and America* and *Negro Year Book* series have been standard reference sources for years, and remain so today. Linda McMurry's book is a biographical sketch of Work (1866–1945), a quiet, scholarly man who devoted his life to systematically acquiring, organizing, and preserving all available information on the Negro—and making that information available for use.

Born in North Carolina just after emancipation, Work struggled through poverty to attend the University of Chicago. He was ordained in the AME Church and attended Chicago Theological Seminary. Committed to "Christian Sociology" and inspired by the notion that the truth revealed by the compilation of factual data would reform society, he transferred to the Sociology Department. Work was one of a number of black intellectuals who gave themselves to correcting the racial falsehoods assumed and perpetuated by white scholarship. "Both blacks and whites were crippled by popular, erroneous conceptions of black inferiority," Work wrote.

R.R. Wright, Sr., invited Work to Georgia State Industrial College in Savannah where he participated in Du Bois's well-known Atlanta University Studies. An activist, Work was a follower of Du Bois and an original member of the Niagara Movement. Then in 1906 a protest against segregated public transportation in Savannah failed, and a disillusioned Work was receptive to a job offer by Booker T. Washington.

Washington needed information for his varied speeches and writings, particularly data which demonstrated the success of Tuskegee graduates and the Tuskegee approach. The Department of Records and Research established by Work at Tuskegee was supposed to concentrate on records, but Work kept pushing the boundaries into research, and the information he garnered soon began to be circulated widely and to be universally trusted as accurate. Converted to Washingtonian self-help, Work spent forty years at Tuskegee, "the center of all things related to the Negro."

Although best known for his annual year books, begun in 1912, and his massive bibliography (1928), Work had other pioneering interests and accomplishments. Influenced by "folk psychology" at Chicago, he was an early advocate of African Studies and recognizer of African survivals, as well as one of the very few blacks or whites not limited by a European world-view of Africa. Work was active in the anti-lynching movement and his reliable statistics on lynching contributed to its decline. Perhaps least known and appreciated is Work's role in the black health movement. Due in significant measure to his agitating, organizing, and supplying of data, black life expectancy rose from age 35 in 1913 to age 52 by 1941.

A fellow sociologist, Du Bois believed that knowledge of facts would change things. He discovered that not to be the case in Atlanta and so shifted his focus to propaganda and political activism. Work shared his premise, but began as an activist, and when protest did not work in Savannah, moved to the compilation and presentation of data. Both made their mark, and it is interesting to see why and how they differed, and what ideological and practical roles Work played in the space between Du Bois and Washington.

Personally, Work was indefatigable, persistent, efficient, methodical, a perfectionist consumed by his endeavors. He was a fount of scholarship and information in service against racism.

He built a foundation for successors like Dorothy Porter Wesley and Ernest Kaiser. This book is a tribute to an under-appreciated man and a record of his accomplishments. There are a few photographs and an index, but—how inappropriate!—no bibliography of Work's extensive publications.

—*Newsletter* of the Afro-American Religious History Group of the American Academy of Religion 10:2 (Spring 1986), 13–14

Mabee, Carleton. *Black Education in New York State, from Colonial to Modern Times.* Syracuse: Syracuse University Press, 1979.

This book chronicles the efforts throughout New York State of black parents, children, teachers, and community leaders—and their few white friends—to secure education on all levels. It begins in the days of the Dutch colony, when conditions were better than one might suppose, and runs to the Second World War. Since then things have been worse than one might suppose.

Students of black religion will be interested in the significance of Sunday Schools and the active role of black churches and church people, like James W.C. Pennington, in the struggle to educate a people. Here, too, is a discussion of leaders like James McCune Smith, Charles L. Reason, Sarah J.S. Garnet, and William H. Johnson.

Mabee describes two abolitionist institutions which deserve a good deal more attention than they've heretofore received: the Presbyterian-related Oneida Institute at Whitesboro and the Baptist-related New York Central College at McGrawville. These schools pioneered in the education of women as well as blacks and in work-study, also. Central was the first college anywhere to appoint a black faculty member. There are tempting references to the black-sponsored Toussaint L'Ouverture College in Poughkeepsie, a fruitful subject for further research.

A theme that runs through *Black Education in New York State* is the conflict within the black community between integrated and separate education. While this "two-ness" is hardly a new idea, the dichotomy is illuminated by Mabee's study.

—*Newsletter* of the Afro-American Religious History Group of the American Academy of Religion 4:2 (Spring 1980), 9-10

Microfilming Corporation of America. Eight Archives

The Microfilming Corporation of America (MCA), a subsidiary of *The New York Times*, makes commercially available several large and important collections of black papers and archives. While expensive, they do provide a unique way for college libraries to acquire really significant primary source material that would otherwise be inaccessible. In brief, the MCA collections are as follows:

1. *Black Abolitionist Papers, 1830-1865.* 15,000 documents by 300 Afro-American anti-slavery spokespersons, with emphases on the convention movement, the black anti-slavery press, and sermons, religious tracts, and missionary documents. 17 reels.

2. *The Papers of George Washington Carver, 1864-1943.* Memorabilia, correspondence, and writings by and about Carver. 67 reels.

3. *The Tuskegee Institute News Clippings File, 1899-1966.* Hundreds of thousands of clippings from 300 periodicals arranged first by year and then alphabetically by subject within each year. 252 reels.

4. *The Papers of William E.B. Du Bois, 1877-1965.* Correspondence from the UMass archives. 76 reels.

5. *Slavery.* Pamphlets, books, periodicals. 5939 titles on 6668 microfiche.

6. *The Papers of Daniel Murray, 1881-1955.* Correspondence, personal papers, and material from Murray's unpublished encyclopedia. 27 reels.

7. *The Gerrit Smith Papers, 1775-1924.* In addition to abolitionist material, there are Smith documents on women, the anti-Masonic movement, etc. 77 reels.

8. *The Papers of the Congress of Racial Equality, 1941–1967.* CORE documents from the civil rights movement. 49 reels.

These notes of course are only suggestive in describing such large and complex archives. For each collection there is a printed guide with appropriate indexes, biographical notes, information on the history and organization of the material, etc. These may be purchased separately, and several, particularly the one on Du Bois, are rather important publications in their own right. Descriptive brochures and answers to questions may be requested from Microfilming Corporation of America, 1620 Hawkins Ave., P.O. Box 10, Sanford, NC 27330.

—*Newsletter* of the Afro-American Religious History Group of the American Academy of Religion 8:1 (Fall 1983), 13–14

Miller, Randall M., and Jon L. Wakelyn, eds. *Catholics in the Old South.* Macon: Mercer University Press, 1983.

Everyone knows that a comprehensive work on black Catholics and black Catholicism is one of the most-needed books in Afro-American religious studies. *Catholics in the Old South* is not that book, but it is one of the specialized studies that will make a broad survey possible. Surprisingly, virtually half of *Catholics in the Old South,* a collection of essays, deals with Afro-Americans.

One may be startled to learn that in 1860 there were in the South 100,000 black Catholics composed of slaves, free blacks, and "Creole free persons of color." Divided by culture, circumstances, and geography, they were concentrated in Maryland, western Kentucky, Charleston, Florida, and New Orleans. If there is a single generalization in this diversity, it is that white Catholics, no less than white Protestants, identified their religion with Southern culture in sanctioning slavery, states' rights, and the Lost Cause. For Catholicism this tendency seems to have been accentuated by the Church's growing domination by anti-democratic and anti-intellectual Tridentine Irish immigrants.

This book's essays directly relevant to Afro-Americans are: Randall Miller's "The Failed Mission: The Catholic Church and Black Catholics in the Old South" (the book's only reprinted article); R. Emmett Curran's "'Splendid Poverty': Jesuit Slaveholding in Maryland, 1805–1838"; Gary Mills' "Piety and Prejudice: A Colored Catholic Community in the Antebellum South" (Natchitoches parish, Louisiana); Jon L. Wakelyn's "Catholic Elites in the Slaveholding South." And the book's half-dozen other essays all touch on the Afro-Catholic experience, sometimes at length.

Catholics in the Old South is full of unexpected, even astonishing, discoveries. It explores with precision and balance a field largely ignored despite both its inherent interest and its significance for wider studies.

> —*Newsletter* of the Afro-American Religious History Group of the American Academy of Religion 8:1 (Fall 1983), 13

Morrison-Reed, Mark D. *Black Pioneers in a White Denomination.* Boston: Skinner House, 1980.

When Mark Morrison-Reed graduated from Meadville Theological School in 1979, he was the tenth black to have studied at that Unitarian seminary. This book, originally a thesis, is a study of two of his predecessors, Egbert Ethelred Brown (1875–1956) and Lewis Allen McGee (1893–1979), both of whom tried to introduce liberal religion to the black community. They were unsuccessful, and Morrison-Reed analyzes their failures as well as telling their stories.

Brown was a Jamaican who began a Unitarian church in Montego Bay, and in 1920 moved to this country to found the Harlem Community Church in New York. While blacks were largely indifferent to his efforts, Brown's real struggle was with the Unitarian hierarchy. He was, in Morrison-Reed's phrase, "abandoned and humiliated" over and over again by whites unaware of their racism. If portraits of Louis A. Cornish and Samuel A. Eliot hang in the corridors of 25 Beacon Street, someone ought to turn their faces to the wall; they treated Brown shamefully and interpreted his stubborn zeal for Unitarianism as additional evidence that he was a troublemaker and a nuisance who didn't fit in.

Brown worked as an elevator boy and as a speaker for the Socialist Party in order to support himself while he watched the Unitarians provide mission funds to Finns, Icelanders, and Italians. Only when Frederick May Eliot took over leadership of the denomination in 1937 did Brown's fortunes begin to change. Today many of his sermons have been collected by Robert Hill as part of the Marcus Garvey project at UCLA, and there is an effort to have Brown's daughter give his papers to the Schomburg Center of The New York Public Library.

Morrison-Reed gives less space to McGee who, like Brown, came out of a black Methodist background. McGee discovered he was a religious liberal when, as a mailman, he read a copy of a subscriber's Unitarian magazine. Unlike Brown, McGee became a humanist, and founded the Free Religious Fellowship among blacks in Chicago. But even McGee, appearing at a later time and with a much more acceptable personality and style, ran into Unitarian elitism and paternalism. It was not until 1961 that he became the first black to serve as senior minister of a white church, the Unitarian Fellowship of Chico, California.

Morrison-Reed raises important questions. Why did Brown's church fail while the Community Church in New York under John Haynes Holmes became 20 percent black? Why was Brown's appeal largely to West Indians? Was left-wing political activity a help or hindrance to Brown's Harlem ministry? Why was there no apparent relationship between the Harlem Community Church and the Harlem Renaissance? Most significant is the question of what liberal religion means in the light of the black experience.

The health of the Unitarian-Universalist tradition is demonstrated by the existence of this book, which shows that people can face the mistakes of the past and ask hard questions about the future. Other white churches need to be confronted by the reality of their own history in the same way. Morrison-Reed's book is important, therefore, not only as an analysis of neglected black pioneers in one white denomination, but as a model of self-examination for others to follow.

—*Newsletter* of the Afro-American Religious History Group of the American Academy of Religion 5:2 (Spring 1981), 12-13

Moss, Alfred A., Jr. *The American Negro Academy: Voice of the Talented Tenth.* Baton Rouge: Louisiana State University Press, 1981.

The American Negro Academy has always been a neglected institution. It was ignored by the public both black and white during its existence (1897 to 1928) as well as by most of its own members, and it has certainly been slighted by historians since. Yet the Academy included some of the most significant Afro-American men (it essentially excluded women) of its day; the presidents were Alexander Crummell, W.E.B. Du Bois, Archibald Grimké, John W. Cromwell, and Arthur A. Schomburg. Alfred Moss's detailed account chronicles the precarious life of the Academy and attempts to show why it never achieved its goal of becoming an influential black learned society.

The Academy grew out of the period Rayford W. Logan calls "the betrayal of the Negro." Leon Litwak and others have described how the failure of Reconstruction, disenfranchisement, the codification of Jim Crow with the blessing of the Supreme Court, "scientific" racism promulgated by the country's leading white scholars, and economic repression by Northern Republican industrialists-philanthropists rationalized by Booker T. Washington all combined to create an Afro-American nadir. Moss points out that in this period the U.S. became a colonial power, and even the Social Gospel did not address the new racism. As a result, blacks began to build more self-sufficient communities, and the Academy sought to be a community of intellectuals leading and protecting their people by opposing racism on scholarly grounds and encouraging prideful consciousness of black history and culture.

From the outset the Academy revealed the inherent tension between, on the one hand, assimilationism, distance from black folk culture, and a certain elitism, and, on the other, maintaining a distinct Afro-American ethnic identity and supporting a definition of American nationality that would encompass it. Crummell's opening address to the first session of the Academy on March 5, 1897, argued that American blacks lacked "civilization," a force producing all the arts, because they had no "sophisticated and regenerative culture" of their own. At the same meeting, Du Bois in his well-known paper on "The Conservation of the Races" described "the great message we have for humanity," and said, "For the development of Negro genius, of Negro literature and art, of Negro spirit, only Negroes bound and welded together, Negroes inspired by one vast ideal can work out" that great message "in its fulness."

The Academy intended to produce a journal, aid bright youth, establish a library, create international ties, have a full complement of fifty members, and exert a strong influence on educated blacks and whites. It never did any of these things, and most of Moss's book is an account of inactivity or laborious dealings over internal organizational matters. There are reasons for the Academy's lack of vigor. It was located in Washington, D.C., and found it difficult to transcend its geography. There was a relatively small pool of proven talent from which to draw and many of the best people, like Du Bois, were already committed to other enterprises and even over-extended. Booker Washington was, of course, opposed to the Academy.

On the positive side, the Academy in later years did attract considerable attention from its exhibitions of rare Afro-Americana. It also supported Kelly Miller's successful effort to have Howard University establish a special library collection of African and Afro-American materials. Most important was the series of scholarly papers originally read at meetings that the Academy published. These were intended to provide information as well as to demonstrate that blacks were capable of intellectual work on a par with whites. There are twenty-two Occasional Papers and five American Negro Monographs. They are, in the main, significant contributions, and a lasting tribute to the idea and ideal of a learned society. Finally, it must be remembered that the Academy began only thirty years after the end of slavery. Most blacks were not writing scholarly papers. Neither were most whites, and the few who were were neither interested in the Academy nor sympathetic to its purposes.

There are fascinating tid-bits in Moss's account: gossipy conflicts, rivalries, and exclusions from membership; the disappointing presidencies of Du Bois, Grimké, and Schomburg; the perseverance of Cromwell, who really kept the Academy going. There are some interesting facts: thirty-one of the Academy's ninety-nine members over the years were ministers and another twenty-nine were active laymen. Moss sheds light on people like Kelly Miller, Alain Locke, and Carter G. Woodson. There are surprises: the Academy came close to inviting Garvey to address a meeting. And amusing insights: the Academy traditionally met in March after national election years to coincide with the inaugurations of Republican presidents.

It is interesting to note that the Academy should finally fail just at the time of the New Negro and the Harlem Renaissance when a great flowering of Afro-American art, literature, music, and dance burst into national consciousness. Perhaps the reason is that the Renaissance drew more upon the uniqueness and vitality of the black folk tradition than it did upon the European academic tradition. At any rate, with the Renaissance, the "sophisticated and regenerative" culture of which Cromwell spoke finally came into existence, Du Bois's hope for "the great message we have for humanity" began to be realized, perhaps in ways he did not expect or approve, and the American Negro Academy died.

The American Negro Academy contains an index and a bibliography, including a listing of the Academy's publications. There are photographs of the Academy's presidents and prominent members.

Newman, Debra L. *Black History: A Guide to Civilian Records in the National Archives.* Washington: National Archives Trust Fund Board, 1984.

Black History is one of the more important and useful reference books to appear in some time. It spells out in detail the Afro-American material contained in the records deposited in the National Archives by some 453 federal agencies. Any researcher who has worked in the Archives knows how rich its black holdings are; this guide is, in effect, a preliminary search that opens up the Archives' vast collections and makes subsequent investigation substantially easier. Perhaps its greatest contribution, however, is its surprises, that is, the listing of archival materials that few realize exist.

The guide is organized by record group and series, just as the papers themselves are arranged in the Archives. Record Group 4, for example, is the archives of the U.S. Food Administration. An introductory paragraph explains the nature of the USFA which existed from 1917 to 1920. Under the Agency's States Administration Division there was a Negro Activities Section which contains one and a half feet of papers documenting food conservation efforts by black clubs and organizations. There was also an Educational Division, under which was a Negro Press section. This is all described as to general content, specific Afro-American inclusions, quantities of material, and arrangement. Under the Press Section's Miscellaneous Data and Correspondence file for 1917–1918 there are long lists of black ministers and churches.

Unless one becomes intrigued enough to read the book through all 453 agencies, which is not a bad idea, the best approach to its contents is via the detailed index. Under "Churches," for example, the reader is led to the Census of Religious Bodies for 1926–1928 in the records of the Bureau of the Census, where there is, among other papers, ten feet of material on "Negro Baptists"; to the Records of the FBI where there is a "Negro Church" file; to the Works Projects Administration where there are records of surveys of Negro churches, church archive inventories, and publications on black religion in the WPA library; to the Records of the Government of the District of Columbia where there is local black church material.

Another approach to the index is through proper names. There is W.E.B. Du Bois material, for example, in the Records of International Conferences, Commissions, and Expositions; in four different sections of State Department files; in the 1919 Records of the American Commission to Negotiate Peace; correspondence in the Records of the Bureau of Labor Statistics; and even a sound recording in the National Archives Gift Collection of Du Bois speaking in 1960 on "Socialism and the American Negro."

These illustrations are only examples. Anyone doing research on any phase of Afro-American history would be wise to consult this guide to the vast and varied holdings of the National Archives.

> —*Newsletter* of the Afro-American Religious History Group of the American Academy of Religion 10:1 (Fall 1985), 14–15

Paton, Alan. *Towards the Mountain: An Autobiography.* New York: Charles Scribner's Sons, 1980.

If it is possible for any white person to stand with Mahatma Gandhi and Martin Luther King as a true personification of the struggle against colonialism, racism, and apartheid, my nominee is Alan Paton.

This first volume of Paton's autobiography takes him from his birth to an English family in South Africa in 1903 to the spring of 1948. The spectacular success of his first novel, *Cry, the Beloved Country,* then made it possible for him to resign his job to devote the rest of his life to writing. But that same spring saw the political triumph of the extreme Afrikaner nationalists. Everyone knows Paton's brave and lonely stance in that troubled land from that day to the present.

Paton's family was Christadelphian. He moved beyond that limited circle to participate in the larger world of Toc H, the Student Christian Movement, and eventual confirmation in the Anglican Church. But it is not impossible to hear in Paton's writing a lyricism that can only be called biblical, and to see in the simplicity of his life and steadfastness of his belief other traces of his sectarian roots. It is in the largeness of his vision that he transcends, as few others anywhere, the confines of family, class, nation, church, and race itself to see humanity whole.

This book repeats Paton's description of his reaction to Edith Jones's funeral, the "deepest experience," after which "I was no longer a white person but a member of the human race." Edith Jones was a white woman who gave herself to a variety of organizations which worked for the betterment of African and Coloured children. At her death, South Africans of all races, nationalities, and religions came to St. George's Presbyterian Church, Johannesburg, to honor her memory; they were, as Paton saw, for that moment "reconciled under the roof of this church."

Paton writes, "What life had failed to give so many of these people, this woman had given them—an assurance that their work was known and of good report, that they were not nameless or meaningless, and there is no hunger like this one. Had they all come, no church would have held them all, the vast, voiceless multitudes of Africa, nameless and obscure, moving with painful ascent to that self-fulfillment no human being may with justice be denied, encouraged and sustained by this woman who withheld nothing from them, who gave her money, her comfort, her gifts, her home, and finally her life, not with the appearance of prodigality nor with fine-sounding words, but with a naturalness that concealed all evidence of the steep moral climb by which alone such eminence is attained."

Towards the Mountain adds some details to the lives of two men Paton wrote about in other books—Geoffrey Clayton, the Archbishop of Johannesburg, who was persecuted by the government; and Jan Hofmeyr, the liberals' hope, who probably would have succeeded Smuts had the Nationalists not come to power. Both books, *Apartheid and the Archbishop* and *South African Tragedy*, are essential for understanding the country's retrogression. And Hofmeyr is an absolutely fascinating figure who would be unknown in this country were it not for Paton's biography.

Paton is so well known as a novelist and symbol of opposition to "separate development" that it is hard to think of him in the single vocation he held to age 45—superintendent of a reformatory for African boys. Paton of course was a liberalizer who replaced inhumane with decent treatment. Eventually even the fence around Diepkloof reformatory was taken down. Meanwhile, the Afrikaners built a wall around South Africa and turned a whole country into a prison. Ironically, Alan Paton, a reformatory warden, was one of the few who stood fast for freedom.

—*Newsletter* of the Afro-American Religious History Group of the American Academy of Religion 5:2 (Spring 1981), 13–14

Plunkett, Michael, comp. *A Guide to the Collections Relating to Afro-American History, Literature, and Culture in the Manuscripts Department of the University of Virginia Library*. Charlottesville: University of Virginia Library, 1984.

Finding aids for the 10,000 manuscript collections at the University of Virginia Library were scanned for Afro-American material, and the result is this list of 420 collections. Each is described in a paragraph. The collections vary widely: one may consist of a single item; another may comprise thousands of pieces—a family's papers, say. So there is a good deal of variation here, and for the largest collections this *Guide* can only provide hints.

The largest and most numerous collections are family and plantation records that contain information on slaves. Most of the material is comparatively early, but there is some contemporary material, Virginius Dabney's papers, for example. There are some surprises: Cotton Mather's list of marriages (including blacks) and 4700 letters to and from William Stanley Braithwaite somehow found their way to Virginia. There is some material on black churches as well as white churches with black members.

This is all not only a helpful source of information on manuscripts in a major university library, but also a model other institutions might well follow in making their collections better known and more usable. A rather detailed index makes access easy, and the *Guide* is illustrated with several striking photographs from the collections.

—*Newsletter* of the Afro-American Religious History Group of the American Academy of Religion 10:2 (Spring 1986), 14–15

Richardson, James C., Jr. *With Water and Spirit: A History of the Black Apostolic Denominations in the U.S.* Washington: Spirit Press, 1980.

Twenty-five years ago while on a Caribbean holiday Henry Pitney Van Dusen, the president of Union Seminary, ran across a pentecostal church. His popular article about this visit became, difficult though it is to believe, the first introduction to the existence of the pentecostal movement for the majority of mainstream American church members. Van Dusen's role in the World Council of Churches had sensitized him to the authenticity and promise of the "younger" churches, so he treated his subject seriously and sympathetically, and predicted pentecostalism's increasing importance.

Much has taken place since that article, including the Catholic charismatic phenomenon, but probably the most interesting development is the fact that a number of pentecostal churches themselves are now mature, secure, and self-conscious enough to begin to explore their own history with disinterest and their current status with objectivity. The increasing awareness of the significance of this movement for American church history in general (and its neglect by establishment historians) means that names like Charles F. Parham and William J. Seymour, places like Topeka, Kansas, and Azuza Street, and dates like 1901 and 1906 will begin to find their way into the standard histories and be taken with the seriousness they deserve.

James C. Richardson's book deals with the black Apostolic denominations, those churches which came out of the Holiness movement, emphasize speaking in tongues as the one normative charismatic experience for all Christians, and repudiate the Trinity by their doctrine of the necessity of water baptism in the name of Jesus only.

Following Vinson Synan's earlier work, Richardson traces these "Oneness Pentecostals" from their origins in Wesleyan sanctification, and neatly spells out the Biblical authority for the Apostolic theological positions on repentance, spirit and water baptism, Jehovah-is-Jesus, and personal holiness.

The bulk of the book, however, is an extremely useful catalog and description of the 21 oldest black Apostolic denominations which represent nearly 3,000 congregations and a million and a half members. Richardson untangles the genealogies of these churches by identifying their founders and leaders, sketching their histories, and summarizing their strong and weak characteristics. Most new bodies have come into existence by splits within existing Apostolic churches, and Richardson is frank in pointing out that desire for the bishopric and personal leadership is a primary reason for division, along with doctrinal disputes over such issues as divorce, jewelry, and women preachers.

Richardson is deeply distressed by the Apostolic churches' divisiveness, and pleads for their greater unity. It would be useful, I should think, to consider the Apostolic movement sociologically as a group of sects well on their way to becoming churches. From this perspective, headquarters establishments, an educated clergy, and routinized stability are all acquired at considerable expense, not least of which is jeopardizing the open arena where charismatic individuals rise up and are recognized as leaders. In other words, the Apostolic churches are going the way of the Methodists and all other enthusiasts who became "respectable," and Richardson's study unknowingly documents this predictable change.

The Apostolic movement is vital, however, in part because it is still young, in part because of West Indian and African missions, in part because of its unique openness to the spirit. James C. Richardson, who is himself a product and a part of the Apostolic church as well as a professor at Virginia Seminary, has done us an enormous favor by bringing to our attention a group of

churches whose history, doctrine, and place in black religious life
deserve much more recognition than they have received.

—*Newsletter* of the Afro-American Religious History Group of the American Academy of Religion 6:2 (Spring 1982), 10–11

Richardson, Joe M. *A History of Fisk University,
1865–1946.* University: University of Alabama Press,
1980.

Fisk University was created by a triumvirate of freed slaves who
believed education would bring full humanity to themselves and
their children; self-sacrificing if grim Yankee missionaries; and
students who sold the irons from Nashville's slave market to raise
money to buy books. Congregational missionaries and freedmen
were a coalition with a lot of grit, and they built a great university.

Unlike many of the newly created schools, Fisk was able to
survive the failure of Reconstruction because of the Jubilee Singers. They began by singing white music to prove that Negroes
could do so. They were not well received, however, until they
began singing spirituals, and when they did, they became an
immediate and sensational success. The choir moved audiences
all across Europe and America and raised the money which
literally kept Fisk's doors from closing. The Jubilee Singers not
only saved a university, they helped preserve the slave songs by
writing them down and by making it respectable to sing them.

In the controversy between industrial versus liberal arts education, Fisk came to symbolize the latter as much as Tuskegee did
the former. In fact, the real story of Fisk is its dogged and
ultimately successful struggle over many years and against great
odds to construct, inch by inch, an academically first-rate institution without compromising a commitment to full civil rights.

Incidentally, anyone who still thinks of Booker T. Washington as a one-dimensional figure may be interested to learn that
his third wife was a Fisk graduate, that he became a Fisk trustee

and money-raiser, and that Booker, Jr., was sent to Fisk. So much for stereotypes.

Students of Afro-American religious history will welcome the light this book sheds on the American Missionary Association, on Fisk's short-lived divinity school, on missionaries to Africa, and on alumni like Henry Hugh Proctor, William N. DeBerry, and William Lloyd Imes, who became preeminent church leaders. All in all, this is an important and useful book, and one regrets only that the story ends with the Second World War.

> —*Newsletter* of the Afro-American Religious History Group of the American Academy of Religion 5:1 (Fall 1980), 11–12

Ripley, C. Peter, ed. *The Black Abolitionist Papers, Volume 1, The British Isles, 1830–1865.* Chapel Hill: University of North Carolina Press, 1985.

This is an extraordinary book in terms of content, scholarly apparatus, and the magnitude and significance of the project of which it is the first published volume. The Black Abolitionist Papers Project began in 1976 with private and public funding to collect and publish the documents of Afro-Americans involved in the anti-slavery movement from 1830 to 1865.

Scattered primarily in various manuscript collections and newspapers, the documents include letters, speeches, essays, debates, pamphlets, editorials, resolutions, autobiographical sketches, and personal papers. The Project located some 14,000 such records of 300 black women and men in 110 newspapers and over 200 libraries. All these primary documents were filmed unedited and are available on 17 reels from Microfilming Corporation of America and University Microfilms International. Many papers of course were previously uncollected, unidentified, and unavailable. Frederick Douglass was not included since his papers are being edited and published at Yale.

The next phase of the Project was the selection of the most important documents—less than 10 per cent of the total—for publication in book form in five volumes. This first book covers the British Isles; there will be one subsequent one on Canada and three on the United States. In the difficult assignment of selectivity, the most important criterion was to include documents "that fairly represent the anti-slavery goals, attitudes, and actions of black Americans and, to a lesser extent, that reveal their more personal concerns."

The schema for the introductory volume is exemplary. The Board of Editorial Advisors is listed and includes such respected names as Dorothy Porter and George Shepperson. A table of contents lists the 102 documents in the book. They are arranged chronologically, from Nathaniel Paul's letter to William Lloyd Garrison of 10 April 1833 to Sarah P. Remond's letter to the editor of the London *Daily News* of 7 November 1865. There are acknowledgments, a list of newspapers and journals, and another list of manuscript depositories. There is an editorial statement on methodology, and an excellent 32-page historical introduction. Each document has an explanatory head-note and long, careful, brilliant footnotes, including bibliography. The appendix consists of a chronological list of black Abolitionists in Britain from 1830 to 1865. There is a detailed index. In the light of this splendid, even ideal, apparatus, it becomes carping to complain that there are only nine illustrations.

The schema as well as the Project itself are of course only means for making accessible the material itself. First of all it must be said that with such giants as Garrison, Phillips, John Brown, Harriet Beecher Stowe, and others active in the American anti-slavery movement, it is sometimes easy to forget that abolition was the overwhelming black passion of the period and it commanded the best of Afro-American thought, energy, oratory, and leadership. Here these men and women speak for themselves. In this light it is probably a good thing that Douglass is not included since his omission allows other blacks who deserve to be better known to have a place on center stage. Here are the voices of William Wells Brown, Charles Remond, J.W.C. Pennington, Henry Highland Garnet, William Craft, Samuel Ringgold Ward, J. Sella Martin, and scores of other less-familiar names.

It is also important to know the role Britain played in the American anti-slavery movement as dozens of American blacks went there, especially after 1850, to lecture, raise money, publish books, extend the Abolitionist network, or simply live and work free from Southern slavery and Northern prejudice. The black mission to Britain cannot be overestimated for its impact on British public opinion, especially by the authoritative testimony of those who had actually lived in slavery. The documents throw light on a number of issues: the importance of black women like Ellen Craft, the Garrisonian split, opposition to the Colonization Society, the church as an ally of slaveholders, the Boston Anti-Slavery Bazaar, and the settlement of fugitive slaves in Canada. Not least important, in Britain "For the first time blacks found a national audience genuinely interested in supporting black causes," that is, churches, schools, newspapers, and vigilance committees in the U.S. and Canada. And blacks' reception on more egalitarian terms than they experienced at home helped them see more clearly the racist character of American society, including the anti-slavery societies themselves.

—*Newsletter* of the Afro-American Religious History Group of the American Academy of Religion 10:2 (Spring 1986), 12–13

Robinson, William H. *Phillis Wheatley: A Bio-Bibliography.* Boston: G.K. Hall, 1982.

At the 1898 auction of the James A. Bancker estate, a manuscript copy of Phillis Wheatley's poem "On Being Brought to America" sold for $1. In 1982 at the auction of Gerald E. Slater, a printed copy of Phillis Wheatley's "Elegy Sacred to the Memory of . . . Samuel Cooper" sold for $3,800. So, symbolically, we have learned to appreciate and value America's first great black woman poet.

Interest in Phillis Wheatley has increased so substantially that for some time scholars have needed a comprehensive bibliography of works by and about her. That need has now been met by William H. Robinson's book. Robinson, professor of English and director of the Black Studies Program at Rhode Island College, is our leading Wheatley scholar and interpreter. His compilation is definitive, and his evaluation is authoritative.

Robinson first lists Wheatley's poems published during her lifetime. He then records and describes chronologically virtually every book, article, and dissertation that treats Wheatley and her poetry from 1761 to 1979. Bringing together so many diffuse and elusive references is an impressive achievement. All subsequent work on Wheatley will have to begin with Robinson's study.

Phillis Wheatley has had many critics. Some have accused her of romanticism and sentimentality, of glorifying her enslavement (it brought her to Christianity), and of not being self-consciously black. But no one ever questioned her genius.

A useful feature of Robinson's bibliography is that it is possible to trace the critical response to her poetry over the years and watch the opinions change. Robinson's annotations are especially helpful. He provides excellent summaries and corrects innumerable errors written about her life and her poems. A careful reading of Wheatley finds her to be something more than the docile slave she is usually depicted as.

The Schomburg Center is one of the institutions Robinson thanks for providing help with his work. The Rare Books, Manuscripts & Archives Section holds rare copies of her published poems, and the Reference & Cooperative Services Section has the major critical studies of her poetry.

—*The Schomburg Center Journal* 2:2 (Spring 1983), 4

Robinson, William H. *Phillis Wheatley and Her Writings*. New York: Garland Publishing, 1984.

Phillis Wheatley may well be America's most durable author. Apart from poems in newspapers, pamphlets, and broadsides, she published only one book, *Poems on Various Subjects, Religious and Moral*, in London in 1773, yet in some two dozen editions over the years it has remained in print ever since. Not a minor accomplishment for an adolescent African slave girl in colonial Boston.

What is the secret of Wheatley's continuing appeal? She is not so profound an American poet as Edward Taylor, nor so signifi-

cant a woman writer (though Robinson disagrees) as Ann Brad-
street. Compared with her fellow blacks, Wheatley is not the
intellectual equal of Lemuel Haynes, she lacks the political consciousness of David Walker, and her poetry lacks the spontaneity
that characterizes George Moses Horton. Yet Wheatley has always been a powerfully symbolic figure for Afro-Americans and
sympathetic whites. More dormitories, libraries, YWCAs, and
housing projects have been named for her, probably, than any
other Negro woman.

Perhaps the appeal is that her very existence demonstrates that
the presuppositions of American racism, from slavery through
segregation to sociobiology, are simply not true. Perhaps the
appeal lies in the personal triumph of the woman herself. She
was stolen from family, country, and culture (including language), and subjected to the horrors of the Middle Passage. As a
sickly, naked child of seven (so it was thought because she was
missing her front teeth) she was bought cheap out of a "parcel of
small negroes" on a Boston dock in 1761. In a final humiliation,
she was given the name of the ship that had delivered her into
slavery.

But through her own extraordinary gifts Phillis Wheatley rose
to become a correspondent of George Washington, a guest of
British nobility, and a writer we have taken seriously for over 200
years.

Professor William H. Robinson of Rhode Island College is the
leading Wheatley scholar and interpreter, and we have in his
newest book a veritable one-volume Phillis Wheatley encyclopedia. There is a first-rate essay "On Phillis Wheatley and Her
Boston" that spells out what is known about her life (patiently
corrected of accumulated biographical errors) set in the framework of the city where she lived. There is a critical analysis of her
work. There is a facsimile reproduction of the first London
edition of her book. There are printings of her earlier and later,
i.e., before and after 1773, uncollected poems. Her known letters
are here, as are photographs of extant manuscripts. There are
variant poems, an early biographical sketch, illustrations, a bibliography, with everything fully and carefully annotated and
documented.

Robinson makes a number of important points about Wheatley's life and work. He shows how Mrs. Wheatley recognized
Phillis' talent, treated her as a privileged child rather than a

slave, and actively promoted her career. Despite the encouragement of her mistress, it is clear that Phillis' own natural abilities made her a writer; "her own curiosity led her to it," John Wheatley said. Speaking of curiosity, Phillis became something of a literary one; Thomas Wooldridge testified, apparently with some surprise, "I was present while she wrote." Robinson explains how the evangelical piety of the Wheatley family influenced Phillis; it was her poem on the death of the "Great Awakener" George Whitefield that established her reputation, and, in the international Evangelical network, the sympathy of the Countess of Huntington that opened doors for her in England.

Robinson persuasively argues that Wheatley displayed broader interests than evangelical piety, however, in her work. With pioneering tributes to black Africa, an expose of the hypocrisy of Christian slaveholders, and encomiums to liberty, she was racially more self-conscious and less accommodationist than has been generally supposed. Robinson also says she is a better poet than she has been given credit for being, though he admits her work is uneven. She has been underrated in terms of her stylistic talent, the imitative nature of her poems, and her ability to transcend the heroic couplet.

With all its strengths, there are two things I find wrong with this book. Even though it contains everything you always wanted to know about Phillis Wheatley, it is necessary to exert considerable energy and ingenuity to find anything. The index is inadequate, and some of the most informative gems of Robinson's scholarship are carefully concealed in the footnotes. Another problem is that the book is not designed with the practical needs of collectors and dealers in mind. It would have been helpful to have a separate section where information about editions, variants, etc., was brought together for easy reference.

Of the eighteenth-century editions of *Poems on Various Subjects*, the most common is the first edition published in London in 1773. There are four states with minor differences, Robinson points out, a fact, so far as I know, not previously noticed. These appear regularly on the market and now sell from $1250 to $1500. Wheatley imported copies to sell herself and signed a number of these on the verso of the title page, which of course makes them particularly desirable today. The most recent signed copy I've noticed in a dealer's catalogue mistakenly suggested that the signature might mean it was her own copy; it was priced at

$3500. A Philadelphia edition of 1774 was once advertised, but this appears to be a ghost. The first American edition was printed by Joseph Crukshank in Philadelphia in 1786 and is, as they say, "excessively rare." One was offered for sale in New York several years ago at $4000. Crukshank published another edition the next year that is equally hard to find, as is another reprint in 1789, and an Albany edition of 1793. Perhaps the scarcest edition is an undated (1787) London "second edition" printed for J. French which is essentially the same as the London first except for a new title: *Poems on Comic, Serious and Moral Subjects*. In 40 years Dorothy Porter of Howard was never able to locate a copy. One does exist at the Schomburg Center, however, and according to *NUC* there is another at the University of Texas.

The most startling copy of the London first is one "bound in negro skin" which Charles F. Heartman owned in the 1930s. In a November 14, 1935, letter to Arthur A. Schomburg, Heartman offered it on approval to The New York Public Library for $35 with the chilling aside, "If you knew how much trouble I had to get this binding done. . . . " Mr. Schomburg declined the offer.

Phillis Wheatley's broadsides have virtually disappeared from the market, although a copy of her pamphlet "Elegy Sacred to the Memory of . . . Samuel Cooper" brought $3800 at the Slater auction in 1982. There are a great many lost Wheatley manuscripts, but these do surface occasionally, particularly in the Philadelphia area where it is presumed they were sold after her death by an impecunious John Peters. Peters was the brash and restless free black whom Phillis married after the Wheatleys died. Phillis herself died in poverty and obscurity exactly two hundred years ago, December 5, 1784, at the age of 31.

The late Prof. Charles Davis of Yale has pointed out that Wheatley is not representative of Afro-American literature as genre, and that literature reflecting blacks as a particular people begins only with the slave narratives. Amiri Baraka elaborates this idea by suggesting that Wheatley, a protected house servant, "a pet of the slave society," represents the dialectical opposite of the black masses from whom she was isolated.

But Phillis Wheatley has had her uses. The Abolitionists used her to demonstrate black humanity. The New England primers designed to teach Freedmen to read used her as an example of the piety to which ex-slaves should aspire. Above all, Afro-Americans themselves have used her in the struggles to counter the racist American belief in black inferiority, and to construct a meaningful history. "The African Muse" has served them all faithfully, and William Robinson serves well Phillis Wheatley, her memory, and her continued significance with this monumental book.

—*American Book Collector* 5:6 n.s. (November-December 1984), 40–44

Russell, Lester F. *Black Baptist Secondary Schools in Virginia 1887–1957.* Metuchen: Scarecrow Press, 1981.

Russell begins his study with a survey of education for blacks in Virginia prior to 1861. He claims that from the beginning many slaves received religious and apprenticeship training and were even taught to read and write, but that Nat Turner's revolt of 1831 was a turning point. After the insurrection, owners agreed that it was impossible to cultivate slave minds without raising expectations, the fulfillment of which the master class had no intention of permitting.

The Civil War disrupted the old order, and freed slaves found modest opportunities for learning as contraband, as soldiers in the Union army, and from the American Missionary Association, the American Baptist Home Mission Society, and the U.S. Bureau of Refugees, Freedmen, and Abandoned Lands. The Radical Republican Congress did make an attempt, through the Freedman's Bureau, to protect the freedmen from the vicious efforts of white Virginia to return blacks to near slavery. But at the failure of Reconstruction, the Virginia Baptist State Convention realized that blacks themselves must be responsible for whatever education was going to take place.

The bulk of Russell's book is the narrative story of the thirteen secondary schools established in Virginia by Baptists, from Virginia Union, founded in Richmond in 1865 (and which became a major university), to the little-known, struggling high schools and industrial institutes which subsisted on hard-earned black dollars—some into the 1950s. These schools would be pathetic were it not for the strength of those dedicated souls who, against all possible odds, kept them going, and the fact that not a few distinguished black Americans came out of them.

Russell's book is enriched by splendid photographs and a map, an appendix of source documents and biographical sketches, a bibliography, and an index. The import of his subject is communicated by his restrained conclusion: "Had it not been for the church, the education of the Black race in Virginia would have been practically nonexistent. . . ."

—*Newsletter* of the Afro-American Religious History Group of the American Academy of Religion 7:2 (Spring 1983), 8

Shockley, Ann. *Say Jesus and Come to Me.* New York: Avon Books, 1982.

Readers of this journal know Ann Allen Shockley as Head of Special Collections at the Fisk Library, and as the author of a number of important works on black librarianship. Not everyone may know, however, that throughout her distinguished library career, Ann Shockley has also been publishing fiction, most notably *Loving Her* and short stories with a lesbian theme.

Her new, nationally distributed novel is the story of a black woman, Myrtle Black, a preacher who has an affair with Travis Lee, a prominent black woman singer. But neither publicly nor privately do things go smoothly: "Black people had not yet come fully to grips with homosexuality. For these reasons [Myrtle] had to conceal her sexuality. Religion and race mattered first to her."

Myrtle's public racial and religious task is leading a historic demonstration in Nashville against exploitation, the first women's march in the South. She is also building a church. Scattered throughout the novel are striking and insightful sketches of the black bourgeoisie, the black underworld of pimps and prostitutes, black church services, black music, black gay life, and white leaders of the women's movement. It would all make a marvelous movie. *Lady Chatterley's Lover* is not really a book about gamekeeping, as a famous review in a British gamekeepers' journal implied by ignoring everything in the novel except Mellors' occupation. So *Say Jesus and Come to Me* is not firstly a book about religion. It is a novel about sisterhood. At the same time it is neither incidental nor accidental that the leading character is a minister and that the physical love she discovers with another woman is set within the context of the spiritual love proclaimed by the black church.

—*Newsletter* of the Afro-American Religious History Group of the American Academy of Religion 7:1 (Fall 1982), 13

Shreve, Dorothy Shadd. *The AfriCanadian Church: A Stabilizer.* Jordan Station: Paideia Press, 1983.

Everyone knows of substantial black movement to Canada—loyalists during the American Revolution, passengers on the Underground Railroad, participants in various settlement schemes. But we know a good deal less about black life in Canada since these migrations, or about the people Dorothy Shadd Shreve calls AfriCanadians to differentiate them from Afro-Americans and to satisfy the needs of Canadian nationalism.

This book is essentially the story of the Amherstburg Baptist Association, a confederation of black churches in Upper Canada, i.e., Ontario. They had problems with whites, other Baptists, and among themselves, but they struggled along, many successfully into the present. The book takes a brief look at AME and British Methodist Episcopal churches as well as C.H. Mason's pentecostal Churches of God in Christ, all also in Southwestern Ontario.

This kind of local and regional history is of course unobtainable elsewhere, and so the book is a real contribution. There is an index, a bibliography, and many valuable photographs. The book is best ordered directly from the author (a descendant of

Mary Ann Shadd Carey) at P.O. Box 30, North Buxton, Ontario, Canada NOP 1YO.

—*Newsletter* of the Afro-American Religious History Group of the American Academy of Religion 8:2 (Spring 1984), 14

Smith, Dwight L. *Afro-American History: A Bibliography.* Vol. II. Santa Barbara: ABC-Clio, 1981.

This annotated bibliography contains over 4,000 entries selected from the *America: History and Life* database, a collection of abstracts of articles from 1,900 historical periodicals published from 1974 through 1978. The coverage is comprehensive, the annotations are consistently useful, and access is provided to a variety of American and foreign journals it would be impossible to keep track of otherwise.

The topical arrangement is admittedly arbitrary, but the 55 entries under "Religion and the Churches" can be greatly supplemented by scanning the detailed index. Because of the range of periodicals covered, even the most resolute bibliographer will find something new in his own area of interest.

—*Newsletter* of the Afro-American Religious History Group of the American Academy of Religion 6:1 (Fall 1981), 15

Thurman, Howard. *With Head and Heart.* New York: Harcourt Brace Jovanovich, 1979.

During the Great Awakening an advertisement appeared in the *Boston Weekly News-Letter* of April 15, 1742, for a runaway slave who could be recognized because he was "very forward to mimick some of the strangers that have been of late preaching among us." No one could ever accuse Howard Thurman of mimicking anybody. He stands unique in American religion: the last of the great preachers of a generation ago; a pioneer in transcending boundaries of race, class, nation, culture, and religion; and, most interestingly, an authentic holy man, a mystic in the midst of American religious activism who has explored the deep inner life of the spirit.

Howard Thurman was born in a Florida which had, state-wide, only three public high schools for Negroes. At Morehouse College the library was such that he could, and did, read every book in it. The political machinations he engineered to get the first black student admitted to Vassar were worthy of Adam Powell, Jr. The dialectic between these political realities and the spiritual reality discovered by Thurman on his true, inner journey constitutes the real substance of his autobiography.

Outwardly as well, however, Thurman's pilgrimage took him to interesting places: Atlanta, Oberlin, Howard, the Church for the Fellowship of All Peoples in San Francisco, Marsh Chapel at Boston University (to which Harold Case invited him despite both racial and theological pressures). As a visitor to Asia and Africa, Thurman struggled with reconciling his commitment to the Christian faith with the racist and colonialist culture in which that faith was located.

Christian that he is, Thurman pays his debts, from John Hope through Rufus Jones to Mahatma Gandhi. (Gandhi once asked him why the Negro slaves in America had not become Muslims, since Islam is the only world religion without internal discrimination.) Even though one can see the influence of these people, and others, on Thurman, they do not alone account for his spirituality. This is a product of his radical self-understanding and his realization that the truth he found in himself is universal.

"A man's life is a single statement," Thurman writes. Having had revealed to him, as other mystics, a glimpse of the unity of the universe, he goes on to say, "The Head and the Heart at last inseparable; they are lost in wonder in the One." Beyond everything else Howard Thurman is a humble seeker who has never been without wonder; that may be his secret.

—*Newsletter* of the Afro-American Religious History Group of the American Academy of Religion 4:2 (Spring 1980), 9

Wagner, Clarence M. *Profiles of Black Georgia Baptists.* Gainesville: Author, 1980.

In 1774 in Burke County, Georgia, a slave named George Liele was converted, baptized, and began to preach. Today there are nearly 12 million black Baptists in the United States alone, making the Baptist Church, of which Liele was the first black leader, the largest single movement in Afro-American history. Clarence Wagner is Executive Secretary of the General Missionary Baptist Convention of Georgia, and pastor of the First Baptist Church of Gainesville. His book is a collection of sketches of local church and association histories, as well as of the Georgia state convention. A number of documents are reproduced, including convention programs and some material on the National Baptist Convention, U.S.A., Inc. There are particularly interesting biographies and photographs of the seventeen state convention presidents since 1870, and of the presidents of the Women's Auxiliary.

Given the extraordinary influence and importance of the Baptist Church, it is always surprising to realize how little attention has been paid to recording its history and understanding its role. Historians like Wagner who focus on state and local records are not only telling accounts fascinating in and of themselves, but they are also compiling the kind of data it is necessary to have before larger generalizations can be drawn.

—*Newsletter* of the Afro-American Religious History Group of the American Academy of Religion 6:1 (Fall 1981), 14

Webb, Lillian Ashcroft. *About My Father's Business: The Life of Elder Michaux.* Westport: Greenwood Press, 1981.

When Randall K. Burkett and I edited the first volume of *Black Apostles*, we noted with regret that there was no serious biographical or analytical account of Elder Lightfoot Solomon Michaux, the flamboyant radio evangelist who flourished in Washington, D.C., in the 1930s and '40s. That gap is now filled by Lillian Webb's excellent study.

Michaux (1884–1968) was one of the first to use what is now called the mass media for religious programming, and his "Happy Am I" broadcast attracted literally millions of listeners. He skillfully used radio not only for his famous "War on the Devil," but also to attack Herbert Hoover and help elect and re-elect Franklin D. Roosevelt. Michaux's political influence, in turn, was helpful in supporting his extensive relief programs during the Great Depression, and, later, in keeping his various business and real estate ventures afloat and out of trouble.

In an insightful analytical chapter on the nature of cults, Webb argues persuasively that Michaux was more prophet than cult leader, and that his Church of God and Gospel Spreading Association was more consistent with the black Christian church than has been previously supposed. Early in his career Michaux split from the Church of Christ (Holiness) U.S.A. of Bishop C.P. Jones, but in a good many ways he remained faithful to that tradition despite his authoritarianism and showmanship.

In its first-rate synthesis of history and analysis, this book is something of a model. Like Robert Weisbrot's study of Father Divine, it elevates an often disparaged religious leader to a place where his ministry can be more objectively seen, understood, evaluated, and appreciated. There is a bibliographic essay, an index, and a marvelous collection of photographs.

—*Newsletter* of the Afro-American Religious History Group of the American Academy of Religion 8:2 (Spring 1984), 14–15

Willan, Brian. *Sol Plaatje: South African Nationalist, 1876–1932*. Berkeley: University of California Press, 1984.

A number of years ago when I first read Sol Plaatje's *Native Life in South Africa*, I was struck by the persuasiveness of its evidence, the eloquence of its presentation, and the moral strength of its argument on behalf of South Africa's blacks in the face of white oppression. I found it, too, depressingly contemporaneous; in fact, the conditions about which Plaatje wrote in 1916 had grown considerably worse instead of better. As an early and major spokesman for his people in that beautiful but troubled land, Plaatje has deserved a recognized place in the larger history of the freedom movement of colonized people of color. Brian Willan's long-anticipated biography now firmly establishes Plaatje's stature as a remarkable person as well as his significance as an African nationalist pioneer.

Solomon Tshekisho Plaatje was born in 1876 to a Christian family of the Barolong people at Doornfontein, an outstation of the Berlin Mission Society in the Orange Free State. A bright and hardworking child with a gift for languages, he received a mission school education, and worked for the Kimberley Post Office and then as a court translator. In Kimberley, Plaatje was part of a small group of Europeanized Africans self-confidently bent on "progress" and "improvement." They deeply believed in the superiority of English culture, especially its promise of "Equal rights for all civilized men," interpreted as equality of opportunity and parity before the law.

In Mafeking during the Boer War, Plaatje conducted himself ably throughout the famous siege, "the necessary myth," Willan calls it, to rally public support for Britain's imperialist war. Even at this early date, however, signs began to appear that England would deal more equitably with her white enemies the Afrikaners than she would with her faithful subjects the black Africans. As editor of Native newspapers in Mafeking and Kimberley, Plaatje worked against the decline of liberal English influence in government and the erosion of Native rights as Afrikaner nationalists came to power through the Act of Union. The major African response was the creation in 1912 of the South African Native National Congress with the Rev. John Dube as president and Plaatje as secretary.

The Natives' Land Act of 1913 mobilized the Congress movement since the Act legislated segregation and allowed white capitalist agriculture to turn Africans from peasants into farm laborers. Willan rightly calls the Act "one of the most important pieces of legislation in South African history," for it struck at the heart of the decency in which progressive Africans like Plaatje had been taught to believe. "A deliberate scheme for partial enslavement," Plaatje called the Act in a reaction which combined disbelief with a sense of betrayal.

Plaatje travelled to England with other Congress delegates in an attempt to mobilize public opinion against the Act. They were of course unsuccessful, but Plaatje entered into a variety of wider circles and won friendship and respect throughout the country, especially through his association with the Brotherhood Movement and with Left politicians. He was particularly aided by a number of sympathetic English women, notably the daughters of Bishop Colenso. In London, too, despite the constant crisis of insolvency, Plaatje saw to the publication of *Native Life in South Africa* in 1916 and made academic connections regarding his lifelong interest in Native linguistics and orthography.

From 1920 to 1922 Plaatje visited Canada and the United States where his oratorical genius and firsthand accounts of life in Africa made him a favorite of black audiences. He seems to have met and captivated everybody: Ida Wells Barnett, J.E. Bruce, John Cromwell, W.E.B. Du Bois, Jessie Fauset, Marcus Garvey, and Robert Russa Moton. Plaatje became especially friendly with Moton, probably because they understood each other well: in the Washington tradition each was an eminently respectable broker across racial lines dependent for his position of black leadership on the charity and good will of kindly but condescending whites—whom they were not above manipulating within the little space where they were allowed to operate.

In South Africa itself the situation moved from bad to worse as a calculated series of legislative enactments hacked away at black rights and opportunities: the Native Affairs Act of 1920, the Colour Bar Bill of 1926, the Native Administration Act of 1927, etc. Plaatje and his colleagues struggled against each one to no avail. Through it all, Plaatje never lost sight of the Cape ideal of a common society, nor did he ever consider avenues of resistance other than those conformable to the highest English ideals: personal diplomacy, influencing opinion, and responsible voting. In this light, the fight to save the Cape franchise becomes particularly symbolic and sad. For those who know South African history, it is interesting to see familiar names appear in Willan's book as they touch upon Plaatje's life and work: Abdullah Abdurahman, Clements Kadalie, Jan Hofmeyr, Z.K. Matthews, Olive Schreiner and her husband, and A.B. Xuma.

In his later years Plaatje concentrated on the languages and literature which had always fascinated him and at which he had always been such a master of subtlety. He was the first to translate Shakespeare into an African language, publishing *The Comedy of Errors* in 1930 as *Diphosho-phosho* (literally "Mistake upon Mistake"). In 1930 also he published *Mhudi*, the first novel in English by a black South African. His writing, like his politics, sought to wed European and African traditions. Plaatje died in Kimberley in 1932.

Sol Plaatje was caught throughout his life in a number of paradoxes. He was a thoroughly Westernized African deeply concerned with preserving Native languages, history, and folklore. He was a gentleman dependent upon personal relationships with other gentlemen who found himself spurned by racist whites and increasingly separated from the black masses who were evolving into a working class. Most of all, he was a profound believer in Christian faith and Victorian liberalism, a great tradition upon which the British turned their backs and the Afrikaners brutally trampled.

Willan's book is a model of scholarly research, elegant writing, and, most difficult to achieve, brilliant illumination not only of its subject but of that subject's larger context. This is the "life and times" genre at its best. The book is strengthened by the extraordinary collection of over 100 photographs Willan has unearthed and assembled and which, happily, the University of California Press has reproduced.

South Africa is daily in the news and current events there bear out the worst of Plaatje's fears—and beyond. South Africa has its contemporary heroes, but it also has its historical ones. When South Africa is free, Plaatje will be recognized as a national founding father; until then Willan's book holds him up for all the world to see how decent and reasonable men who sought only simple justice were pushed aside by ruthless white racists in control of a minority government.

—*Newsletter* of the Afro-American Religious History Group of the American Academy of Religion 9:2 (Spring 1984), 11–13

Index

Darwin, Charles, 100 n5
Dathorne, O. R., 64 n9
Davids, Joel, 128 n42
Davie, K. U., 126 n6
Davis, Charles, 173-177, 217
Dean, Jacob, 144 n5
Dean, John, 144 n19
De Berry, William N., 211
Delany, Martin, xv, 66
Dennis, Walter D., 171
Diagne, Blaise, 49
Dibble, J. Birney, 174-176
Diop, Alioune, 50, 51
Diop, David, 50, 53-56, 60
Dithebe, M. J., 118
Divine, Father, 156, 176-177, 224
Divine, Mother, 176-177
Dodd, Thomas J., 44
Douglass, Frederick, 23, 65, 174, 211-212
Drake, St. Clair, 62-63, 64 n15
Dube, John, 225
Du Bois, William E. B., xvi, 50, 65-72, 173, 177-179, 179-180, 185, 187, 191, 192, 195, 197, 201-203, 205, 226
Dudley, Edward, 157
Dunbar, Barrington, 182
Dunbar, Paul Laurence, 191
du Plessis, Izak D., 125 n2
Dwight, Timothy, 150, 181

Eason, James W. H., 87, 103 n19
Edwards, Paul, 174
Eikerenkoetter, Frederick J., 156-157
Elaw, Zilpha, 163-165
Eliot, Frederick May, 200
Eliot, Samuel A., 200
Ellis, Joseph H., 150
England, William, 37
Equiano, Olaudah, 174, 190, 193
Essig, James D., 180-181

Fanon, Franz, 29
Farmer, E., 109
Farson, Negly, 128 n49
Fauset, Jessie, 226
Feuser, Willfried, 64 n9
Fisher, Mary, 144
Fleisch, Sylvia, 33
Fletcher, James A., 182
Foner, Philip S., 183-184
Foote, Julia A. J., 163-165
Ford, Arnold J., 137
French, J., 217
Fuller, Latimer, 109
Fuller, Thomas, 156
Gacokia, Harrison, 128 n51
Gandhi, M. K., xix, 50, 205, 222
Garnet, Henry Highland, 160, 212
Garnet, Sarah J. S., 196
Garrison, William Lloyd, 151, 212
Garvey, Amy Jacques, 91, 104 n26, 104 n33, 127 n15, 131
Garvey, Marcus, xii, xv, xvii, 49, 83, 86, 89, 90-91, 96, 99, 100 n1, 102 n16, 103 n19, 104 n26, 104 n29, 106 n54, 111-113, 121, 124, 126 n15, 127 n20, 128 n44, 131-132, 134-135, 142, 144 n6, 145 n29, 145 n33, 186-188, 188-189, 192, 203, 226
Gates, Henry Louis, 173-174
Gathuma, Arthur, 129 n54
Gatung'u, Arthur, 128 n51
Gerloff, Roswith, 184-185
Gide, Andre, 51
Goldthorpe, J. E., 130 n66
Goodwin, W. A., 109
Gordon, John Dawson, 89
Grafton, Charles C., 93, 94, 105 n43
Green, Claude, 133
Gregg, John A., 156

Saunders, C. C., 126 n10
Schomburg, Arthur A., 185-186,
    191, 201, 203, 217
Schreiner, Olive, 126, 226
Schreiner, W. P., 126
Sears, Ernest, 140, 142, 145 n27
Sedgwick, Adam, 75
Selleck, Charles A., 144 n18
Senghor, Leopold, 50-52, 54,
    58, 61-63, 64 n8, 64 n9
Seymour, William J., 208
Shaw, Oliver Wendell, 192
Shepherd, William Henry, 190
Shepperson, George, xvii, 126
    n15, 212
Shick, Tom, 190
Shockley, Ann Allen, 219-220
Shreve, Dorothy Shadd, 220-221
Sibley, John Churchill, 129 n59
Sigmund, Paul E., 64 n3
Skinner, Richard, 152
Skota, T. D. Mweli, 125 n1, 126
    n7
Slater, George W., Jr., 183-184
Slater, Gerald E., 213, 217
Smith, Dwight L., 221
Smith, Edwin W., 64 n11
Smith, Gerrit, 197
Smith, James McCune, 196
Solomon, Job ben, 165
Soyinka, Wole, 61
Spartas, Reuben Mukasa, 97-98,
    106 n58, 119-120, 128 n44,
    128 n45
Spencer, Peter, 166
Spingarn, Joel Elias, 178
Stepto, Robert, 174
Stevens, Thaddeus, 5
Stokes, Albert, 133
Stowe, Harriet Beecher, 212
Stuart, Bertie A. Cohen, 167
Sundkler, Bengt G. M., 106 n52,
    126 n11, 126 n14
Sweetwater, Charles, 116
Synan, Vincent, 209

Taylor, Edward, 214
Taylor, Gardner C., 156-157
Taylor, Simon W., 64 n6
Terry-Thompson, Arthur C.,
    100 n1, 102 n14, 102 n15,
    105 n38, 105 n45, 125 n2,
    127 n17, 128 n41
Theresa, Angelina, 114
Thorez, Maurice, 51
Thurman, Howard, 221-222
Tile, Nehemiah, 126 n10, 126
    n11
Tobitt, Richard Hilton, 87, 103
    n21
Toure, Sekou, 50
Trotman, Arthur S., 97, 119
Truman, Harry, 22
Turner, Franklin D., 171
Turner, Harold W., 106 n51,
    160
Turner, Nat, 218
Tuttle, Charles E., Jr., 152
Van Dusen, Henry Pitney, 76,
    208
Vassa, Gustavus. See Olaudah
    Equiano
Vilatte, Joseph René, 93-96, 105
    n41, 111-112, 127 n18, 127
    n19, 129 n59
Vincent, Theodore G., 103 n23,
    104 n31
Vladimir, Bishop, 94
Von Grunebaum, G. E., 64 n13
Wagner, Clarence M., 223
Wakelyn, Jon L., 198-199
Walker, David, 215
Walker, Eric A., 126 n9
Walker, Williston, 105 n47
Wallace, George, 22
Wallace, Henry A., xviii
Wallerstein, Immanuel, 64 n4
Walls, W. J., 156
Walshe, Peter, 126 n7
Walters, Harold A., 167

About the Author

Richard Newman taught at Vassar College, Syracuse University, and Boston University, where he was Chairman of the Social Sciences Department. He was Senior Editor at G. K. Hall & Co., Boston, and Executive Editor at Garland Publishing, Inc., New York. Since 1981 he has been at The New York Public Library.

He is the author of several recent works in Afro-Americana: *Black Access: A Bibliography of Afro-American Bibliographies* (Westport, 1984); *Lemuel Haynes: A Bio-Bibliography* (New York, 1984); and *Afro-American Education, 1907–1932: A Bibliographic Index* (New York, 1984). With Betty K. Gubert he compiled *Nine Decades of Scholarship: A Bibliography of the Writings 1892–1983 of the Staff of the Schomburg Center for Research in Black Culture* (New York, 1986).

Robert A. Hill, who wrote the foreword, is a professor in the Department of African Studies, UCLA, where he is editor of the *Marcus Garvey and Universal Negro Improvement Association Papers.*